AMC'S BEST
SEA KAYAKING
IN THE MID-ATLANTIC

40 COASTAL PADDLING ADVENTURES
FROM NEW YORK TO VIRGINIA

Michaela Riva Gaaserud

Appalachian Mountain Club Books
Boston, Massachusetts

AMC is a nonprofit organization, and sales of AMC Books fund our mission of protecting the Northeast outdoors. If you appreciate our efforts and would like to become a member or make a donation to AMC, visit outdoors.org, call 800-372-1758, or contact us at Appalachian Mountain Club, 5 Joy Street, Boston, MA 02108.

outdoors.org/publications/books

Distributed by National Book Network.

Front cover photograph © Peter Gaaserud

Back cover photograph © Michaela Riva Gaaserud

Interior photographs by © Michaela Riva Gaaserud, unless otherwise noted.

Maps by Ken Dumas © Appalachian Mountain Club

Cover design by Athena Lakri

Interior design by Abigail Coyle

Library of Congress Cataloging-in-Publication Data

Names: Gaaserud, Michaela Riva, author.
Title: Best sea kayaking in the Mid-Atlantic : 40 coastal paddling adventures from New York to Virginia / Michaela Riva Gaaserud.
Description: Boston, Massachusetts : Appalachian Mountain Club Books, [2016] | "Distributed by National Book Network"—T.p. verso. | Includes bibliographical references and index.
Identifiers: LCCN 2015046383| ISBN 9781628420319 (paperback) | ISBN 9781628420326 (ePub) | ISBN 9781628420333 (Mobi)
Subjects: LCSH: Sea kayaking—Middle Atlantic States—Guidebooks. | Middle Atlantic States—Guidebooks.
Classification: LCC GV776.M5 G33 2016 | DDC 797.122/40974–dc23
LC record available at http://lccn.loc.gov/2015046383

Printed in the United States of America, using vegetable-based inks.

21 20 19 18 17 16   1 2 3 4 5

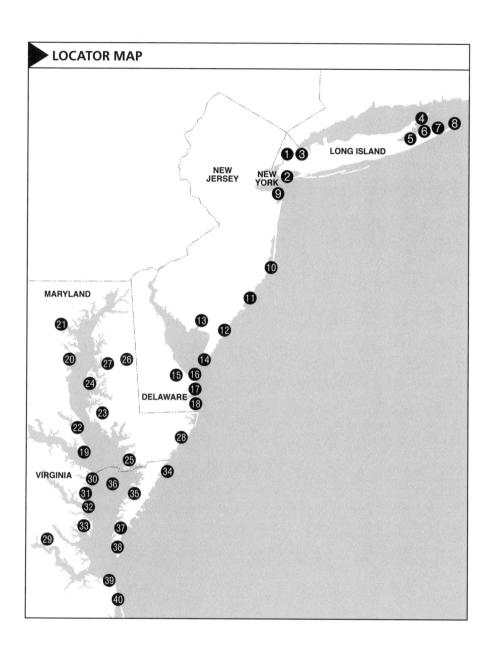

LOCATOR MAP

NEW JERSEY

NEW YORK

LONG ISLAND

MARYLAND

DELAWARE

VIRGINIA

▶ CONTENTS

Essays

▶ AT-A-GLANCE TRIP PLANNER

trip number, trip name	primary launch	distance
NEW YORK		
1 Pelham Bay Park to New Rochelle	Bronx, NY	7.0 nm
2 Jamaica Bay Wildlife Refuge	Brooklyn, NY	3.5, 5.0, or 10.5 nm
3 Oyster Bay Harbor	Oyster Bay, NY	5.4, 6.5, or 7.4 nm
4 Shelter Island–Coecles Harbor Marine Water Trail	Shelter Island, NY	5.6 nm
5 Bullhead Bay to Scallop Pond	Southampton, NY	7.0 nm
6 Sag Harbor	Sag Harbor, NY	4.5 or 9.5 nm
7 Three Mile Harbor	East Hampton, NY	7.0 nm
8 Lake Montauk	Montauk, NY	6.0 nm
NEW JERSEY		
9 Navesink River	Red Bank and Rumson, NJ	2.5, 4.5, 6.5, and 7.0 nm
10 Island Beach State Park	Berkeley Township, NJ	2.0 or 3.0 nm
11 Great Bay	Tuckerton, NJ	7.0 or 9.0 nm
12 Ocean City	Ocean City, NJ	3.5, 4.0, or 4.5 nm
13 Egg Island–Glades Paddling Trails	Downe and Port Norris, NJ	2.6, 6.1, 6.7, or 9.1 nm
14 Cape May	Cape May and Lower Township, NJ	2.2, 4.5, 7.0, or 12.5 nm
DELAWARE		
15 Broadkill River	Milton and Lewes, DE	11.0 nm
16 Cape Henlopen State Park	Lewes, DE	1.5 or 4.0 nm
17 Delaware Seashore State Park	Bethany Beach, DE	3.5 and 4.0 nm
18 Assawoman Canal	South Bethany, DE	5.5 nm

water type	trip highlights	fee	skill	work boats	lighthouse	camping
open/protected	Paddle past islands, through lagoons, and into Long Island Sound	$	⚠			
protected	Enjoy peaceful paddling in the heart of New York City					▲
protected	Paddle past gorgeous estates in a bay adored by Theodore Roosevelt	$				
protected	Paddle a scenic, protected harbor	$	(ALL)			
open/protected	Enjoy a peaceful paddle among wildlife		⚠			
protected	Rub elbows with the rich and famous in a historic harbor	$	(ALL)	🚢	☀	
protected	Bird-watchers shouldn't miss paddling this popular harbor			🚢		
protected	An active lake with pockets of serenity		⚠	🚢		
protected	A tidal estuary with sandbars, forest, and grand properties			🚢		
protected	Enjoy undeveloped shores in a beautiful state park	$	⚠			
open/protected	Protected marsh, open water, and birding on the Atlantic Flyway		⚠			
protected	Paddle bays and creeks in a vacation community			🚢		
protected	A peaceful maze of creeks runs through this large marsh		⚠			
open/protected	Enjoy many paddling options in this popular beach community		⚠	🚢		▲
protected	Enjoy a relaxing paddle down a scenic tidal river		(ALL)			
open/protected	Historic lighthouses and dolphins highlight this challenging paddle	$	⚠	🚢	☀	▲
open/protected	Paddle through marsh and around islands in a beautful setting			🚢		▲
protected	A peaceful oasis in a busy vacation community		(ALL)			

(ALL) = good for novices;   ⚠ = expert only
▲ = camping on-route;   ▲ = camping nearby

trip number, trip name	primary launch	distance
MARLYAND		
19 Point Lookout	Scotland, MD	1.5, 3.0, and 4.6 nm
20 Annapolis	Annapolis, MD	11.0 nm
21 Baltimore's Inner Harbor	Baltimore, MD	4.5 nm
22 Solomons Island	Solomons, MD	5.0 or 9.5 nm
23 Blackwater National Wildlife Refuge	Crapo and Church Creek, MD	6.6, 7.0, or 8.0 nm
24 Tilghman Island	Tilghman Island, MD	up to 8.7 nm
25 Janes Island	Crisfield, MD	1.0 to 11.0 nm
26 Choptank River	Denton, MD	7.0, 14.0, or 30.0 nm
27 Wye Island	Wye Mills, MD	11.7 nm
28 Assateague Island	Berlin, MD	4.0 or 9.0 nm
VIRGINIA		
29 Jamestown Island	Williamsburg, VA	8.5 nm
30 Reedville	Reedville, VA	6.0 and 8.0 nm
31 Fleets Island	White Stone, VA	8.0 nm
32 Milford Haven/Gwynn's Island	Diggs and Gwynn, VA	7.0, 8.0, or 12.0 nm
33 East River	Mathews, VA	5.0 or 11.0 nm
34 Chincoteague Island	Chincoteague Island, VA	9.5 nm
35 Onancock Creek	Onancock, VA	8.0 nm
36 Tangier Island	Tangier, VA	2.0 or 8.0 nm
37 Oyster Harbor (Cape Charles)	Cape Charles and Marionville, VA	4.8, 5.5, or 22.0 nm
38 Eastern Shore of Virginia National Wildlife Refuge	Cape Charles, VA	2.5, 5.2, or 10.0 nm
39 First Landing State Park—Virginia Beach	Virginia Beach, VA	11.7 or 19.0 nm
40 Back Bay National Wildlife Refuge	Virginia Beach, VA	7.4 or 12.6 nm

water type	trip highlights	fee	skill	work boats	lighthouse	camping
open/protected	Many options await in this historic Civil War park	$	⚠	🚢	🗼	▲
open/protected	Experience the fun vibe of Maryland's capital city		⚠	🚢		
protected	The busy Inner Harbor is energizing and fascinating		⚠	🚢		
protected	A kayaker's paradise on a tidal river and creek			🚢	🗼	
protected	Solitude and silence await in this pristine refuge		ALL			
open	Take on long stretches of shoreline and challenging water		⚠	🚢		▲
open/protected	Six paddling trails await with views of bald eagles		ALL	🚢		▲
protected	Take a long journey or brief paddle on this pretty river		ALL	🚢		
protected	A leisurely circumnavigation yields great wildlife viewing			🚢		
open/protected	Paddle past wild ponies in this pristine state park			🚢		▲
open/protected	Paddle past one of the country's most historic sites		⚠	🚢		▲
open/protected	Paddle through a charming fishing community			🚢		
open/protected	Tackle challenging waters around this beautiful island		⚠	🚢		
open/protected	Explore beautiful and often empty waterways			🚢		
open/protected	Peaceful scenery and the potential for seeing dolphins		ALL	🚢		
open/protected	Paddle between islands and look for herds of wild ponies	$		🚢		▲
open/protected	A picturesque paddle along the shores of a nature preserve		ALL	🚢		
open/protected	A unique island that may soon disappear		ALL	🚢		
open/protected	Take a short round-trip paddle or a long one-way trip			🚢		
open/protected	Paddle in an important bird migration locale	$	ALL	🚢		
open/protected	Paddle in the Atlantic Ocean along the Virginia Beach shoreline	$	⚠	🚢	🗼	▲
open/protected	Bask in the peacefulness of this remote wildlife refuge		⚠			▲

ALL = good for novices;   ⚠ = expert only
▲ = camping on-route;   ▲ = camping nearby

▶ ACKNOWLEDGMENTS

Regardless of how involved the process for writing a guidebook is and the great number of people who helped along the way, it is really you, the reader, who is seldom acknowledged. The truth is that without you, there would be no demand for this book, and as a result, no book at all. So it is all of you: the ones who have a passion for the sport of sea kayaking and an interest in exploring the mid-Atlantic coastline that I acknowledge and thank for making this book possible.

On a personal level, I want to thank the staff at Appalachian Mountain Club Books for approaching me to write this book, and for their dedication to the freedom and exhilaration of the outdoors. I also want to thank my travel companions (Pete, Ann, and my mom) who kayaked alongside me or supported me while I was on the water to make all the hours of research extra enjoyable.

▶ INTRODUCTION

As a lifelong resident of the mid-Atlantic coast, I've spent many years exploring the incredible shoreline between New York and Virginia. You could potentially paddle from New York to the Virginia–North Carolina border in roughly 428 miles, but if you take into account all the tidal shoreline along the mid-Atlantic coast, the number jumps to an astonishing 10,528 miles. To put this into perspective, the distance around the world at the equator is 24,902 miles.

Although many major coastal features characterize the mid-Atlantic, including bays, harbors, tidal rivers, and islands, one in particular deserves a mention up front. The mighty Chesapeake Bay, which is the nation's largest estuary, extends 200 miles, from Havre de Grace, Maryland to Virginia Beach, Virginia. Approximately 150 rivers and streams flow into the Chesapeake Bay, including the three largest: the Susquehanna, Potomac, and James Rivers. The Chesapeake Bay is the dominant feature along the Maryland coast and throughout much of Virginia. It divides the mainland from the Delmarva Peninsula and is a very important ecological and economic feature in both states.

As one of the most populated coastal regions in the country, the mid-Atlantic offers paddlers a wide variety of environments. With major cities such as New York; Philadelphia; Baltimore; Washington, DC; and Richmond located in this region, it might seem as though it would be difficult to find solitude and nature while paddling this stretch of coastline. I've found the opposite to be true. While areas of heavy congestion can certainly be found on the mid-Atlantic waterways, there are many avid paddlers on the east coast, and many convenient access points in the tidal waterways have been established as a result.

In addition, many local kayaking organizations throughout the region have developed kayaking trails and have been instrumental in lobbying for the protection of natural areas and wildlife habitat. As such, many excellent resources are available to paddlers in the mid-Atlantic and visitors can often join local paddling clubs for outings.

Designating the "best" kayaking trips in the mid-Atlantic is a tricky business. One paddler's ideal route could be considered boring by another and too advanced for a third. I wish I could boast that I have personally paddled the entire 10,528 miles of tidal shoreline in the region—if you have, I'll gladly turn the reins over to you—but I have completed extensive research to come up with 40 routes that offer something unique. So what locations made the final cut? I selected places that would appeal to a broad range of paddlers. There are some city routes, some isolated wilderness routes, and many routes that fall somewhere in between. Some of the features I assessed include the scenery, accessibility, wildlife, and unique history surrounding a location. I also did my best to balance open water routes with protected shorelines, since we all have our own idea of what constitutes an ideal paddle. I also included a mix of point-to-point routes and round-trip routes.

For many locations, I've included several routes, offering options of both differing lengths and differing difficulty levels. This was done to allow for a wide variety of skill levels and weather conditions, while also taking into consideration just plain how much time you have to paddle on a particular day.

One thing all the routes have in common is that the launch site is easy to find and easy to use. Good public access is important, especially when traveling to a place for the first time. You want to be able to launch easily and know that your vehicle will be waiting for you when you return.

I hope you get as much enjoyment out of reading this book and paddling the routes detailed in it as I did writing it. It was truly a pleasure kayaking up and down the beautiful mid-Atlantic coastline, and I will continue to explore new places in this fascinating region.

►HOW TO USE THIS BOOK

Although at first glance this book looks like a solid "roadmap" to paddling the vast mid-Atlantic coastline, in fact it is far from that. There are countless opportunities for exploration and even I, as a lifelong resident and avid paddler, have just scratched the surface of all there is to see along this beautiful and diverse shoreline.

In addition, the routes I've set forth for you are suggestions for where to begin in each area. I don't think I've ever paddled the exact same route in one location twice, and I encourage you to use my suggestions as a starting point for building your own route based on your interests, weather conditions, and most importantly, your skills.

If you are already familiar with parts of the mid-Atlantic coast, you can use the At-a-Glance Trip Planner to refine your options.

While some areas may always be appropriate only for advanced paddlers, there are no locations that are always appropriate for the novice. Too many variables come into play, including but not limited to conditions, tides, weather, your personal skills, skills of those paddling with you, and equipment. Each trip highlights key information to help you evaluate the known elements on the routes.

Where possible, multiple launch sites are listed, but the route described generally leaves from the launch that will be easiest for most people to use. Maps, a compass, and a GPS device are necessary when paddling. When planning your route, keep in mind bailout points, rest stops, and camping areas.

Cautions include particular hazards rather than every potential problem waterways can bring your way. This is where you should look for information about which areas are only suitable for those with strong skills or where wind, currents, and fog are known issues.

Overviews discuss the history of a location and any other information that make it noteworthy. Route descriptions provide details about the paddle trip and one or more suggested itineraries. Where practical, multiple routes of different lengths are provided as options.

If you're looking for a more strenuous day than the suggested routes describe or need to adapt to difficult conditions, feel free to lengthen or shorten your route.

▶ TRIP PLANNING AND SAFETY

This book is not intended to be used as a how-to guide for sea kayaking. It assumes no liability for the safety or skill level of the reader and assumes that those embarking on trips referenced in this book take proper safety precautions while kayaking, are comfortable with paddling safety and rescue techniques or are paddling with a professional.

Although every effort was made to ensure that the information contained in this book was correct at press time, the author and publisher do not assume and hereby disclaim any liability to any party for any loss or damage from negligence, accident or any other cause. All forms of exercise pose inherent risk. The author, editors, and publishers advise readers to take full responsibility for their safety and to know their limits. Before sea kayaking, be sure your equipment is well maintained and do not take risks beyond your level of experience, aptitude, training, and fitness. As with any exercise program, yours should be prepared in consultation with a physician or other qualified professional person.

The best and safest trips begin long before you launch your boat. These plans include strategic preparation to determine a route, weather monitoring, the selection of paddling buddies, and the gathering of appropriate gear. Preparation should also include making sure you have enough to eat and drink and that you have warm clothing to change into should you get wet. Often, the most important decision you make is whether or not you want to be on the ocean on a particular day based on all the available information and your ability to plan. It is far better to be on land wishing you were on the water than the reverse.

RISK FACTORS ON THE WATER
Even with the best planning, risk is inherent to sea kayaking. We take a small boat out onto the water, and despite the feeling that our boats turn us into amphibious creatures, we rely on our boat, gear, and ability to return us safely to dry land.

Risk can be a good thing in moderation. It gives us that tingle in our nerves that makes us feel alive and reminds us of what we have to lose; it also keeps us alert and vigilant to danger. But the bottom line is we want to live to paddle another day, so we accept that risk is inevitable and learn how to manage it.

Before you head out, consider the following risk factors for your trip.

Wind Everyone has a different definition of acceptable wind speeds for paddling, and wind interacts with other factors like tide and the availability of sheltered areas to change the experience of a paddle. Novice paddlers should have little or no difficulty in winds under five knots. Winds up to 10 knots are generally still accept-able for most paddlers, but novices may get frustrated as boats become harder to control. From 10 to 15 knots, a little more skill is necessary, while winds over 15 knots can become hazardous. Going into the wind tends to reduce paddling speed by about a knot for every 10 knots of wind.

The easiest way to mitigate the effects of wind is to avoid it. Launch only after you've checked the weather forecast, and monitor conditions as your trip progresses. In the summer, winds are often strongest in the afternoon and pop-up thunder-storms are common throughout the region. Plan alternate routes that take advantage of sheltered areas you can default to if conditions deteriorate. Always be careful of heading downwind if you ultimately have to turn around and paddle into it on your way back.

Waves and Swell Waves bounce back when they hit a steep shoreline, creating a confused state called clapotis, which can be quite challenging to negotiate. Avoid this hazard by paddling farther from shore, where the swells tend to be more orga-nized and are less likely to break.

While waves are wind-dependent, swells march across the ocean—sometimes for thousands of miles—on their own accord. While they tend not to be as steep as waves, a steeper incline creates steep, dumping waves. When studying a chart be-fore an excursion, look for areas with submerged rocks or ledges exposed to incom-ing swell. If the swell happens to hit a rock or a ledge, it may rise abruptly and break just as abruptly, expending its stored energy onto the obstruction, which could be devastating to a kayak. As you paddle, watch for texture in the water surface that might indicate submerged obstacles and remember that there's always a bigger wave out there.

Be aware that the forecast and buoy measurements are for "significant wave height" (the average height of the highest one-third of the waves) in open ocean. When those open-ocean waves roll into more shallow water, such as near beaches and ledges, they will grow even higher. Conversely, protected areas will have smaller waves than the forecast or buoy readings.

Tidal Current Be aware of the tidal current movement on your route and predict places where it may create hazards. Plan ahead, not only to use current to your ad-vantage, but to negotiate potentially rough areas at slack tides. Tidal rips are some-times identified on charts, but most are not. You will need to develop a sense of where tidal currents will accelerate, anticipate the possibility, and be observant as you paddle.

When crossing open stretches of water, monitor tidal draft and watch for telltale signs of strong current, like submerged buoys.

When wind opposes tidal current, the friction on the water surface steepens waves. When wind and current move in the same direction, waves may be dimin-ished, but a dramatic change may occur as quickly as the tide changes.

When paddling in an inlet, estuary, or a gap between islands, know that the water in the middle of a channel is the fastest moving, with slower water near the edges. Eddies may also form along the edges, spiraling back against the current. Use these to paddle against prevailing current or as a respite from conditions in the main current. In some cases, however, eddies may create rough conditions of their own as the two opposing currents collide.

The National Oceanic and Atmospheric Administration (NOAA) maintains tide stations and creates computer-generated tide calculators for just about anywhere you need them. They also generate current stations in the more obvious places where currents increase. The NOAA website has tide and tidal current predictions. Weather radios broadcast times and heights for high and low tides, and phone apps are also available.

Lightning There are no safe places on the water when lightning is near. If you can hear thunder, you are within striking distance. The most effective way to mitigate lightning risk is pure avoidance. Monitor weather forecasts and if possible, watch the weather radar on your cell phone. As you paddle, keep an eye out for the tall, billowing, anvil-shaped cumulonimbus clouds that produce thunderstorms.

If you do hear thunder, get off the water—period.

Once on land, if you cannot find shelter in an enclosed building or vehicle, avoid open areas and seek low, rolling terrain. Avoid caves or rocky overhangs where lightning may arc across the gap. When risk is higher, perch on a foam pad or a life jacket, assuming "the lightning position" by squatting, feet together, arms wrapped around your legs, and eyes closed. Space group members at least 50 feet apart to reduce the chance of multiple injuries.

Hypothermia If you paddle during the summer in the mid-Atlantic, you'll likely be much more susceptible to heat stroke than hypothermia, but never underestimate the dangers of cold water or even cool water.

Preparedness, constant attentiveness, and some background knowledge are your best defenses against hypothermia. Often enough, hypothermia is subtle and goes unnoticed until the victim starts showing more advanced symptoms.

Symptoms of moderate hypothermia include shivering, impaired speech and movement, lowered body temperature, and drowsiness. Be on the lookout for the "umbles": stumbles, mumbles, and bumbles. This amounts to the loss of agility, an inability to speak clearly, difficulty with knots and zippers, and similar issues that indicate a loss of control over normal muscular and mental faculties.

A victim should be given dry clothing and placed in a sleeping bag or blanket, if available, then given quick-energy food and something warm (not hot) to drink.

To prevent hypothermia, dress for the water. For water in the mid-50s Fahrenheit or lower, this usually means wearing a wetsuit or drysuit. In midsummer, when mid-Atlantic temperatures are hot and the air is humid and you can reliably get back into your boat quickly, you should wear something lighter (you don't want to overheat). In cool weather, have extra hats and gloves in a dry bag where you can reach them from the cockpit. A loose fitting outer layer that goes over a life jacket can quickly help a chilled paddler. Keep snacks and water easily available as well since fuel helps your body stay warm.

The biggest way to keep hypothermia at bay is to avoid prolonged exposure to cold water. While 60-degree air might feel comfortable, 60-degree water rapidly cools your body temperature. Learn to roll your kayak and self-rescue techniques. You should be able to reliably get out of the water in less than two minutes.

Cold Shock A capsize in cold water presents the risk of cold shock and can produce a gasp reflex that could lead to drowning. Sudden immersion in cold water increases blood pressure, heart rate, and adrenaline levels, which could lead to cardiac arrest. There is no reliable way to prevent this, but wearing warm enough clothing is a good start.

Wildlife On the water there are few wildlife hazards. Sharks are becoming a more common visitor to the mid-Atlantic coastline, including great white sharks. Sightings do happen, but they are not a common occurrence. A more common hazard is jellyfish stings. They are always a possibility, especially in warm water.

On land it is very common to see snakes around the launch areas and on shallow water. Most of the snakes in this region are not poisonous. However, the Copperhead (entire region) and Cottonmouth (southern Virginia only) can be found and the latter can be aggressive.

ON-SHORE HAZARDS

For most, driving to and from the launch is probably more risky than anything you'll encounter while launching, but it's easy to overlook on-shore hazards when we're out paddling. Following is a high-level list of dangers to be aware of:

- ▶ Falling on slippery rocks or ramps
- ▶ Leaving your boat too close to the tide line at low tide
- ▶ Poison ivy
- ▶ Ticks
- ▶ Bee stings
- ▶ Sunburn (on the water, too)
- ▶ Snakes
- ▶ Bears

BAILOUTS, DIFFICULT LANDINGS, AND ESCAPE ROUTES

When planning a trip, be wary of areas with limited landing spots and be aware that conditions may make some landing areas difficult or dangerous to access. Identify possible landing areas on your chart, map, or GPS device before setting out. The ability to land in some areas is dependent on the abilities of the least skilled member of your paddling group. Be wary of trips that commit you to an area that might make it difficult to retrace your route in the event you cannot continue forward into hazardous conditions. It helps to have an alternate route in mind.

COLLISION AVOIDANCE

The prospect of being struck by a larger boat is a real hazard in most coastal kayaking locations. Avoidance is the most likely way to control this risk. Increasing your visibility to larger boats is also a good idea, but not a foolproof one.

The first rule of collision avoidance is to assume that no one can see you.

Kayaks ride low in the water, sometimes disappearing behind small waves, so we don't usually appear on radar. We also become even less visible when weather or even sunshine reduces visibility. Also take into account that captains of larger vessels have numerous distractions to deal with and they often can't see over the bow of their own boat. Right of way is completely irrelevant when you see a boat bearing down on you. Always defer to the "law of gross tonnage" and let the larger boat have its course.

The second rule is to just plan to avoid the path of larger boats. Minimize the time you spend in boat channels, understand the routes larger boats will likely take, and paddle in shallow areas if there is any doubt.

In marked channels, make sure to visually line up buoys to understand the channel location and cross at a right angle. In channels or open areas, kayaks should maintain a tight formation to give larger boats plenty of operating space. Don't spread your group out all over the water; remember: There is safety in numbers and this very much applies to kayaking.

To determine if you are on a collision course with a vessel, note the angle it makes on your bow and watch to see if that angle changes. If the boat moves forward of that angle, it will pass ahead of you; if it drops behind that angle, you will pass ahead of it. If the angle does not change, you are on a collision course and need to adjust your heading.

STAY IN TOUCH

Leave a written float plan with someone on shore before you launch. This plan should include details about group members, itinerary, specifics about when you will check in and expected time of return, and clear instructions to call the Coast Guard for help should you fail to check in or return when expected.

Many paddlers now use cell phones on overnight trips to check in with someone at home. It's a great idea, but be sure to leave specific instructions about what to do if you fail to check in, keeping in mind that you might not have cell service everywhere you go. If the plan is to check in, don't fail to do so unless you want to be rescued. If you get stuck at your check-in time without cell service, contact the Coast Guard on your Very High Frequency Radio (VHF) to relay a message home.

INCIDENTS ON THE WATER

Accidents happen and sometimes things go wrong. Coming through a kayaking accident in the best shape possible begins before you launch. Be sure you bring appropriate safety, first aid, and boat repair equipment with you and practice rescue skills regularly. If you are paddling with a group, hold a pre-trip briefing or discussion to clarify protocol for different scenarios such as capsizing or getting separated. Also establish a channel for VHF communication between group members other than channel 16 (which is for distress and hailing only).

Making a Distress Call Keep in mind that many islands and geographic features have duplicate names. Thus, latitude and longitude is the best way to communicate your location. The Coast Guard would rather be called and decide they aren't needed than learn about an incident late in the day, making their job more difficult. If you call for help on the radio and do not receive a response it is possible that the Coast Guard heard your call, either directly or through other boaters' relays.

You can call for help on your cell phone if you have a signal and the appropriate number.

GROUP PADDLING

The need for leadership skills can sneak up on you; one day you're the inexperienced paddler in the group, counting on others for guidance, and soon enough you may realize that people are looking to you to ensure their safety. This is certainly the case if you learn to paddle and then take your family out for a trip. To be an effective leader, you need to have solid enough personal skills to be able to focus your attention on your group members rather than yourself.

Small groups of similarly-skilled, self-sufficient paddlers may decide each member is equally responsible for all group decisions. This may work with the right group, but there is a fine line between "everybody is responsible" and "no one is responsible." If everyone is truly dependent on no one else and with no expectations from the group, it makes perfect sense. If this is not the case, an effort to reach consensus about an important decision may undermine quick and efficient action. If you happen to be one of the more experienced members of the group, you may feel powerless to establish a safe and manageable routine, and if things get out of hand, no matter what anyone says about shared responsibility, it will still be your problem.

Another approach is to choose a leader. Among small groups of two to three paddlers with similar skills, a loose, "co-leader" approach may work, but as the group gets larger, it will operate most effectively with one designated leader. Before you head out, know your fellow paddlers' preferences and your own comfort level with the leadership style to which you all agree.

On the water, it can be a challenge to keep the group together. Occasionally groups spread over large distances, faster paddlers getting way ahead while others dawdle behind. There are times—perhaps while following a shoreline—where getting spread apart has low consequences, and might even be preferable. Most of the time though, sticking together makes the most sense. In open water or in channels, a tight group makes for a "smaller target" for powerboats and doesn't block channels. Ideally, your group should paddle close enough together to easily communicate without shouting.

SELF-SUFFICIENCY

While not everyone should paddle alone, having the ability to do so greatly increases your safety and confidence in every paddling experience. If you become separated from your group but were relying on others for skills or equipment, you're no better off than if you had launched solo. If you do choose to rely on others, crucial questions ensue. Is the person you are relying on truly self-sufficient, or is he or she also relying on you? If that person is not hired as your guide or instructor, is he or she aware of your dependence?

For many, a sense of autonomy is an attraction of sea kayaking. You can carry in your boat everything you might need for a long journey and you can carry within yourself the knowledge and skills to make such a journey possible. Unlike larger boats, the sea kayak is most often designed for one person, small enough to be portable and big enough to allow the paddler to pack along the essentials.

Becoming a self-sufficient paddler, though, takes more than a well-packed boat; it is a gradual process of learning through formal instruction and through picking up bits and pieces of information, advice, and gear from friends and fellow paddlers. Those most able to paddle alone—by choice or chance—are those who realize that preparation and skill are always more reliable than luck.

Paddling alone can be quite different from sharing the experience with others. Stretches of ocean that might otherwise be dominated by talk turn quiet. There's no one to speed ahead or lag behind and you may alter your pace at will. By setting your own pace, you may be more attuned to sounds and smells and the subtle information coming to you in the feel of the water through your hull. Without the distraction of other people, you're more likely to notice the environment around you. Group dynamics are greatly simplified when you have only yourself to manage and decisions are yours alone. With only yourself to rely upon, you should give risks more thought, asking yourself "what would I do if?"

Solo paddling isn't for everyone, even for those who have become truly self-sufficient. You may not be comfortable with the risks you assume alone on the ocean. You may prefer the company of others, no matter the weather or the route.

If you do choose to paddle alone, plan every element of your excursion with extra care and plan to be off the water long before dark. Always leave a detailed float plan with someone on shore and prepare yourself well with navigation tools including charts, a compass, and GPS. Also bring emergency gear, bail-out plans, and a method for calling for help if you need it.

BASIC VHF PROTOCOL

At first, using the Very High Frequency Radio (VHF) may seem a bit mysterious, with unfamiliar etiquette and language. Add to that the notion that anyone could be listening, including the Coast Guard, and you could be easily intimidated by talking into this little device. But with practice, talking on the VHF may come as easily as using the phone, but there is protocol to be followed:

▶ Only use channel 16 for hailing and emergencies. Any talk on channel 16 should be brief; if needed, switch to a different channel.

▶ Before pressing the transmit button to speak, listen and make sure the channel is free. After transmitting, wait a reasonable period for a response since you won't be able to hear a response if you are trying to transmit again.

▶ Engage the transmit button for a moment before you speak. Speak clearly, making an effort to enunciate each word. Say "over" when you are done speaking and then disengage the transmit button

▶ Keep calls brief, with no unnecessary talk.

Aside from general communication, there are three types of calls you need to know how to make on channel 16:

▶ **The Sécurité call** (pronounced "say-CUR-i-tay") is used to advise other vessels of your presence. Most commonly, paddlers use a Sécurité call before crossing a channel in the fog. To properly make the call, say "Sécurité, Sécurité, Sécurité," then identify your group by the leader's name, give your location, and state the reason for your call (such as you are about to make a crossing of a particular channel and the expected time it will take you to cross). Then state "Standing by on one-six. Over." Wait to hear a response before you cross.

▶ **The Pan-Pan call** (pronounced "pahn-pahn") is used to alert other vessels of an urgent situation regarding the safety of a vessel or person so they can avoid interfering. This might be used to request medical help, if a kayaker flips his/her boat but is in the process of recovering, or if danger is not as imminent as that of a Mayday call. The correct usage of the call is three "Pan-Pans" followed by the name of the intended recipient (this could be a particular Coast Guard station or simply, "all stations"), followed by the identification of the vessel (kayak), its position, the nature of the issue, and the type of assistance required (if any).

▶ **The Mayday call** is a call for help in case of imminent danger that could result in loss of life or vessel. To make this call, state "Mayday, Mayday, Mayday, all stations." Then identify your group by the leader's name and state the emergency and your location. Then identify how many people are in your group and specifics about the person in need (age and specific condition). Then state, "Standing by on one-six. Over."

Check the batteries on your VHF before you leave by pressing the transmit button to see if the battery level drops. Listen to others on the radio to become familiar with radio etiquette.

EDUCATION

On the water, you must always be attentive to numerous details such as zipping your life jacket, making sure grab loops are outside your sprayskirt, your hatch covers are properly closed, and you are warm. No detail is too small to be given consideration. In addition, you need to be acutely aware of your surroundings. This includes monitoring boat traffic, watching the weather, and knowing what the tides and currents are doing and where they want to take you.

Unfortunately, it is impossible to gain wisdom from reading a book, and good paddling skills are not acquired quickly. Most sea kayakers gradually gain perspective by paddling with more experienced peers and getting guidance from qualified instructors. Too often, paddlers overrate their abilities and as such find themselves in uncomfortable or even threatening situations.

While these early sections offer a foundational review of kayaking best-practices and technique, if you are new to sea kayaking seek out hands-on experience through trusted sources. The good news is that the mid-Atlantic offers many opportunities to learn to paddle. The guidance of a good coach will help you ascend the learning curve more quickly and more importantly, safely. Pool sessions are also an excellent way to learn safety skills, especially when repeated throughout the off-season.

▶ EQUIPMENT

The correct gear is required to be safe and self-sufficient on the water. There isn't one equipment list that is right for each paddling itinerary, environment, or weather condition, but the following equipment is generally necessary for a safe paddle.

PERSONAL EQUIPMENT
Every paddler should be equipped with this gear, even when paddling with a group.

Kayak For most of the destinations covered in this book, a touring sea kayak is most appropriate, but there is no perfect boat for all areas and conditions. If you have not yet purchased your kayak, it's easy to be overwhelmed by the vast variety of boats on the market. Don't be. This is the fun part.

Start by trying out as many as you can and see what feels the most comfortable. Some kayak stores offer demo days or the opportunity to try out boats before you purchase them.

Consider each kayak's shape, dimensions, and cargo space. Generally speaking, the longer and more narrow the boat, the faster and more unstable it will be. Shorter, wider boats are the most stable, but you will give up performance and speed in trade.

Consult other paddlers and instructors for advice and talk to experts at your local shop for suggestions for boats that meet your needs. As someone who owns more than a dozen kayaks, I can definitively say that no two are alike and no two handle the same. The most important factor in purchasing the right boat is whether or not you're comfortable in it. Remember, a 10-minute paddle at a store may feel different than a three-hour paddle fully loaded, so if there are any red flags of discomfort, take them seriously.

Paddle Most kayakers have a personal attachment to their paddles. They've spent hours holding them and they feel the most comfortable with them in hand. The bottom line is, a paddle is only as effective as your stroke, but weight and design do play a factor.

Good paddles are worth the money. Generally speaking, the lighter the paddle, the better. Look for a good carbon paddle if that fits within your budget and consult an expert in your local kayak shop to help select the correct length for you and your boat.

Personal Flotation Device (PFD) A properly fitting life jacket is extremely important and should not be skimped on. It could, quite literally, save your life. Be sure to purchase a Coast Guard-approved type III or V life jacket with multiple adjustment points. The jacket should fit snugly so it doesn't ride up when in the water.

Remember, life jackets don't do anything for you if they aren't on you. Wear your life jacket rather than tucking it behind your seat or under your deck bungies. According to the Coast Guard, less than 10 percent of people who drown in boating accidents are wearing life jackets.

Spray Skirt Spray skirts are designed to keep water out of your cockpit. This could be water from breaking waves, paddle drips, or even rain. This is especially important in cold weather and rough water (at any temperature). Be certain that the grab loop is positioned at the front of the skirt, is outside the boat, and is within easy reach should you need to exit your boat. Tight neoprene spray skirts are more water-resistant but can be difficult to remove, while looser-fitting nylon skirts are easiest to remove but aren't as water-resistant.

Tow Systems Short, quick tows are sometimes needed to help a fellow kayaker out of danger, while longer tows are at times necessary to help an injured or otherwise incapacitated paddler.

Tow belts are the most common tow system for touring paddlers. They consist of a pouch worn around the paddler's waist that has a quick release buckle. A floating tow-line with a clip on the end is located inside the pouch.

Lights I don't recommend paddling at night, but you should be prepared in case of an unforeseen delay on your route. The Coast Guard requires kayakers to have a light and three flares on board after dark. A waterproof headlamp and bright LED lights that mount to your kayak's deck with suction cups are good options. Lights that clip to your life jacket are good to have in an emergency so you can be seen in the water.

Water and Food Always bring water and food along when paddling. How much you bring will depend on the length of your trip and how hot it is. The general rule is to bring one gallon of water per person per day. This is a good start. You will need more water than you think. As for food, be sure to bring more than you anticipate you will need during your trip. You can burn calories quickly while paddling, especially if it's cold or the conditions are challenging.

Other Personal Gear A bilge pump and sponge are a must for emptying water from your boat. Also bring a paddle float so you can use your paddle as an outrigger in the event you capsize and need to reenter the boat from the water if other rescue techniques fail.

CLOTHING
The clothing you bring along will vary greatly for each paddle, depending on the air temperature, water temperature and length of your trip. The best advice is to bring

clothing for all possible conditions. It's usually better to be a little warm than not warm enough. Also take into account the strength of the sun and wear protective clothing if necessary. Dress in layers and remember that conditions on the water in the summer in the mid-Atlantic can be very hot (with no shade). Try to avoid wearing cotton and select quick-drying fabrics.

NAVIGATION

A chart and compass and the skills to use them are essential before heading out for a paddle. Even if you know an area well, you might need a chart to find a bearing and a compass to stay on a straight line if it suddenly becomes foggy or night falls before you reach your destination. A baseplate compass is versatile enough to help find bearings on your chart and to reference while following a bearing. A deck compass makes it easier to follow a bearing.

GPS units should not be considered replacements for non-electronic navigation tools and skills. They are certainly nice to have, but batteries can run out and electronics can fail. If you carry a GPS unit, do so in addition to a chart and compass.

COMMUNICATION

A cell phone and a VHF (Very High Frequency) radio are the two most basic communication tools, each with its own benefits and limitations, but having both makes it likely that you'll be able to summon help should you need it.

Invest in a waterproof container or case to protect your cell phone on the water. Cell phones do not work everywhere, but coverage in the mid-Atlantic is fairly consistent. In addition to making calls and texting, many phones have GPS units, can track weather and tides, and perform other useful functions.

Handheld, waterproof VHFs are necessary. If you call for help on Channel 16 on a VHF radio, odds are good that the Coast Guard will hear and respond, but closer boaters may also hear it and respond first. The signal is limited, but the Coast Guard uses repeater towers along the coast, so they will probably hear your call. In addition, the VHF may be used to communicate within a group and to access NOAA weather channels.

It may seem simple, but it's also important to wear a loud whistle on your life jacket. This can help get the attention of those paddling with you and will carry much farther than your voice.

You can also get attention and summon rescuers to your position with small pencil flares that can be carried in a life jacket. Other tools to direct rescuers to your location include hand flares, signaling mirrors, sea dye, strobes, and reflective tape.

FIRST AID

More important than any equipment, first aid training will prepare you for mishaps. Basic first aid is a start, while a two-day Wilderness First Aid course will cover most of the situations likely to occur on the water. This training needs to be updated at regular intervals.

At a minimum, carry a first aid kit in your day hatch with all the essentials, including adhesive bandages, gauze, tape, sunscreen, nonprescription pain relievers, moleskin, and any needed personal prescription medications.

REPAIR KIT

A small repair kit can go a long way if your boat gets damaged. It should contain electrical tape, duct tape (formulated to adhere while wet), epoxy putty, a fiberglass repair kit (for longer trips with fiberglass boats), a large flotation bag (in case compartments are compromised), and tools to fix a skeg or rudder.

▶STEWARDSHIP AND CONSERVATION

Kayakers in the mid-Atlantic are fortunate to have hundreds of miles of beautiful coastline to explore with easy access to the water in many areas. Through the hard efforts of conservation organizations, state parks, and local volunteers, there are many places in our region with mapped kayak trails and public launch sites.

Like all people who enjoy the outdoors, sea kayakers should be respectful of the privilege to enjoy protected outdoor spaces and do our part to take care of them. This could be as simple as picking up any trash you find while paddling, to organizing public clean-up events. In addition, always park in legitimate parking spots, obtain any needed launch permits, and be courteous to local residents and watermen.

LEAVE NO TRACE

The Appalachian Mountain Club (AMC) is a national edu-cational partner of Leave No Trace, a nonprofit organization dedicated to promoting and inspiring responsible outdoor recreation through education, research, and partnerships. The Leave No Trace program seeks to develop wildland eth-ics—ways in which people think and act in the outdoors to minimize their impact on the areas they visit and to protect our natural resources for future enjoyment. Leave No Trace unites four federal land management agencies—the U.S. Forest Service, National Park Service, Bureau of Land Management, and U.S. Fish and Wildlife Service—with manufacturers, outdoor retailers, user groups, educators, or-ganizations such as AMC, and individuals.

The Leave No Trace ethic is guided by the following seven principles:

1. **Plan Ahead and Prepare.** Know about public access, campsite limitations, and areas that are closed for seabird nesting. Small groups have less impact on re-sources and on the experiences of other visitors.

2. **Travel and Camp on Durable Surfaces.** Many islands are vegetated thanks to a thin layer of soil that collected there over many years, despite the forces of wind and water working to erode it. Stepping on plants can kill them and compact the soil beneath, rendering it lifeless. Dunes are similarly fragile, held together by grasses that could easily be killed by human impact. Whenever possible, walk on durable surfaces such as granite ledges and cobble beaches. Follow established trails and camp in established sites. Good campsites are found, not made.

3. **Dispose of Waste Properly.** Pack it in, pack it out. Inspect your camp for trash or food scraps, even small bits of biodegradable waste. Leave your site cleaner

than you found it. Cook in the intertidal zone if possible, or on a ledge if not. Soap is usually unnecessary to clean, which can be done with hot water and a handful of sand to scour pots. Urinate below high tide line and pack out solid human waste and all toilet paper. It is illegal to dump it in the ocean, and the "cat hole" method favored by backpackers doesn't work on a small island with little soil. Commercially available systems make packing out human waste easy, but any method of securing the waste and removing it from islands and the water is acceptable.

4. **Leave What You Find.** Cultural or historical artifacts, and natural objects such as shells, rocks, and plants, should be left as found.

5. **Kindle No Fires or Minimize Campfire Impact.** Cook on a stove. Use established fire rings, fire pans, or mound fires. Aside from the threat of wildfires, campfires scar rocks and other features, leaving charred remains. Always check island regulations—whether it's private or public—before building a fire. If you build a campfire, keep it small, burn driftwood but not downed wood or wood from elsewhere, and build it in the intertidal zone. Allow a fire to burn down to the smallest coals and scatter them below the high tide line when fully extinguished. If possible, pack out the remains.

6. **Respect Wildlife.** Observe wildlife from a distance, paddling quietly and using binoculars. Extra care should be taken near seals. Feeding animals alters their natural behavior. Store your rations and trash securely. Adhere to warnings— posted on islands, near the shore, or online—about nesting birds in season, roughly April 1 through August 31.

7. **Be Considerate of Others.** Be courteous, respect the quality of other visitors' experiences, and let nature's sounds prevail. Share boat ramps and launches graciously. Store boats and other gear inconspicuously. Use the smallest campsites available in case a larger group arrives.

AMC is a national provider of the Leave No Trace Master Educator course. AMC offers this five-day course, designed especially for outdoor professionals and land managers, and the shorter two-day Leave No Trace Trainer course. For Leave No Trace information contact the Leave No Trace Center for Outdoor Ethics, 800-332-4100 or 302-442-8222; lnt.org. For a schedule of AMC Leave No Trace courses, see outdoors.org/education/lnt.

NEW YORK

The New York coastline may seem like an unlikely place to find good kayaking. When you look at a map, only the southeastern tip of the state, around New York City and Long Island, border the Atlantic. This busy area may not look inviting at first, but the contrary is true. There are 127 miles of coastline in New York, and you can find numerous great places for a few hours of relaxing fun or full-day outings.

There is a large network of kayakers in and around New York City. In fact, the city is so kayak-friendly that there is even an organization called The Downtown Boathouse (downtownboathouse.org) that offers two places (Pier 26 and Governor's Island) where the public can borrow kayaks and paddle for 20 minutes at a time for free. The Downtown Boathouse is run by volunteers and is dedicated to offering free public access to the New York City harbor for recreational use.

New York City Water Trail (see Trip 2) is also a labor of love from local kayak enthusiasts. This system of 160 square miles of ocean, inlets, bays, creeks, and rivers runs through the five boroughs and provides many opportunities for paddling. The scenery varies from city skyline panoramas to tranquil tidal marshlands.

A New York City Parks permit is required to launch in many parks in and around the city (including Pelham Bay Park). Permits are valid for one season and can be used to launch at all city-owned kayak and canoe launches. They cost $15 and can be purchased in person at one of the New York City Department of Parks and Recreation permit offices (located in the Bronx, Brooklyn, Manhattan, Queens, and Staten Island), or they can be purchased by mail. Applications can be downloaded at nycgovparks.org.

1

PELHAM BAY PARK TO NEW ROCHELLE

Paddle past islands, along shorelines, and through lagoons for beautiful views of Long Island Sound.

Distance ▶	7.0 nautical miles
Cautions ▶	On windy days, the waters in the area around Spindle Rock can be rough. At low tide, some places can be rocky. Boat wakes can make for challenging paddling in the Sound.
Charts and Maps ▶	NOAA Electronic Charts US5NY15M and US5NY16M / Paper Chart #12364

LAUNCH

Pelham Bay Park, the Bronx The launch is located off Park Drive near the exit in the back left (northwest) corner of the parking lot (on the opposite side of the lot from the beach). From I-95 North, take Exit 8A in New York. Follow signs to Orchard Beach. As you approach the entry gates (before turning right to the gate), the launch is straight ahead. *GPS coordinates: 40° 52.343′ N, 73° 47.845′ W.*

ROUTE DESCRIPTION

Pelham Bay Park is a primary feature in the Bronx. It is New York City's largest park and is more than three times bigger than Central Park in Manhattan. Most people know Pelham Bay Park for its gorgeous Long Island Sound shoreline and popular Orchard Beach. Others come to play golf on two courses or to use the playgrounds, bridle paths, and ball fields. What some people don't know is that Pelham Bay Park is a favorite among the local paddling crowd. It offers a scenic launch on a protected lagoon with easy access to Long Island Sound. It is also home to a diverse population of animals and plants. This is a lovely urban paddling route that offers a great variety of water conditions and scenery.

A New York City Parks permit is required to launch at Pelham Bay Park. The permit is good for one season and can be used to launch at all city kayak and canoe launch facilities. The permit can be purchased by mail or in person at one of the City of New York Parks and Recreation permit offices in the Bronx, Brooklyn, Manhattan,

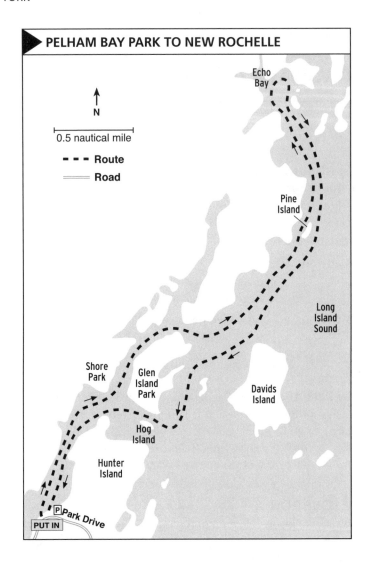

PELHAM BAY PARK TO NEW ROCHELLE

Echo
Bay

N

0.5 nautical mile

- - - Route
===== Road

Pine
Island

Long
Island
Sound

Shore
Park

Glen
Island
Park

Davids
Island

Hog
Island

Hunter
Island

P Park Drive

PUT IN

Queens, and Staten Island. Applications can be downloaded at nycgovparks.org. The cost is $15 per permit.

There is a huge parking lot for the beach, and you will have to pay to park between Memorial Day and Labor Day, but it's free to park in the off season. There are no bathroom facilities near the kayak launch, but there is a large public restroom complex at the beach.

You can unload your kayak near the ramp before parking. There are signs regarding use of the ramp and a park bench located in front of a short path that leads to the ramp. Make sure you have your permit with you when you launch.

You'll likely share the ramp with other kayakers, rowers, stand-up paddle-boarders, and people fishing. It's a popular spot, yet once you launch and slip into the protected waters of the lagoon, you'll feel like you're in a remote area. The water may be very low at low tide, but you can follow the lagoon to the left a short distance to explore the marsh. This area is perfect for beginner paddlers to learn boat-handling skills and become comfortable on the water. Once you've had your fill of the salt water marsh shoreline, turn around and head north toward the mouth of the lagoon.

Hunter Island will soon be on your right. You may not notice you've reached Hunter Island, because it isn't actually an island. Originally, it was part of a group of islands located in the western portion of Long Island Sound called the Pelham Islands. They were named for their owner, Thomas Pell, Lord of Pelham Manor (who, among other accomplishments, founded the town of Westchester). Hunter Island was purchased in 1804 by a politician and businessman named John Hunter, who built a magnificent mansion on the island. His home was said to have original artwork by Rembrandt, Rubens, Raphael, and Van Dyke. After Hunter's death in 1852, New York City purchased the island. In 1937, the city filled LeRoy's Bay while constructing Orchard Beach and connected the island to Twin Island and Rodman's Neck to form part of Pelham Bay Park. Adjacent land had already been designated as parkland in 1888, but the newly created shoreline brought a 1.0-mile crescent-shaped beach and many of today's amenities to the park. Today, Hunter Island is a marine zoology and geology sanctuary and has a large forest of white, red, and black oak.

Just past Hunter Island is the first of two inlets to Long Island Sound. In the middle of the inlet you'll see Hog Island. This small park was once an area where American Indians raised pigs that were originally introduced by Europeans and left behind as a feral population. The island is only a fraction of the size it was at that time, since a Category 2 hurricane that made landfall on the New York coast in 1893 took out much of the island.

Skip the inlet for now and paddle straight into the narrow passage between Glen Island Park (on your right) and Shore Park (on your left). A few beautiful homes line the left shore prior to Shore Park, and just after the park you'll pass by the New York Athletic Club—the large white mansion with the red roof. A large marina dominates the left shoreline, and the area is very busy during the summer season.

As you paddle past Glen Island Park you'll likely see many people fishing, walking, and otherwise enjoying themselves in this popular park. At 105 acres, it covers the entire island and borders Long Island Sound. It is the second most popular park in the county park system and was originally a private summer resort. The resort consisted of a handful of islands that have since been connected with fill. Remains of the resort include castles you can see from the water, cannons, sculptures, and round towers. The castles were constructed in the late nineteenth century and were used as a German restaurant and beer garden.

Glen Island Park is connected to the mainland in New Rochelle by a drawbridge that was built in the 1920s. As you pass under the bridge, you'll see the second inlet to Long Island Sound. If you continue straight you'll paddle into New Rochelle Harbor, but you'll have to turn around shortly thereafter as there is no outlet to the Sound. Turn right instead, and if weather conditions permit, paddle through the inlet (Beckwith Point will be on your left) toward Long Island Sound.

As you make the turn, you'll notice numerous rock outcrops. Be very careful, especially at low tide, and stay to the right of the large rock, called Spindle Rock. On windy days, the water will be noticeably rougher than it was in the protected waters of the harbor. There will also likely be a lot of boat wakes to contend with. If you are skilled enough to handle the conditions, proceed north along the shoreline.

The paddle up the shoreline can be quite beautiful. Numerous islands dot the Sound and interesting houses line the waterfront. Less than 1.0 mile up the shoreline is Davenport Park. This pretty 20-acre park juts outs out into the Sound and provides wonderful views of the water. It is a recreation area with a Shakespeare garden.

Continue paddling, and in less than 0.5 mile you'll pass Pine Island. The island has an older home on it and a rocky shoreline. It provides a bit of protection from wind and waves and is a good place to make any needed equipment adjustments.

Cormorants at the inlet to Long Island Sound.

As you continue up the coast, the shore will make a turn to the left and lovely Echo Bay will come into view. Paddle through the bay and around its northern point. Just beyond the bay is the entrance to the protected harbor in New Rochelle. There are a handful of islands (many of them parks) around the harbor that make for interesting paddling. New Rochelle is the seventh largest city in New York and is known nationally as a pedestrian oriented city. Take some time to paddle around this beautiful area before turning around for the return trip.

As you paddle back to Pelham Bay Park, take the outer route around Glen Island Park and slip back in to the protected lagoon behind Hunter Island, past Hog Island. Look for osprey as you re-enter the calm waters of the lagoon; the area is known for its thriving population of these beautiful birds.

The launch might look a little different when you return. There are rapid tide changes throughout the marsh, but you should be able to enter and exit with your kayak at both high and low tide. The water is very clear, so it's easy to see how deep the water is while you're paddling.

MORE INFORMATION
Pelham Bay Park (nycgovparks.org/parks/pelham-bay-park; 718-430-1891). New York City Department of Parks and Recreation (nycgovparks.org; 212-NEW-YORK). Yearly paddling permits are available from the Department of Parks and Recreation and cost $15.

NEW YORK CITY WATER TRAIL

Most people don't associate New York City with miles of tranquil kayaking and a thriving paddling community. But amidst the blocks of high-rise buildings, traffic, technology, and industry, are hundreds of New Yorkers with a thirst for the outdoors and a passion for kayaking. Out of this motivated community sprouted an idea, a movement, and eventually the development of an extensive water trail system through all five of the city's boroughs.

For more than a century, New York City's vast shoreline has been a foundation for industry and a jumping-off point for commerce. As such, access to the waterfront for recreation was limited. In recent years, however, efforts to re-connect the community to the water and provide easy access to kayaking routes inspired the establishment of new and revitalized parks that offer convenient launches for non-motorized boats. As a result, both novice and advanced paddlers can experience hours of superb kayaking from safe, legal, and easily accessible launch sites that connect 160 square miles of ocean, bays, inlets, rivers and creeks.

New York City Water Trail was first established in 2008 with 28 launch sites. Its creation was made possible through the help of many volunteers who collected and shared data on the featured sites, paddling conditions, facilities, and hazards in each area. The trail now boasts double the original number of sites and is growing all the time. Kayakers can enjoy panoramic views of the city's skyline, waterfowl sanctuaries, tidal marshlands, and even the city's famous harbor.

Efforts to expand the water trail are part of an ongoing movement to make New York a premier waterfront city. It boasts more miles of waterfront than Portland (Oregon), San Francisco, Seattle, and Chicago combined. The success of this movement is dependent on the health of New York Harbor. Fortunately, the city has invested billions of dollars to improve the quality of its waterways and as a result, they are healthier now than they've been in the past hundred years.

The very active New York City Water Trail Association (nycwatertrail.org) is a not-for-profit stewardship group with 20 community non-motorized boating organizations. It provides many resources for the New York City paddling community including trip planning assistance, a calendar of organized events, safety information, and local paddling news.

A $15 permit is required to use the city launches and can be requested by mail or in person at locations in the Bronx, Brooklyn, Manhattan, Queens, and Staten Island. Details can be found at nycgovparks.org.

Printed maps are available, as is an online version that shows launch locations.

2
JAMAICA BAY WILDLIFE REFUGE

Enjoy the national park system's only national wildlife refuge, and check out hundreds of species of birds, right in the heart of New York City.

Distance ▶ 3.5, 5.0, or 10.5 nautical miles

Cautions ▶ If the wind is calm, beginners can enjoy paddling the protected waters of the bay. As with most coastal destinations, if the wind picks up, so can the waves. Be sure to assess the water conditions before you head out to make sure your skill level matches the conditions.

Charts and Maps ▶ NOAA Electronic Chart US5NY50M / Paper Chart #12350

LAUNCHES

Floyd Bennett Field seaplane ramp, Gateway National Recreation Area, Brooklyn Kayakers can launch for free from Floyd Bennett Field at 50 Aviation Road in Brooklyn. From the Belt Parkway, take Exit 11S/Flatbush Avenue south. Follow Flatbush Avenue to the main entrance (on the left side of the road) just before the toll booth. After entering the grounds take the first left onto Aviation Road. Turn right to follow signs to the car-top boat launch. Additional details can be obtained at the Ryan Visitors Center (open daily 9:00 A.M.–4:30 P.M.) or by calling 718-338-3799. There is no launch fee or parking fee. Restrooms are located in the visitor center. *GPS coordinates: 40° 35.748' N, 73° 52.892' W.*

Sebago Canoe Club dock, Paerdegat Basin, Brooklyn An additional seasonal launch site is located at the Sebago Canoe Club dock on Paerdegat Basin. Take the Belt Parkway to Exit 13 (Rockaway Parkway) and turn left onto Avenue M. Turn left onto Paerdegat Avenue North to the gates for the canoe club. Kayakers are welcome to use the launch during open hours at the club between Memorial Day and Labor Day. A NYC Parks permit is required to launch from the club. For more information send an email to contact@sebagocanoeclub.org. *GPS coordinates: 40° 37.584' N, 73° 54.280' W.*

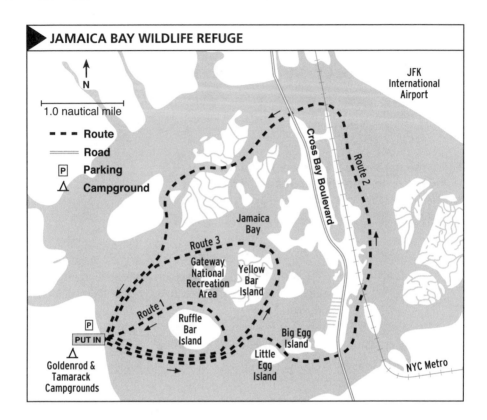

Alternative Launches There are a handful of other public launch sites with parking around the bay at North Channel, Canarsie Pier, Plumb Beach, and Mill Basin Inlet (all in Brooklyn). Free parking and launching is allowed from dawn to dusk at these locations.

ROUTE DESCRIPTION

Jamaica Bay sits on the southwestern side of Long Island in the boroughs of Brooklyn and Queens, and there's a small piece in Nassau County. The bay runs into Lower New York Bay to the west (through Rockaway Inlet) and offers a beautiful natural escape from the city streets.

One of the first things you should know about Jamaica Bay Wildlife Refuge is that it is very large. The bay is nearly 8 miles long and 4.0 miles across. It includes 9,000 acres of beach, islands, marsh, and ponds. Jamaica Bay is part of New York City Water Trail, but unlike most of the other paddling spots on the trail, it provides a much less urban feel. This is partly due to its size and partly because it contains many marshy islands and intertidal flats. As such, it has become a popular spot for the city's paddling crowd.

Jamaica Bay is the only wildlife refuge in the national park system. It's part of the Gateway National Recreation Area, a 26,000-acre area of military sites, city parks, and undeveloped land that extends from Sandy Hook, New Jersey to Jamaica Bay and Breezy Point in New York.

The bay is a saline to brackish estuary and is one of the few remaining sections of the estuarine ecosystem that once thrived in New York City. The shoreline is mostly developed and contains urban residential, commercial, and industrial buildings. The largest feature on the bay is John F. Kennedy International Airport, which sits on its eastern shore. In sharp contrast, you may also see people riding horses on a 3.0-mile stretch of beach that is specifically designed for equestrian use near the Jamaica Bay Riding Academy.

The shoreline along the bay has been repeatedly dredged, filled, and developed. As a result, much of the original wetlands around the bay have been altered or filled in. Even so, the bay offers countless low-lying marsh islands that are great for exploration by kayak and also help control shoreline erosion and provide some level of flood protection to nearby neighborhoods. The original name of the bay was Grassy Bay and the reason for this is evident despite all the shoreline development.

The bay is known for its fantastic bird-watching, and more than 330 species of birds have been recorded there. Thousands of feathered travelers stop in Jamaica Bay every year during their migrations. The area is part of an avian superhighway called the Atlantic Flyway that stretches from the northern Atlantic Coast to South America. Millions of birds migrate on the Atlantic Flyway each year, and more than 500 species have been recorded along it.

Several types of turtles live in the bay, including diamondback terrapins and an endangered species of sea turtle called the Atlantic ridley. Horseshoe crabs and blue crabs are also abundant in the bay, and its waters once supported a thriving fishing industry that had a worldwide reputation for oysters. Unfortunately, although the problem has improved in recent decades, pollution in the bay closed the area to shell fishing in the early part of the twentieth century and remains so today.

Cross Bay Boulevard runs through the bay. It is connected to the mainland and the Seaside Beach area by bridge and runs directly through the largest island on the bay (there is even a large neighborhood on the island).

My personal choice for launching is at Floyd Bennett Field. Floyd Bennett Field was New York City's first municipal airport. It opened in 1931 and launched many record-breaking flights by famous aviators such as Howard Hughes, Wiley Post, and Jacqueline Cochran. The United States Navy took over the airfield in 1942, and it became the busiest airport for military use in the country during World War II. Today, the concrete runways remain a sturdy reminder of the field's heyday and the old seaplane ramp is a great jump-off point for exploring the bay by kayak.

Stop by the beautiful visitor center on your way to the launch. The staff there is exceptionally friendly and helpful. They are happy to share information about the field and the bay, and they can also provide information on kayak tours that are led by the National Park Service. These tours are great for beginner paddlers and offer a chance for prospective kayakers to get their feet wet under the supervision of a guide. They also offer advanced tours for experienced paddlers. With dozens of kayaks in their fleet, the National Park Service is a great resource for paddlers of all abilities.

The visitor center has clean restroom facilities, which I highly recommend over the pit toilets located closer to the launch area.

There are two launch sites in Floyd Bennett Field. One on the northern side on Mill Basin Outlet and one at the old seaplane ramp on the eastern side of the field. I prefer the seaplane launch. This launch provides good access to the many islands on the bay and any number of routes can start and end from this point.

A few words of caution include avoiding the boundary of the Gateway NRA, since a permit is required for paddling in this area. This means you shouldn't paddle near the Rockaway Peninsula (the land mass that borders the bay to the south). To be extra certain, stay to the northeast side of Little Egg Island and pass Subway Island on its northern side. Also, be sure to wear a personal floatation device (yes, wear it—don't just carry it in your boat), and do not enter the salt marshes, which is prohibited.

Floyd Bennett Field visitor center

Around Ruffle Bar Island

A pleasant 3.0- to 4.0-mile route is a circumnavigation of Ruffle Bar Island. Ruffle Bar Island was once home to a booming clam and oyster industry. Unfortunately, as pollution levels rose in the bay, the water was determined to be unsafe for breeding shellfish and the Department of Health closed the industry down. The island is now uninhabited and is a designated bird sanctuary. This is a nice way to get acquainted with the bay without committing to a longer route.

Past JFK Airport

For a nice 12.0-mile route, head straight out past Ruffle Bar (the island directly in front of you at the launch). Pass to its right and head southeast, between Little Egg and Big Egg islands. From there, paddle underneath the southern portion of Cross Bay Bridge, and continue around the large island. Turn left around the tip of the large island, opposite JFK Airport. You should have some pretty good views of aircraft landing and taking off. I've even had a V-22 Osprey fly overhead. If you need a restroom break, take a rest at the North Channel launch, on the northern tip of the large island. Continue by making your way past the small group of islands, heading back southwest toward the launch site any way you choose, staying to the south side of Canarsie Island. Paddle back to the seaplane launch site through the Mill Basin Outlet.

Around Yellow Bar Island

For something in between, paddle a lovely 6.0-mile route that starts from the seaplane launch and makes a large circle around Ruffle Bar Island, Yellow Bar Island (a 40-acre marsh island that will benefit from a multimillion-dollar project recently launched by the United States Army Corps of Engineers to rebuild marsh islands in Jamaica Bay), and Stony Creek Island, before returning to the launch.

MORE INFORMATION

Jamaica Bay Wildlife Refuge (nyharborparks.org/visit/jaba.html; 718-318-4340). Gateway National Recreation Area (nps.gov/gate/index.htm; 718-354-4606). Floyd Bennett Field (nyharborparks.org/visit/flbe.html; 718-338-3799). New York City Water Trail Association (nycwatertrail.org). Sebago Canoe Club (sebagocanoeclub.org; 718-241-3683).

3
OYSTER BAY HARBOR

Adored by Theodore Roosevelt, Oyster Bay features an abundant number of birds, gorgeous estates, and several paddling options.

Distance ▶ 5.4, 6.5, or 7.4 nautical miles

Cautions ▶ In West Harbor, if the wind is moderate or strong and is coming from the west, the waves may increase significantly and can make it a challenge to paddle down the eastern side of the harbor. Long Island Sound is very open and can have wind gusts and high waves. Rocky Point is aptly named and has large rocks.

Charts and Maps ▶ NOAA Electronic Chart US5NY14M / Paper Chart #12365

LAUNCH

Theodore Roosevelt Memorial Park, Long Island There is a public beach with boat ramps where you can launch kayaks and park (it is best to launch from the sandy beach). There is a $20 daily parking fee ($60 for the season, free for seniors) between Memorial Day and Labor Day. After Labor Day there is no fee. To reach the launch from the Long Island Expressway (I-495), take Exit 41 N (NY 106/107). Continue on NY 106 north for 6.3 miles. Once you arrive in the village of Oyster Bay, turn left on Audrey Avenue and follow the signs to the park. At the entrance to the park, turn left onto West End Avenue. Follow the road to the end. There are restrooms in the park. *GPS coordinates: 40° 52.584' N, 73° 32.161' W.*

ROUTE DESCRIPTION

Oyster Bay Harbor is located on the north shore of Long Island, approximately 20 miles east of Manhattan. Most of the harbor is located within the Oyster Bay National Wildlife Refuge, a 3,209-acre refuge and the largest in the Long Island National Wildlife Refuge Complex.

Oyster Bay is known for having the healthiest waters in Long Island Sound and is home to the popular Pine Island oysters, which have been farmed since 1887. The

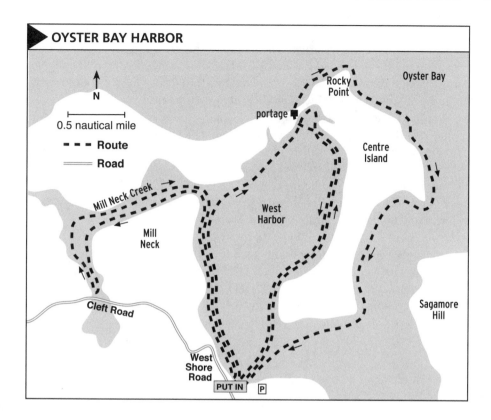

bay produces up to 90 percent of the oysters and 40 percent of the clams harvested in New York.

Since Oyster Bay is very sheltered, it provides essential winter habitat to many types of waterfowl, including multiple varieties of diving ducks, terns, wading birds, and shorebirds. More than 20,000 ducks have been reported in the bay at one time, and over 126 types of birds have been recorded in the refuge. It is also home to harbor seals, sea turtles, diamondback terrapins, and shellfish. As such, Oyster Bay has been designated a Significant Coastal Fish and Wildlife Habitat by the state of New York.

Oyster Bay was a favorite vacation spot of Theodore Roosevelt. He fell in love with the harbor in 1874 when he spent a summer there with his family. By 1887, he had built a house on the harbor and named it Sagamore Hill (sagamore is an Algonquin term for a chieftain). The large Queen Anne style home became known as the "Summer White House" while Roosevelt was president. He died there in 1919. Today, Sagamore Hill is a National Historic Site and the grounds include the Theodore Roosevelt Museum.

One look at Oyster Bay Harbor makes it easy to see why Roosevelt was so enamored with it. This charming deepwater harbor is surrounded by beautiful woods, glacial hills, and impressive mansions.

The harbor's shape resembles that of a tilted horseshoe, with the left side holding the official name of West Harbor. The landmass that makes up the middle of the horseshoe and divides Oyster Bay and West Harbor is known as Centre Island. Not a true island, it is connected to the mainland by a thin strip of land and a causeway. At the top of West Harbor, Mill Neck Creek flows in from the west. The creek is also a great place to paddle and offers some protection on windy days.

Oyster Bay Harbor offers many scenic options for paddling routes. There are three in particular that I enjoy and all begin at Theodore Roosevelt Memorial Park, in the village of Oyster Bay. Kayakers can explore the perimeter of West Harbor (5.4 nautical miles), take a quiet paddle up the western side of West Harbor and into Mill Neck Creek (6.5 nautical miles), or incorporate some open water and a short portage to their route by circumnavigating Centre Island (7.4 nautical miles).

Regardless of the route you choose, be aware that the south side of the harbor (at the launch) is a very popular mooring spot during the summer and produces heavy boat traffic. This area is the former site of Jakobson's Shipyard, which was the center of the shipbuilding industry in Long Island during World War II and produced minesweepers, mini-submarines, and tugboats for the United States Navy. The site of the shipyard is now home to the WaterFront Center (1 West End Avenue, Oyster

A kayaker paddles past a resident's boat moored in Oyster Bay. Photograph by Peter Gaaserud.

Bay; 516-922-SAIL), a hands-on education and recreation facility that also rents kayaks. The center is home to the oldest oyster sloop in North America.

West Harbor

If you choose to explore the perimeter of West Harbor, start by paddling in a clockwise direction from the launch in the southern part of Oyster Bay Harbor and up the western side of West Harbor. As you make your way northwest between the moored sailboats, you'll paddle parallel to West Shore Road. This road runs all the way to the Bayville Bridge (approximately 2 miles away) and is the only object that provides a distraction to the beauty of this charming harbor. The shoreline on the west side has a lot of riprap that helps prevent erosion but also makes it difficult to land a kayak.

At the north end of the harbor is a neighborhood of nice homes and the Centre Island Beach Village Park. The private properties continue along the east side of the harbor. The end of the route offers a nice open water paddle through Oyster Bay Harbor. Be on the lookout for heavy boat traffic in the summer.

If the wind is moderate or strong and is coming from the west, you will likely experience smooth, calm waters along the western shoreline. Be aware that once you round the top of the harbor, the waves may increase significantly, and can even make it a challenge to paddle back down the eastern side. I have matching blister scars on my thumbs that can attest to this.

Mill Neck Creek

If Mill Neck Creek is your destination, from the launch at Roosevelt Memorial Park paddle up the western side of West Harbor. At the Bayville Bridge, turn left to paddle under it and into the creek. There will likely be at least a dozen boats moored here, with many more docked in a marina just west of the bridge.

Mill Neck Creek is a natural breeding ground for black duck, osprey, and clapper rail. The northern shore of the creek is low-lying and has private homes that stretch about a mile to the west, where the creek makes a sharp left bend. The southern shore also has private homes, but it is a high bluff into which the houses fade into a wall of oak trees and mountain laurel about halfway to the bend. At the bend, it's possible to explore a finger-like cove to the right. Take the time to explore both sides.

After you make the left turn, some stunning houses with large, sprawling properties will dominate your view. About 0.5 mile farther south, you'll see a dam that manages the flow of water from Beaver Lake. There is no easy way to get to Beaver Lake, so this is your turnaround point.

Around Centre Island

If you choose to circumnavigate Centre Island, you're in for a fun, varied 8.0-mile journey into the open waters of Long Island Sound and Oyster Bay and a short portage near Goose Point. From the launch at Roosevelt Memorial Park head across the open water of the harbor to the southern tip of Centre Island, being careful while crossing the boat channel. Kayak along the island's western shore, where you'll pass beautiful homes spread across large estates. At the northern tip of the harbor is Turtle Cove and the causeway where Bayville Avenue and Centre Island Road meet. A convenient portage area is located just east of a big parking lot on the causeway. Take out on the sandy beach and walk your boat through the short tunnel that goes under the road. You'll emerge on a beach overlooking Long Island Sound.

Be sure to assess the water conditions before launching into the sound. Since Long Island Sound is very open and not nearly as protected as the harbor, it can have wind gusts and high waves. If your skills match the conditions, launch into the Sound and head immediately northeast (right) around the northern tip of Centre Island at Rocky Point. Rocky Point is aptly named so be diligent about looking for large rocks both under and above the surface (depending on the tide). After rounding the point, head south into Oyster Bay.

Paddle southeast into Oyster Bay, keeping the eastern shore of Centre Island on your right. While making your way down the shoreline, it will swing westward, and you'll pass by the beautiful and historic Seawanhaka Corinthian Yacht Club. The club was founded in 1871 and is a full service year-round yacht club.

The remaining 2.2 nautical miles (approximately) takes you past more opulent homes and the southern tip of Centre Island. Be careful crossing the boat channel as you paddle back to the launch area.

MORE INFORMATION

Theodore Roosevelt Memorial Park (516-624-6202); Oyster Bay National Wildlife Refuge (fws.gov/refuge/oyster_bay; 631-286-0485); Long Island National Wildlife Refuge Complex (fws.gov/northeast/longislandrefuges; (631) 725-7598). Sagamore Hill National Historic Site (nps.gov/sahi; 516-922-4788).

4
SHELTER ISLAND–COECLES HARBOR MARINE WATER TRAIL

Explore a scenic, protected harbor at an island accessible only by ferry.

Distance ▶ 5.6 nautical miles

Cautions ▶ Boat traffic is quite heavy, especially during the summer months.

Charts and Maps ▶ NOAA Electronic Chart US5NY1IM / Paper Chart #12358

LAUNCHES

Burns Road Ramp, Long Island Kayakers can launch from the end of Burns Road, into Coecles Harbor. If you're coming from the south side of Long Island (NY 27), take Sandy Hollow Road (CR 52) to the left and then go left again onto North Sea Road (CR 38). Turn right on Noyack Road. Noyack Road turns into Noyac Road. Turn left on Noyack Long Beach Road (CR 60) and exit onto Ferry Road (NY 114). This will take you to the South Ferry, the Shelter Island–Sag Harbor route. The ferry runs daily every 10 to 15 minutes. The price for one ticket is $17 round-trip, with each additional person costing an extra $2. They don't take reservations and only accept cash. From the ferry on Shelter Island, go northwest on S. Ferry Road (NY 114). Turn right onto Saint Mary's Road and then take the second right onto Burns Road (CR 117). Follow it to the launch.

If you're taking US 25 from the north side of Long Island continue until you reach Greenport and turn right onto 3rd Street. Take the North Ferry, the Greenport–Shelter Island route. Ferries run every 10 to 20 minutes. The price for one ticket is $16 round-trip, with each additional person costing an extra $2. They don't take reservations and only accept cash. From the ferry on Shelter Island, go east on Summerfield Place (NY 114) and take the first right onto Grand Avenue. Turn left onto Chase Avenue, which turns into North Ferry Road. Stay straight on Manwaring Road, and take the second right onto Saint Mary's Road. Take the first left onto Burns Road (CR 117) and follow to the launch. There is no fee to launch and there are no restroom facilities. *GPS coordinates: 41° 4.447' N, 72° 19.039' W.*

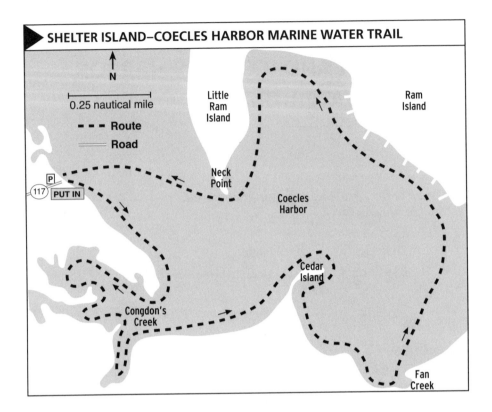

SHELTER ISLAND–COECLES HARBOR MARINE WATER TRAIL

Alternative launch Off US 114 at the end of Thompson Road (Long Island). *GPS coordinates: 41° 3.134′ N, 72° 18.989′ W.*

ROUTE DESCRIPTION

Shelter Island is a beautiful town and an island located in eastern Long Island between the north and south forks. No bridges connect the mainland to the 8,000-acre island, but it can be reached from both forks by ferry.

Around 2,200 residents live on Shelter Island year-round. This number increases to around 8,000 during the summer since, like most of Long Island, Shelter Island includes a mix of full-time and seasonal residents. Some residents are descendants of people who lived on the island during the American Revolution, while some seasonal residents' families have been part-timers for five generations. Parts of the island have appeared in movies such as *Margot at the Wedding* (2006) and *Masquerade* (1987), as well as in television shows such as *Will & Grace* and *How I Met Your Mother*.

Much of Shelter Island consists of nature preserves and protected wetlands. The Nature Conservancy owns the Mashomack Preserve, which covers almost one third of the island (approximately 2,100 acres). It was established in 1980 to prevent development on the island's pristine southeastern peninsula and to protect a large breeding population of osprey.

The Mashomack Preserve includes 10 miles of gorgeous coastline, tidal creeks, salt marsh, fields, and forest. An important wildlife habitat, it is home to several endangered birds (including the piping plover) and rare plants.

Arriving on Shelter Island on one of the two ferry systems is part of the fun. The trip from the north fork is approximately eight minutes and the trip from the south fork is approximately five minutes. Both ferry routes are part of Route 114. I usually come from North Haven via the South Ferry. From the seat of your car on the small ferryboat, you can already get a good feel for how unspoiled the shoreline is. The Mashomack Preserve is across the cove to your right, and one look at it should be enough to whet your appetite for a day of paddling. If Smith's Cove looks too enticing to pass up, it is possible to paddle there and explore the beautiful shoreline. There's a launch site off US 114 at the end of Thompson Road.

My first choice for kayaking on Shelter Island is on a great paddling trail established in a joint effort between The Nature Conservancy, the town of Shelter Island, and Shelter Island Kayak Tours. Called Coecles Harbor Marine Water Trail, it was created in a very protected harbor on the east end of the island. A map of the water trail is available at the launch site or online at taylorsisland.org/documents/20060500Trail.pdf.

Coecles Harbor is the largest harbor on Shelter Island and is also the most protected. This makes it attractive not only to kayakers, but also to pleasure boaters. As such, you will have plenty of company if you paddle during the peak summer season, whereas in the spring and fall you may very well have the harbor to yourself.

The round-trip trail begins at the end of Burns Road. It is worth noting that it's called Burns Road in all written directions I've seen, as well as on maps. However, when I arrived at the launch, the street sign said Burns Avenue. Either way, it's the only "Burns" on the island, so it isn't hard to find.

The launch is located on a delightful little sandy beach. There is parking on the side of the road and a welcoming sign that discusses safety and the water trail. There are no restroom facilities or amenities at the launch, but there is also no launch fee or parking fee.

To the left of the launch is a marina and mooring field. During the summer this area is thick with boats, so be alert as you enter the harbor. The land rimming the harbor to the northeast is a thin strip that buffers the harbor from Gardiners Bay. It connects Ram Island and Little Ram Island. (They are not actually islands.) The tip of Ram Island marks the entrance to the harbor and the end of its protected waters.

The water trail meanders along the shore of the Mashomack Preserve. As you begin your paddle south down the western shore of the trail, you will pass the first of 13 points of interest. White buoys placed approximately 20 feet from shore mark points of interest along the trail, so be sure to bring along a copy of the trail map. Looking down, you'll notice how clear the water is. The bottom is mostly sandy, with the exception of a few large rocks that are easily visible when the water is calm.

A sandy beach at Coecles Harbor makes for an easy boat launch.

The trail runs south across the mouth of Congdon's Creek and into Foxen Creek, where you can expect to see osprey, cormorants, and peat that was built up by grass in the marsh. The trail officially bypasses Congdon's Creek, but it's worth exploring if you have the time. The northern shore is primarily undeveloped, with grass, marsh elder, and bayberry bushes, while the southern branch is home to a small fleet of local fishing boats.

If you paddle at low tide, be careful of shallow water and sticky mud. If your boat gets stuck, do not leave your boat. The mud is extremely soft and you will sink into it. Instead, use your paddle to gently work your way out of the mud. As you continue east along the southern border of the harbor and the Mashomack Preserve, you will notice that private homes border the harbor. Beyond the homes is a maritime forest of oak, hickory, sassafras, and shad.

The trail swings north around Taylor's Island. At low tide the island is connected to the rest of the preserve by a sandbar, but at high tide it barely is an island. Since the water is so shallow (even at high tide), paddle around the island instead of trying to paddle over it. The depth of the water can look deceiving.

Taylor's Island is a town park. Originally named Cedar Island for the eastern red cedars that grew there, it was renamed for S. Gregory Taylor, who bought the island in 1937. The unusual log cabin that sits on the island was built at the beginning of the twentieth century and was expanded in the 1940s. It now functions as a navigation landmark in the harbor. Kayakers are welcome to land on the island, so consider packing a lunch and making a stop on this gorgeous little sandbar.

Continue around the point of Taylor's Island and head south to continue paddling along the Mashomack shoreline. When you reach Fan Creek, turn into it and enjoy a few hundred feet of serenity. The undisturbed shoreline of this narrow waterway offers a glimpse into the shoreline of decades past. It is too bad the creek isn't longer, but it's worth checking out.

The water trail officially ends at this point, but that doesn't mean you need to turn around. A nice route through some open water takes you north to Ram Island and Little Ram Island. Both are within the confines of the harbor and allow you to avoid retracing your steps by providing a circular route. From the southern point of Little Ram Island (Neck Point), continue directly west to the launch. The entire trip following this route will be approximately 5.6 nautical miles.

MORE INFORMATION

Mashomack Preserve (nature.org/mashomack; 631-329-7689). North Ferry Co., Inc. (northferry.com; 631-749-0139). The South Ferry Company Inc. (southferry.com; 631-749-1200).

5
BULLHEAD BAY TO SCALLOP POND

Paddle peaceful, lovely waters to find ducks,
green herons, terns, snowy egrets, piping
plovers, and a historic home.

Distance ▶ 7.0 nautical miles

Cautions ▶ Great Peconic Bay can have standing waves at its entrance and should only be done by experienced paddlers or in very calm conditions.

Charts and Maps ▶ NOAA Electronic Chart US5NY1IM / Paper Charts #12352 and 12358

LAUNCHES

Barkers Island Road, Southampton The launch is located at the end of Barkers Island Road, is free of charge, consists of a small parking area, and has a small, rutted pebble beach. A permit is not required to park, and there are no restrooms. From Route 27, go north on Tuckahoe Road. Tuckahoe Road winds to the left and becomes Barkers Island Road. Follow Barkers Island Road to the end. *GPS coordinates: 40° 54.684' N, 72° 26.494' W.*

Sebonac Inlet Road, Southampton An alternative launch spot is on Sebonac Inlet Road. From Route 27, go north on Tuckahoe Road. Turn left onto Sebonac Road. Sebonac Road becomes Sebonac Inlet Road. Follow the road to the water. Park along the guardrail on the bridge, and launch from the reeds below. A permit is not required to park, and there are no restrooms. *GPS coordinates: 40° 54.447' N, 72° 26.641' W.*

ROUTE DESCRIPTION

Despite all the natural beauty of Long Island, it can be difficult to find a slice of solitude. Harbors are shared with fishing boats, yachts, and jet skis, while pristine beaches are either private or reserved for those willing to shell out big bucks to use them.

This spot is a rare diamond among paddling routes, starting in the Southampton area not far from US 27. It passes through the contiguous waterways of Bullhead Bay, Sebonac Creek, Little Sebonac Creek, West Neck Creek, and Scallop Pond. The

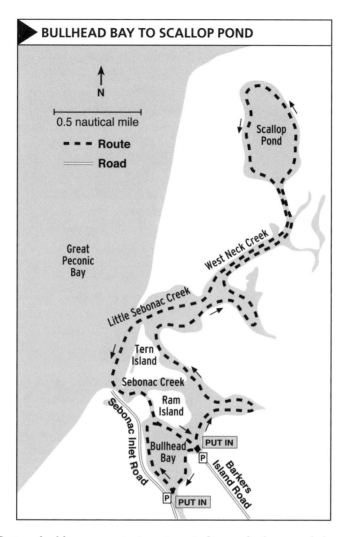

area was first a valuable resource to American Indians, who harvested clams, oysters, scallops, and finfish there. Later, European colonists used it as a prime hunting ground for deer and waterfowl. Today, it is perhaps best known as one of the prime locations in New York State for bird-watching.

Sebonac Creek is one of my favorite kayaking spots in coastal New York. It has easy access, is protected enough for beginner paddlers (when the wind is calm), and offers a variety of beautiful scenery and many types of waterways. Above all, part of the route is accessible only to paddlers, especially at low tide, when the water is very shallow. The last time I paddled this route, on a sunny weekend in early October, I did not encounter another boat the entire way.

The route starts on Bullhead Bay, a pretty little gem that provides access to Great Peconic Bay through Sebonac Creek. The bay is surrounded by a golf course and a few private homes. Mute swans often glide on the lake, which makes it all the more picture-perfect.

There are two launch sites on Bullhead Bay. My choice is the one at the end of Barkers Island Road. The launch is from a small pebble beach that faces north and is tucked into a very small cove. If the wind is blowing from the northeast, this spot is a little more sheltered than the alternative launch site on Sebonac Inlet Road. The Sebonac Inlet Road launch also requires parking along a guardrail on a small bridge and launching between the reeds below.

Check the tides before you set out on this paddle. If the tide is low, make sure you don't park too close to the water's edge. The tides are fairly high in this area, and you don't want to return to any surprises.

As you enter Bullhead Bay from the Barkers Island Road launch, you face a beautiful large private home. Most of the bay will be behind you and to the left. Take some time to paddle around the main part of the bay. Its shoreline is primarily unspoiled cordgrass (both smooth and saltmeadow varieties), and this is a prime area to spot osprey.

Bullhead Bay is bordered to the west by a nationally renowned private golf course, the National Golf Links of America. This prestigious course was opened in 1908 and was designed to include the highly desired qualities of British courses. It hosted the inaugural Walker Cup in 1922 and then again in 2013.

Ram Island borders the bay on the north side. This is a private island with a gated entrance. To the right of Ram Island is a protected bay with a marina and a mooring field. In the summer the field is thick with boats, but it can be quite empty in the off-season. Cormorants frequent this area and can often be seen resting on the mooring balls. Take the time to paddle into this little bay; it is very pretty and peaceful.

Once you've finished exploring the bay, you will see two potential paths as you enter Sebonac Creek. To the left, the creek flows past the southern side of Tern Island, into Great Peconic Bay. Because it can have standing waves at its entrance, the bay should be entered only by experienced paddlers or when the conditions are calm. To the right is Sebonac Creek; choose this route and paddle to the east of lovely Tern Island.

At the end of Tern Island is a very small inlet to Great Peconic Bay that is visible only during high tide. Stay to the right and paddle into Little Sebonac Creek, from where the National Golf Links of America's iconic windmill (located between its second and sixteenth holes) can be seen in the distance. Little Sebonac Creek will soon end at a fork. To the right is a cove with a few homes on the shore and a marsh most everywhere else. The shoreline of the cove runs approximately 1 mile and borders the Wolf Swamp Sanctuary (operated by The Nature Conservancy), to the north and east. This cove makes for a lovely side trip. To continue, stay to the left at the fork, and paddle into pristine West Neck Creek.

West Neck Creek is a paddler's paradise. The water is too shallow for powerboats but is perfect for shorebirds. As such, it's a spectacular area for bird-watching. The majority of the shoreline is tidal marsh. Some of the resident birds include ducks, green herons, terns, snowy egrets, and piping plovers.

The shoreline here is protected, so paddlers will be able to enjoy it for years to come. As you wind your way through the marsh, be aware of sandbars as you paddle, especially if the tide is low. Many mud flats and clam beds can also be seen at low tide. Should you become stuck in the mud, don't exit your boat. Use your paddle to gently push yourself out.

Continue to the end of the creek, where you'll find an oval-shaped secluded lake called Scallop Pond. Scallop Pond is part of the Scallop Pond Preserve, one of the most pristine salt marshes on eastern Long Island. The preserve is an important spawning ground for finfish and shellfish. It also supports 144 bird species.

An interesting house is located on the right side of the lake. It was owned by the oil tycoon Henry Huddleston Rogers II and was inherited by his fashion icon grand-daughter, Millicent Rogers. The home was named the Port of Missing Men, honoring 17 sailors whose lives were lost in a shipwreck in the port in the early 1800s. It was designed as a hunting lodge and was used as a retreat from the formality of the family's large beach mansion in Southampton Village. The family entertained members of European royalty for pheasant hunting parties. The home originally sat on 1,200 stunning acres on a peninsula on Peconic Bay (known as Cow Neck), which was the largest tract of land on Long Island until 1998, when a financier purchased

A cormorant rests its wings atop a buoy in Bullhead Bay.

almost half the land for $25 million. Millicent's daughter-in-law still owns the estate and its remaining acreage, and it is used for family gatherings.

After exploring Scallop Pond, you can start your return trip by heading back the way you came. If the inlet next to Tern Island is open, an alternative route is through the inlet and out into Great Peconic Bay if the conditions are calm or you're an experienced paddler. Paddle left along the western shore of Tern Island and through the inlet back into Sebonac Creek. Remember, standing waves are sometimes found at the Sebonac Creek inlet.

You can skirt past Ram Island on its western side to get back to Bullhead Bay. You'll pass under a small wooden bridge that joins the island to Sebonac Inlet Road. The round-trip route is approximately 7 nautical miles.

MORE INFORMATION

Scallop Pond Preserve (nature.org/ourinitiatives/regions/northamerica/unitedstates/newyork/places-preserves/long-island-scallop-pond-preserve.xml; 631-329-7689).

RIVERHEAD FOUNDATION

Nothing warms the heart like the sweet face of a baby harbor seal. Thanks to the hard work of their staff and the generosity of many private donors, the Riverhead Foundation for Marine Research and Preservation on Long Island rescues dozens of these adorable creatures each year, along with many other types of marine animals.

As the only marine mammal and sea turtle rescue organization in the state of New York, the Riverhead Foundation offers medical attention and rehabilitation to stranded and injured animals along the entire New York coastline. With its 1,850 miles of tidal shoreline, (127 miles of coast), they are a very busy rescue organization, assisting approximately 250 animals annually.

The Riverhead Foundation rescues and rehabilitates marine mammals such as seals, porpoise, dolphin, sea turtles, and even whales. They were the first organization in the world to rehabilitate a Risso's dolphin.

Harbor and gray seals are some of the most common patients rescued and rehabilitated by the foundation. Seal pups often get stranded on the beaches on Long Island during the spring months and are unable to care for themselves. The Riverhead Foundation rescues these pups, assesses their health, and rehabilitates them in their facility in Riverhead. Once the seals are healthy, which can require weeks or months of care, they are carefully returned to the wild. Temporary tracking devices are attached to each released seal so staff at the foundation can learn about their movements and monitor their location. The tracking devices are designed to fall off the seals after a period of time.

The skilled staff at the foundation not only work directly with animals in need, but also spend countless hours doing research. They track populations, research new rehabilitation techniques, and track animals they release to gather important data on specific animals and species as a whole.

The foundation also plays a vital role in educating the public about their local marine environment and informing people on how they can assist with preservation. As part of their strong commitment to education, the Riverhead Foundation offers programs to community schools that allow students to become involved and invested in the rehabilitation process and even witness the release of animals on local beaches.

The Riverhead Foundation is located inside the Atlantis Marine World Aquarium in Riverhead, New York. More information can be found on their website at riverheadfoundation.org.

A rescued seal at the Riverhead Foundation.

6
SAG HARBOR

Rub elbows with the rich and famous while paddling in a historic harbor and find impressive yachts, beautiful homes, and shorebirds in the creeks and coves.

Distance ▶ 4.5 or 9.5 nautical miles

Cautions ▶ Be on the lookout for large yachts, whose captains might not be able to see you.

Charts and Maps ▶ NOAA Electronic Chart US5NY1IM / Paper Chart #12358

LAUNCH

Long Wharf, Sag Harbor The launch is a small, clean, sandy beach at the base of a cute windmill at the end of Bay Street in Sag Harbor. Residents may use the ramp for free, but visitors can expect to pay a $5 fee. (See the harbormaster at 7 Bay Street.) To reach the launch, take US 27 to Bridgehampton and then go north on the Bridgehampton–Sag Harbor Turnpike (CR 79). After approximately 3.5 miles, the road will turn into Main Street. Follow Main Street into the heart of the Sag Harbor village. Look for the windmill by the village beach. Public restrooms are available in the village but not right at the launch. *GPS coordinates: 41° 0.175' N, 72° 17.772' W.*

ROUTE DESCRIPTION

Located on the northern shore of Long Island's South Fork and part of the Hamptons, Sag Harbor itself is about two square miles. There are many historic buildings in the village and Main Street is traditionally known as "Captains' Row," named for the numerous wealthy sea captains who lived there during the height of the town's whaling years.

Sag Harbor was settled in the early 1700s. By 1789 it was an international trading port and was designated New York State's first port of entry. In 1771, Long Wharf was built on the harbor, and since then has been the center of activity in the port.

The town weathered raids during the American Revolution and an attack in the War of 1812, and was the site of a torpedo factory in World War I. (Torpedoes were tested just 0.5 mile north of the village, in the harbor.)

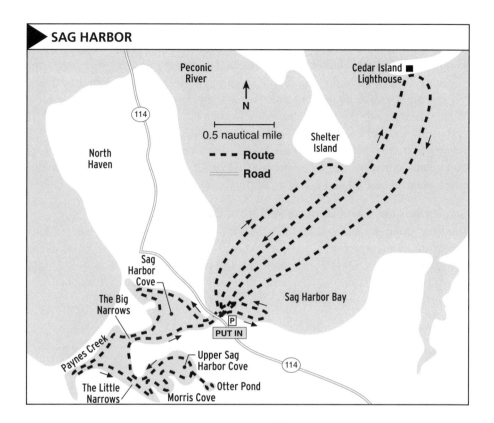

In 1821, the wharf was extended to accommodate the huge whaling trade that developed in the harbor. Sag Harbor was even mentioned several times in *Moby Dick*. At that time, boats were packed six deep into the harbor, and more than 800 men either waited to depart for dangerous voyages lasting up to two years or worked in other facets of the whaling industry.

Today Sag Harbor is a charming seaside village with historic buildings, good restaurants, independent shops, and affluent residents. It has a warm and welcoming vibe and is truly one of my favorite spots on Long Island.

Famous people are evidently drawn to Sag Harbor's charm and reputation. It has been home to authors such as John Steinbeck and James Fenimore Cooper, and also to celebrities such as Julie Andrews, Richard Gere, and Billy Joel (who owns a house just off Bay Street and within walking distance of Long Wharf). Other A-listers who may be spotted in the village include Jerry Seinfeld, Alec Baldwin, Robert DeNiro, and Steven Spielberg.

The only public launch in Sag Harbor is the one located at the end of Bay Street, right next to Long Wharf. Depending on how busy Long Wharf is, you can usually unload your boat and gear in front of the beach and then park on the wharf. The launch site is soft, protected, and easy to launch from. Once on the water, you have several great options for where to paddle. Boat traffic is a big issue everywhere on Long Island, and Sag Harbor is no exception. It is home to countless sailboats and powerboats and a surprising number of mega-yachts. If boat traffic is manageable, I like to start by exploring the protected harbor. Sag Harbor has a large breakwater to the east that shields the harbor from Sag Harbor Bay. From the launch, turn right and paddle around the end of Long Wharf to explore inside the breakwater.

Long Wharf is located next to the Sag Harbor Yacht Club, one of the 100 oldest yacht clubs in the country (established in 1899). Its historic clubhouse has been a village icon since 1914 and is located in the middle of their dock facilities.

Sag Harbor Cove and Upper Sag Harbor Cove

Paddling along the east side of the wharf, it's hard to miss the grand super motor yacht *Intuition II* when she's at anchor. The 193-foot Dutch-built steel boat belongs to the owner of the Sag Harbor Yacht Club and is one of the largest yachts in America. As beautiful as she looks from land, she's even more impressive when looking up at her from the cockpit of a kayak.

The *Intuition II* is a formidable sight from the water. The Sag Harbor beach launch is close by. Photograph by Peter Gaaserud.

Once you're done exploring the harbor, turn back toward the launch and continue paddling under the NY 114 Bridge. You'll enter a series of beautiful coves (starting with Sag Harbor Cove) that are great for exploring. By now, you'll be used to feeling like a peanut in a bowl of apples. Remember this analogy when the behemoth engines of a racing yacht fire up near you, and stay out of their way. They can't avoid you if they can't see you.

The coves near Sag Harbor are lined with residential homes and small marinas. This is definitely not a wilderness paddle, but it can be serene and special just the same. Osprey, terns, and egrets are just some of the residents who fish in the coves' shallow water. Speaking of which, be careful on the southern side of Sag Harbor Cove, where the water can be extremely shallow. It is easy to identify this area because the houses there do not have docks.

Follow the sweeping shoreline of Sag Harbor Cove (it grazes CR 60 in the northwest corner), and then head into the Big Narrows on the southwestern side. The residents here, for the most part, are friendly to kayakers, and boat traffic subsides here just a bit.

The Big Narrows leads into another pretty cove that runs quite a distance along Route 60 on its northwest side. It leads into a small creek called Paynes Creek that can be explored but is less than a 0.5 mile long.

In the southeast corner of the cove is the Little Narrows. The Little Narrows provides access to Morris Cove and the larger Upper Sag Harbor Cove. These coves are at the center of some pricey neighborhoods and are flanked with impressive private estates.

In the southeast corner of Upper Sag Harbor Cove is a small creek that leads under Main Street's Otter Pond Bridge and into Otter Pond. The pond has a fair amount of undeveloped shoreline and is a good place to spot wading birds. The pond and Upper Sag Harbor Cove have even been the temporary home of an intelligent harbor seal, which confirms that fact that they are good places to go fishing.

After exploring Otter Pond, slip back under the bridge and return to Sag Harbor along the opposite shoreline. This route is approximately 9.5 nautical miles, depending on whether or not you explore all the nooks and crannies.

Sag Harbor Bay and the Peconic River

If you're looking for an open water paddle, paddle northeast from the launch through Sag Harbor Bay and into the Peconic River. The river makes a sharp S curve around Sag Harbor before flowing into Gardiners Bay. At the juncture of the two is Cedar Point and the historic Cedar Island Lighthouse.

The original Cedar Island Lighthouse was built in 1839 to help guide whaling ships into and out of Sag Harbor. The current structure has stood since 1868 but was decommissioned in 1934. It originally stood on an island, which became connected to the mainland during a hurricane in 1938 that created a sandbar. The lighthouse is part of Cedar Point Park (in Suffolk County) and is a well-known marker (during the day) for pleasure boaters arriving in the Hamptons.

A direct paddle from the village launch to Cedar Point is 6.0 nautical miles round-trip, but you can also paddle along the Sag Harbor Bay shoreline and then the eastern shore of the Peconic River (western side of Northwest Harbor). Taking the shore route will up your mileage to around 9.5 nautical miles.

Shelter Island
It is also possible to paddle to the southern tip of Shelter Island (approximately 3.5 nautical miles round-trip). You can choose from countless possible routes from Sag Harbor, depending on the boat traffic and weather.

No matter where you decide to paddle, a good post-workout lunch spot for diehard seafood fans is the iconic restaurant right on the wharf called the Dock House. They serve fresh local seafood (including lobster rolls and chowder) and killer waffle fries. They are also a seafood market. The restaurant has limited seating, but most people order and then take their food to the wharf or the picnic tables by the beach launch for authentic waterfront dining.

If you're lucky enough to be in town for the Fourth of July, you'll be treated to a spectacular fireworks display on the Sag Harbor waterfront, courtesy of the Sag Harbor Yacht Club.

MORE INFORMATION
Village of Sag Harbor, Harbor and Docks (sagharborny.gov/departments/harbor-and-docks; 631-725-2368). Cedar Island Lighthouse (cedarislandlighthouse.org; 516-458-9222).

WINDMILLS OF LONG ISLAND

First timers to Long Island may find it curious that wooden windmills dot the landscape. A handful of these peaceful landmarks have survived centuries of weather and are a reminder of the area's English ancestry.

Wooden windmills have been part of Long Island's culture from the time it was settled and date back as early as 1644. At one point they were considered to be cutting edge "technology" that performed vital functions for the community, such as milling grain, pumping water, and sawing wood. The mills also served as a community center where people gathered to socialize and exchange news while they waited for their grain to mill.

Eleven original windmills still stand today and the majority are located on the east end of the island where they could catch steady winds rolling off the ocean. As such, the south fork of eastern Long Island boasts the largest number of historic windmills in the country.

Early windmills were constructed on exposed wooden structures and were called post mills, but the structures that remain today are primarily tapered octagonal smock mills. Smock mills have wooden shingles all around them that resemble skirts.

After the invention of more modern technology, windmills remained an integral part of the culture on Long Island. Many of the windmills are still well known today, and many have been carefully restored.

One such windmill is the Southampton Windmill, built in 1713 and originally located in modern day Southampton Village, where Hill Street currently is. It was relocated in 1890 to a private estate, which was sold after World War II and run as the Tucker Mill Inn. Tennessee Williams rented the windmill for a summer in the 1950s and is said to have written several of his famous plays there. Today, Stony Brook Southampton is located there.

Another well-known windmill is the Bee-be Windmill, constructed in Sag Harbor in 1820 for a retired whaling captain and shipbuilder. This smock mill has a stone foundation and a four-story tower and is the only windmill in the United States that still has its cast iron gearing, which includes iron shafting, wood, and cog work. The windmill has been moved five times, but currently resides in Bridgehampton, on the corner of Ocean Road and Hildreath Road. It is one of the most recognized landmarks in the hamlet.

There are also plenty of replica windmills on Long Island, including one on top of the tourist welcome center in Sag Harbor. It was built in the 1960s and is an icon at Long Wharf. This windmill is of special interest to kayakers, because the pretty little beach behind it is a public launch site.

Windmill at Sag Harbor visitor information center.

7

THREE MILE HARBOR

*A great place for seeing a variety of birds—
including rare species, Three Mile Harbor
features egrets, osprey, oystercatchers,
plovers, terns, herons, and dunlins—and
diamondback terrapins.*

Distance ▶ 7.0 nautical miles

Cautions ▶ Be cautious of heavy boat traffic.

Charts and Maps ▶ NOAA Electronic Charts US5MA22M and US5NY1IM /
Paper Charts #12358 and #13209

LAUNCH

Will Curl Highway, East Hampton A good launch point for kayaking in Three
Mile Harbor is on the southeast side of the harbor at the end of Will Curl Highway.
It is difficult to find public launch sites on the harbor. Some marinas may let you
launch if you ask politely, but it's a gamble. The launch at the end of Will Curl
Highway doesn't offer much parking, but it is free and public. To reach it from East
Hampton, head north on North Main Street. The road will become Three Mile
Harbor Road. Turn left onto Will Curl Highway. Park at the end of the road
(overnight parking is not allowed). There are no restroom facilities. There's a short
path that leads to the beach. *GPS coordinates: 41° 0.628' N, 72° 10.967' W.*

ROUTE DESCRIPTION

Three Mile Harbor is a beautiful, large protected harbor off of Gardiners Bay. It is
east of Sag Harbor (about 3 miles from East Hampton) and is East Hampton's most
popular port. Three Mile Harbor offers boaters convenient access to anchorages,
marinas, supplies, and restaurants.

At the entrance to Three Mile Harbor, from Gardiners Bay, is a narrow inlet bordered by two parks. On the western side is Sammy's Beach, a 116-acre nature
preserve that separates Gardiners Bay and the Three Mile Harbor Inlet. This approximately 1-mile-long spit of land provides habitat for roughly 50 types of birds, including some rare species. The preserve is one of more than 400 nature preserves that
encompass 3,500 acres of land in the town of East Hampton. Sammy's Beach

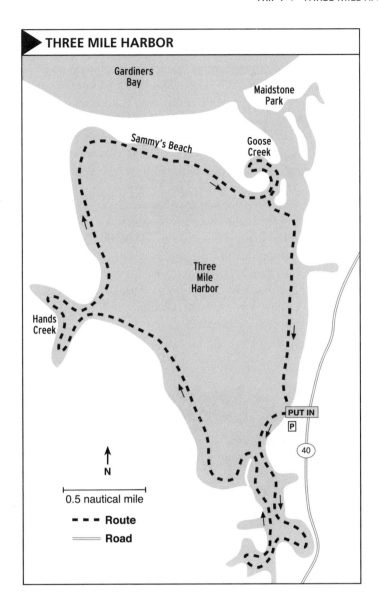

THREE MILE HARBOR

Gardiners Bay

Maidstone Park

Sammy's Beach

Goose Creek

Three Mile Harbor

Hands Creek

PUT IN

P

40

N

0.5 nautical mile

- - - Route

═══ Road

consists of mostly sea grass and sand dunes. Its current topography was formed by a large deposit of sand that was put there in 1999 after the channel was dredged and the subsequent implementation of a revegetation project.

There are two theories for how the reserve was named. The most likely is that it was named after Samuel Parsons, who owned the peninsula in the mid-1700s. The second is that a cargo ship carrying "hope chests" built in New Haven for ladies of East Hampton ran aground near the beach in the 1670s. Many local ladies went to visit the wreck and one, Elizabeth Parsons, fell in love with a survivor of the wreck, Samuel Sherrill. The two married in 1676.

Regardless of the name's origin, Sammy's Beach marks the mouth of Three Mile Harbor on its west side. On the east side, it is Maidstone Park beach.

Maidstone Park is a county park in the town of East Hampton and divides Gardiner's Bay from Three Mile Harbor. It is developed, with a bathing beach, baseball field, restrooms, picnic areas, and parking. The 400-foot beach along Gardiner's Bay is known as a good spot for swimming and kayaking. Many open-water swimmers and triathletes swim along this beach, which traditionally has relatively calm water. In contrast, the inlet to Three Mile Harbor is known for its strong currents. This makes it a great fishing spot, but not so great a kayaking spot.

Because the east side of the harbor has many marinas, you will have to avoid a lot of boat (a.k.a., yacht) traffic when you start. The southern end of the harbor is also very developed, but the environment will get significantly quieter as you make your way around to the western and northern shores.

From the Will Curl Highway launch you can paddle a large loop route around the harbor. The launch is located next to private homes in a beautiful residential section and provides a great view of the entire harbor.

A swan strolls along the beach at Three Mile Harbor.

Last time I launched from this location, I was welcomed by a beautiful swan, who looked as if he'd walked out of a fairytale. It was a breezy day and he stood right on the beach, pruning himself. These elegant ornamental birds have been the subject of a controversy between the New York Department of Environmental Conservation (DEC) and many Long Island residents. The DEC introduced a plan in January 2014 to eradicate the birds because they are considered an invasive species. Hundreds of birds were brought to New York from Europe in the late 1800s and were released to start their own breeding populations. Now, these beautiful white birds, who are considered mute since they rarely vocalize, are blamed for killing vegetation and deterring other native birds from nesting. The plan was met with an outcry from residents and resulted in more than 30,000 people signing a petition to save the birds. This led to a revision of the plan that offers a "commitment to full consideration of non-lethal techniques" for managing the population.

The paddle around the harbor takes you by a mix of residential and commercial property. Multimillion-dollar estates flank portions of the popular harbor, especially near the northern shoreline. Jet skis are not allowed in the harbor, so that helps keep the commotion down, even though the harbor is still busy.

Paddling south along the shore, you'll pass many private homes before reaching Marina Lane Waterside Park. This marks the bottom of the main "oval" of the harbor. Continue paddling into the charming coves at the south end of the harbor. They are located in a protected little arm but are surrounded by marinas so there is a lot of boat traffic in this area. A small creek begins approximately 1 mile south of the launch, but it is accessible only at high tide.

Once you've explored the protected southern arm, continue around the 0.5 mile long spit of land that sticks out at the southern border of the harbor. This area, like most others on the harbor, is private, and landing is not permitted. It is pretty to paddle around, however, and there are often osprey living near the water's edge.

Continue your route toward the western shore. The next section of the harbor is primarily residential. Take the time to explore Hands Creek. The shore near the creek is less developed, and going into the creek will offer an extra 0.5 mile or so of paddling real estate.

The area north of Hands Creek is pristine and sparsely developed. Private homes line the shore, but many are hidden in the trees. At the northernmost point of the harbor, about 1 mile from Hands Creek, is Sammy's Beach.

On the eastern side of Sammy's Beach is a tidal area known as Goose Creek. You will need to round the bend to the left between Sammy's Beach and Dayton Island (which sits in the middle of the mouth of the harbor entrance) to reach the entrance. Once you're inside, the creek provides a sheltered paddle with a plethora of shorebirds to observe. Expect to see egrets, osprey, oystercatchers, plovers, terns, herons, and dunlins. It is also a great area to see diamondback terrapins, horseshoe crabs, and fish. Much of this creek is accessible only at high tide.

When you're finished exploring Goose Creek, skip the busy, long, narrow entrance to the harbor and all the strong currents that come with it. Instead, continue east and then south along the eastern shore of the harbor to return to the launch.

If you're lucky enough to be at Three Mile Harbor during the Great Bonac Fireworks Show, don't miss it! This spectacular tradition, which is not held on the Fourth of July, but usually later in July, has a 30-plus-year history. The show is funded by corporate sponsors and public contributions, and the event benefits local charities. The fireworks are displayed over Three Mile Harbor, and many great places to watch can be found around the harbor, including Sammy's Beach and Maidstone Park. Many people watch from their boats, but I don't recommend taking out your kayak for this event since a large number of boats go out on the water in the dark. It is truly an incredible local event.

MORE INFORMATION
Town of East Hampton (ehamptonny.gov; 631-324-2417).

8

LAKE MONTAUK

Enjoy the fun of an active lake that features a United States Coast Guard station and pockets of serenity.

Distance ▶ 6.0 nautical miles

Cautions ▶ The lake experiences heavy boat traffic and large waves often roll in between the rock jetties protecting the bay at its northern end, especially on windy days.

Charts and Maps ▶ NOAA Electronic Chart US5MA22M / Paper Chart #13209

LAUNCH

Montauk Point State Park, Montauk A good spot to launch is from a quiet little beach on the eastern side of the lake, just off East Lake Drive. To reach the launch, take US 27 and turn north onto East Lake Drive. Continue for about 2 miles until you see Little Reed Pond on your right. A couple hundred yards past the Little Reed Pond parking area is a small dirt pull-off on the left side of the road. If you reach the airport, you've gone too far. There is a nature preserve sign at the pull-off and a short path leading to the water. Park in the pull-off area (there is room for just two or three cars) and walk your boat down to the sandy beach. During a recent conversation with the local chief harbormaster, I was told if no permit signs are posted, it's okay to park. There is also no fee to launch and are no restrooms. *GPS coordinates: 41° 4.321' N, 71° 55.574' W.*

ROUTE DESCRIPTION

Traveling to Lake Montauk will give you an appreciation for why Long Island was named as such. Try driving there on a summer weekend, and this will be a painful realization as you sit in traffic on US 27. Setting all that aside, Lake Montauk is a beautiful paddling destination near the easternmost point on Long Island.

The first time I drove out to Montauk, I was surprised that the terrain at the eastern end of Long Island suddenly becomes rugged and hilly. It seems more to me like northern New England and less like the flat, sandy mid-Atlantic coast we typically see.

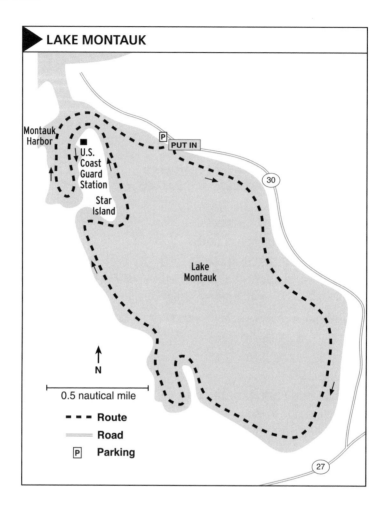

LAKE MONTAUK

Montauk
Harbor

P   PUT IN

U.S.
Coast
Guard
Station

30

Star
Island

Lake
Montauk

N

0.5 nautical mile

- - -   Route
═══   Road
P   Parking

27

If you've never been to Point Montauk, take the time to drive the few extra miles to the end of US 27. It is home to the oldest lighthouse in New York State, Montauk Point Lighthouse. Built in 1796, this 110-foot tall National Historic Landmark is still an active navigational aid and is the fourth-oldest in the country. Its light flashes every five seconds and is visible for up to 19 nautical miles. The road makes a circle at the point, so you can drive past the lighthouse without stopping, or if you want to visit the lighthouse, there's a parking lot that provides access for $8.

Lake Montauk is just down the road from the lighthouse. Originally, Lake Montauk was the largest body of fresh water on Long Island and was often called the "Great Lake." But in 1927 a hole was blasted out of its northern shore to connect it to the saltwater of Block Island Sound and the Atlantic Ocean. So today, it's not actually a lake at all, but instead a 900-acre "embayment."

An entrepreneur named Carl Fisher was responsible for the transformation of Lake Montauk. Fisher was also partly responsible for the development of Miami Beach. His intent was to make Lake Montauk the "Miami Beach of the north," and he opened a yacht club, casino, and several other businesses on the lake once it became connected to the Atlantic. It didn't take long for eelgrass to begin to grow in the newly brackish water, for saltwater species to migrate into the lake, and for new residents to build homes and businesses at the water's edge. Fisher lost his fortune in the stock market crash of 1929, which put an end to his development of the area but the lake was forever changed.

The United States Navy took over the lake during World War II and since then, Lake Montauk has been home to both the largest commercial and largest sport fishing fleets in the state of New York. Fishing charters out of Lake Montauk claim 25 world fishing records, including the catch of a 76-pound striped bass. Yearly shark tournaments are also held at the lake.

Nearly all of Lake Montauk's shoreline is developed. The eastern shore is primarily residential or part of Montauk Point State Park, with the exception of a few small marinas. There is also a small airport near the northern end.

The western shoreline is a mix of residential and commercial development, with the northern portion consisting primarily of commercial marinas, yacht clubs, and restaurants. Ferry service runs from Lake Montauk to Block Island, Martha's Vineyard, and New London, Connecticut. A small land bridge connects the shoreline to Star Island at the northern end of the lake. The island is homeport to countless fishing vessels and the United States Coast Guard.

All this boat activity means paddlers need to be very careful when kayaking near the northern end of the lake. In addition to heavy boat traffic, large waves often roll in between the rock jetties protecting the bay, especially on windy days. Having said this, the lake is still a great place to paddle and can be thoroughly enjoyed from the cockpit of a kayak.

From the launch off East Lake Drive, you can see much of the lake, which is roughly an oval. The launch puts you near the northern end, so I suggest heading south along the eastern shoreline. The paddle south can be surprisingly tranquil. Granted, in nice weather you will have many pleasure boaters, jet skis, and even water skiers to contend with, but the majority of the large marinas are at the northern end.

The southbound paddle can be very peaceful in the off-season, and certainly enjoyable during the summer. A small marina is less than a mile from the launch, followed by private homes and eventually a few spots of undeveloped beach. Near the southern shore of the lake is a small town near which the traffic from boats, stand-up paddleboards, and other watercraft will start to pick up.

When paddling off the shoreline, be on the lookout for areas where shellfish restoration projects are taking place. They will be marked with buoys and may say something like "Clam Farm." These "safe" zones are part of ongoing efforts to

The historic Montauk Point Lighthouse is the fourth-oldest lighthouse in the country.

breed shellfish and to restore depressed populations of species. Give these areas a wide berth.

As you round the southern end of the lake and head up the western shore, stay close to the shoreline. Less than a mile up the west side is a protected cove that has remained relatively undeveloped. Paddle into it for a feel of what the lake looked like prior to development. Enjoy the beach heather and cordgrass because the hustle and bustle of Star Island is in the next leg of your trip.

As Lake Montauk isn't really a lake, Star Island isn't really an island. A causeway runs between it and the shoreline, making it necessary for you to paddle around the island counterclockwise. As you paddle up the eastern shore, you will soon find yourself among fishing boats, mega-yachts, and everything in between. The friendly Montauk Yacht Club, with its resort and marina, is just one of the establishments you'll pass. It is actually a fun place to paddle and the hubbub of the area creates a fun vibe.

As you round the top of Star Island, paddle down its western side and into Montauk Harbor. You will pass a United States Coast Guard station. Its impressive cutter is always ready for action and its location is the perfect jump-off spot for a rescue out at sea.

Just opposite the northern tip of the island on the lake's western shore is the family owned Montauk Marine Basin. Some of the world's best charter boats operate from this establishment, and they hold multiple fishing tournaments each year. Chances are you'll see commercial fishing boats offloading their catch during the season, and you may also see large fish hanging from the dock scales. Many restaurants (with fresh seafood!) are in this area, so make a note of where to return to after your paddle.

The busy harbor inlet is just to your north. It is not advisable to cross the inlet (or to paddle between the rock jetties) unless you have excellent boat handling skills, the weather conditions are good, and the boat traffic is minimal. This is a very congested area with strong currents and waves coming in from the Sound. Instead, you can head back around to the east side of Star Island and make the crossing back to the launch when it's safe.

MORE INFORMATION
Hamlet of Montauk (ehamptonny.gov/HtmlPages/MontaukHamlet.htm; 631-324-4141). Montauk Point Lighthouse (montauklighthouse.com; 631-668-2546). Montauk Point State Park (nysparks.com/parks/61/details.aspx; 631-668-3781).

NEW JERSEY

New Jersey contains approximately 130 miles of coastline. The northern coastline in New Jersey is a mostly ancient coastal plain that is directly exposed to wave erosion. The beaches are located in front of a bluff that varies from just a few feet to 26 feet high.

The southern shoreline is made up of a series of barrier islands that vary in size (5 miles to 18 miles). The barrier islands offer large systems of lagoons, open bays, and salt marshes. The barrier islands are separated from one another by tidal inlets.

The New Jersey shore suffered tremendous damage from Hurricane Sandy in 2012. This stretch of coastline was thrust into national headlines when the most intense storm of the season slammed into the coast on October 29. Economic losses to businesses totaled nearly $30 billion, and more than 2 million homes lost power. Storm surges and flooding had an impact on much of the state.

Although parts of the New Jersey coastline are forever changed as a result of Sandy, the residents were quick to rebuild and just a few short years later things appear to be back to normal, at least to the untrained eye.

Kayakers have many choices in New Jersey. They can wind through large, designated wildlife areas that often consist of pristine marshland, paddle through open bays and tidal rivers, or challenge themselves in open water around Cape May (see Trip 14) and other popular vacation areas.

Wildlife viewing in New Jersey can be particularly rewarding. Not only are there many species of shore and migratory birds, but playful harbor seals also frequent its northern waters.

There are numerous kayaking outfitters along the New Jersey coast. Some offer just rentals, while others offer instruction and tours. Although some public launch sites require permits to launch and/or park, many are free.

9
NAVESINK RIVER

Choose from a variety of routes to explore a tidal estuary with small sandbars, forested shoreline, and grand properties.

Distance ▶ 2.5, 4.5, 6.5, and 7.0 nautical miles

Cautions ▶ The water can get rough at the eastern end of the Navesink River, where it flows into the Shrewsbury River. There are strong currents at the confluence of the rivers, as the water funnels into Sandy Hook Bay, making the area potentially very hazardous. This is also an area of heavy boat traffic on nice days. Unless you are a very experienced paddler, it is best to stay upstream from this turbulent part of the river.

Charts and Maps ▶ NOAA Electronic Chart US5NJ15M / Paper Chart #12325

LAUNCHES

Maple Cove, Red Bank Located in Red Bank at the northern end of Maple Avenue, there is a very small piece of land that is owned by the borough and provides easy access to the Navesink River. To get there from the Garden State Parkway, take Exit 109 to CR 520 toward Red Bank/Lincroft. Merge onto Half Mile Road, and turn left onto West Front Street after about 0.5 mile. Continue approximately 1.5 miles to Maple Avenue, and turn left. The launch is at the end of the road, where you will find a small parking lot. There is no fee, and there are no restrooms. *GPS coordinates: 40° 21.109' N, 74° 4.193' W.*

Victory Park, Rumson There is another beautiful public launch 3.0 miles downriver from Maple Cove in Rumson. To reach it, follow same directions as above, but instead of turning on Maple Avenue, continue on West Front Street. The road will turn into River Road (CR 10). Continue another 3.0 miles and turn left onto Lafayette Street and take it to the end. You'll need to find parking along Lafayette Street. There is no fee to launch or park, and there are restroom facilities. *GPS coordinates: 40° 22.620' N, 74° 0.766' W.*

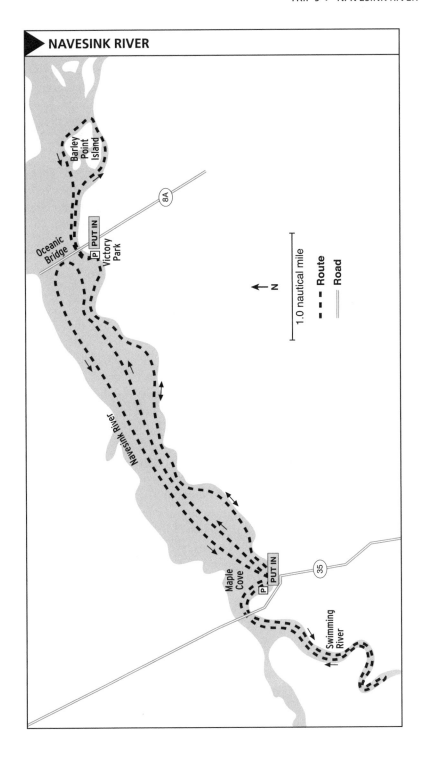

ROUTE DESCRIPTION

New Jersey has approximately 127 miles of coastline on the Atlantic Ocean, stretching from Sandy Hook to Cape May. Although the Jersey Shore is famous for its busy boardwalks, Atlantic City casinos, and oceanfront resorts, it is also a state with many great kayaking opportunities. Numerous coastal bays and rivers combined with areas of protected natural areas provide miles of wonderful waterways to enjoy by kayak. Whether you're a seasoned kayaker or a novice looking to get experience, New Jersey offers a diversity of paddling choices.

The Navesink River is a tidal estuary in northern New Jersey that is approximately 8 miles long. It flows into the Shrewsbury River before reaching Sandy Hook Bay, and ultimately, the Atlantic Ocean. The river is located in Monmouth County and is surrounded by some of the most affluent areas in New Jersey, including Red Bank, Fair Haven, and Rumson.

The river is around the corner (to the southwest) from Sandy Hook, a barrier spit of land that separates Lower New York Bay from the Atlantic Ocean. The Navesink is known to be excellent for crabbing and for fishing for species such as striped bass, fluke, weakfish, and bluefish.

The Navesink River is a natural playground for water-lovers. It is a tremendous resource for sailing, power boating, swimming, rowing, and of course, kayaking. At times ice-skating can be added to the list of recreational activities available on the river since during cold winters, the river often freezes.

You don't need to paddle a specific route on the Navesink River; basically your choices are to paddle up the river or downstream. The bulk of the river is between Red Bank and Rumson. Upstream from Red Bank, the river flows under Route 35 and narrows as it splits into the Swimming River and Shadow Lake.

Downstream from Rumson is an area of islands, the largest of which is Barley Point Island, a private 38-acre island with approximately 57 homes. The island represents a shore life of yesteryear, with mostly small cottages that have been handed down for generations. The island is connected to the mainland by two small bridges, but there are no paved roads past the entrance. Life on the island is a quiet contrast to the neighboring mansions of Rumson, and the landowners are dedicated to their island, their family ties to the sand their homes sit on, and to smartly planning for future generations to also enjoy the island.

Maple Cove to Oceanic Bridge or Swimming Bridge

Two beautiful public launch sites can be found on the Navesink River: in Red Bank at Maple Cove and in Rumson at Victory Park. To reach the launch at Maple Cove, pull into the small parking lot and look closely past the park bench for the small break in the tall grass. There you will see a short sandy walkway to the shore. The first time I went there I completely missed finding the launch because a couple was sitting on the bench eating lunch and blocked the view of the path. So look closely between the tall reeds for the sandy path.

Maple Cove is a pleasant gift to kayakers. The launch is a sandy little beach with nice views of the river and it is usually quiet. There are no restroom facilities at the launch or other amenities, but there is a small parking lot and a trash can.

It is best to paddle on the river at high tide since lower water levels unveil a muddy river bottom. You can paddle either direction on the Navesink River from Maple Cove. If you paddle upstream, you can complete a pleasant 5.25-mile paddle up the Swimming River to Newman Springs Road and back. If you paddle downstream, you can do a lovely 8.0-mile round-trip paddle to the Oceanic Bridge.

Victory Park to Oyster Point or Barley Point

The second launch is a little more than 3.0 miles downriver in Rumson, at Victory Park. Rumson is an upscale area with beautiful estates on the waterfront and a picturesque downtown area. Victory Park is a lovely public park with a long, wide sand beach.

The park has a playground and bandstand that were donated by local families. It also has permanent restrooms and many other facilities, such as a basketball court,

The beach launch at Maple Cove.

tennis courts, and a bocce court. There is a monument in the park dedicated to soldiers from many different wars.

The beach at Victory Park is perfect for launching kayaks. Only car-topped boats are allowed since there is no ramp or place to drive a trailer. Launch to the left of the end of the road on the lovely sand beach. You can drive up, unload your boat, and then park along the street.

A great 7.5-mile out-and-back route goes from Victory Park upstream to the Oyster Point area near the Route 35 Bridge. The scenery, as with much of the river, includes some small sandbars, forested shoreline, and residential properties, some of which are grand on any scale. Sunset paddles are particularly beautiful from the Navesink River.

To take a shorter, 3.0-mile paddle from Victory Park, paddle to the right of the launch, under the Oceanic Bridge, and around Barley Point Island.

The Navesink River has a lot of wildlife, especially near the Oceanic Bridge. In fact, at one time in recent history, it was home to a pod of bottlenose dolphins. The dolphins spent the better part of a year roaming around the river's waters. They are thought to have followed a school of fish into the river from Sandy Hook Bay.

MORE INFORMATION

Borough of Red Bank, Parks and Recreation Department (redbanknj.org/content/parks-and-recreation; 732-530-2782). Borough of Rumson, Parks and Recreation Department (rumsonnj.gov/departments/parksrec.htm; 732-842-3300).

SANDY HOOK ALL WOMEN LIFEGUARD TOURNAMENT

Every year in July, approximately 200 skilled lifeguards come together in Sandy Hook to face off as teams in ten events. These fearless rescuers put their lives on the line every summer to help save dozens of people. They are skilled, they are fit, and they are all women.

The Sandy Hook All Women Lifeguard Tournament is the largest and oldest all-women lifeguard event in the United States. It features teams from Cape Cod to North Carolina and even as far away as Los Angeles. They come to honor their towns, show off their skills, and participate in fierce competition.

The event draws crowds of spectators and includes contests that show how these amazing women save lives through tests of endurance, skill, and strength. Swimming, running, ocean kayaking, and surf rescue are just some of the numerous skills required of lifeguards that are featured in the tournament.

Examples of events featured in the competition include the "ironwoman" event (a 100-yard run, 250-yard ocean swim, 400-yard paddle on a rescue board, and another 200-yard run), the surf rescue event (100-yard offshore swim with a rescue board, followed by a victim rescue in the surf, then a paddle back to shore), and the 1,000-yard Surfboat Challenge.

Many competitors come back year after year to enjoy the great experience this event provides. It's exciting, fun, and challenging.

The event was started in 1985 by a female lifeguard with the National Park Service (NPS). The first tournament drew 55 participants and has been growing ever since. There is no fee to enter the event, hosted by the NPS, and it is open to any women working as a lifeguard (volunteer or paid) at a beach, lake, river, or pool. Swim caps, lunch, and awards are provided. It is held at Gateway's Sandy Hook Unit. Competitors represent state, federal, and municipal lifeguard units.

Sandy Hook All Women Lifeguard Tournament. Photograph by Laura Pedrick.

The tournament is an NPS workforce diversity initiative and is designed to help showcase the high fitness and skill levels required of female lifeguards. Another goal is to encourage other women to consider becoming lifeguards and to act as role models. It also helps the participants maintain their rescue skills.

At the time of the inaugural event, tournaments for lifeguards were mostly geared toward men. They may have included one women's event in each tournament, sometimes calling it the "mermaid relay." Today, it's much more common for lifeguard tournaments to include women, but these competitors are no mere "mermaids."

10
ISLAND BEACH STATE PARK

Enjoy paddling near tidal marsh, freshwater wetlands, maritime forest, and one of the few undeveloped barrier island beaches along the Atlantic coast on this 10-mile stretch of paradise.

Distance ▶ 2.0 or 3.0 nautical miles

Cautions ▶ Currents change with each tide and a nearby inlet creates very strong currents. On the western side of the islands, just outside the conservation zone, is Oyster Creek Channel, which receives a lot of boat traffic during the day and has strong currents that are produced when the tide goes out and water empties from the channels that cut between the islands. At times the water moves so fast it looks like a powerful stream. The currents can be especially strong during tides that occur when the moon is new and full. At low tide, sandbars emerge, sometimes making it impossible to paddle.

Charts and Maps ▶ NOAA Electronic Chart US5NJ30M / Paper Chart #12324

LAUNCHES

Bay Access Road, Seaside Park The first of two launch sites at Island Beach State Park, this provides access to the open bay and is a couple miles north of the Sedge Island area, where the other launch is located. To reach it from the Garden State Parkway, take Exit 98 from the local route to NJ 34 South. It becomes NJ 35. Continue on NJ 35 until it ends at the park entrance. Pick up a park map when you enter the park. Unfortunately, the map isn't great, but since there is only one road through the park it is still useful. There is a daily fee of $12 for non-residents and $6 for New Jersey residents to use the park (which is open 24 hours). NJ 35 becomes Shore Road when it enters the park. *GPS coordinates: 39° 48.471' N, 74° 5.757' W.*

Continue on Shore Road and turn right onto Bay Access Road. There is no sign for it on Shore Road, so it can be difficult to find. As you approach the Interpretive Center, a small gravel/sand-packed road will be to your right. (If you see the sign that

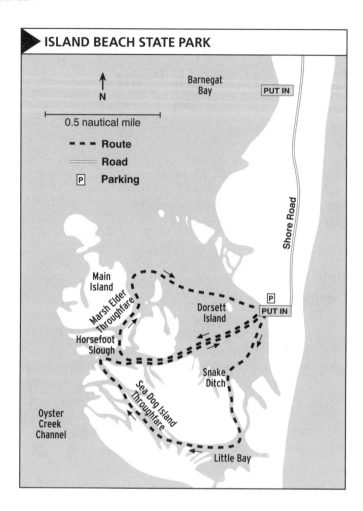

alerts you that the Interpretive Center is ahead, you've gone too far.) Turn onto the gravel road and drive to the end. There is limited parking at the launch, but there is a small sandy beach area that provides access to the open bay. There are no restroom facilities at the launch, but there are several restrooms in the park.

Area 21, Seaside Park A beautiful launch area is located near the end of Shore Road at Area 21 and provides great access to Barnegat Bay and the Sedge Islands Wildlife Management Area. From the first launch, continue on Shore Road, past the Interpretive Center. There is a sign for this launch; you will see it on your right, opposite the parking area. It is clearly marked as a kayak launch. You can either turn right onto Winter Anchorage Access Drive and drive down to the water to unload your boat and return to the parking area across Shore Road to park, or you can carry/wheel your boat from the parking lot (about 275 steps from the road to the launch).

The put-in is sandy and gradual. There are restrooms by the parking area. *GPS coordinates: 39° 47.375′ N, 74° 5.684′ W.*

ROUTE DESCRIPTION

Island Beach State Park is located near Seaside, New Jersey. It is one of a few undeveloped barrier island beaches on the Atlantic coast. It encompasses a thin 10-mile stretch of more than 3,000 coastal dune acres between the Atlantic Ocean and Barnegat Bay. It's representative of how much of the New Jersey coast looked prior to development.

Barnegat Bay is approximately 42 miles long and is fed by several small rivers. It's accessible to the Atlantic Ocean through Barnegat Inlet and is part of the Atlantic Intracoastal Waterway. Barnegat Bay took a beating during Superstorm Sandy in 2012. If you live on the East Coast, it's hard to forget the news footage of the area in the days and weeks following the storm. Luckily, the area has already bounced back considerably and is once again a popular vacation destination, although the devastation left by Sandy will never be forgotten.

Island Beach State Park is known as the launch point for Sedge Island and the Sedge Islands Wildlife Management Area. It has beautiful sandy beaches, a tidal marsh, freshwater wetlands, and a maritime forest. Home to a diversity of wildlife, including waterfowl, songbirds, peregrine falcon, and the state's largest colony of osprey, it also has more than 400 types of plants.

A large marine conservation zone includes all the nearby islands and swings north along part of the park's bay shoreline and also south, near Barnegat Inlet. The group of marshy islands that make up the Sedge Islands are the perfect playground for kayaks. The water is shallow in many places, and narrow marsh channels provide navigable roadways for paddlers. Currents change with each tide, however, and because of the nearby inlet there are some places where the current can be very strong.

The Sedge Islands are forever changing with the wind and tides. Back in the 1860s, there was a wide harbor where the islands are currently located. The harbor was called Winter Anchorage and was home to multiple wooden 75-foot schooners (in the winter). Today, the islands provide habitat for many species of marine animals, including seals. Blue claw crabs, hard clams, and many fish, such as striped bass, flounder, and weakfish, abound there.

The largest island, shown on many maps as Sedge Island, sits just southwest of the Area 21 launch. On its northeastern side is Snake Ditch, one of the deepest areas around the islands, at approximately 30 feet deep. A grove of pine and cedar trees on the islands is a key spot for bird-watching year-round.

Directly west of the launch is Main Island. At the northern end of Main Island is the Sedge House, a renovated duck hunting lodge built in 1909. The lodge drew famous visitors such as presidents, celebrities, and even baseball legend Babe Ruth, who played poker and cooked clam chowder there. Today the house is a camp for future scientists and is maintained by the New Jersey Division of Fish and Wildlife as a Natural Resource Education Center. It has seven bunkrooms, a common room, a full kitchen, and a dining room.

On the north side of the islands is a beautiful spot that many refer to as "the Bahamas" because the combination of healthy eelgrass and sand flats make the water crystal clear. This wasn't always the case, but recent conservation efforts have contributed to the restoration of this important environmental area.

On the southern end of the islands is a dike that was built by the United States Army Corps of Engineers to protect the islands from the eroding effects of Barnegat Inlet.

There are many options for paddling routes, but two good ones (both beginning at Area 21) are detailed on the Island Beach State Park Canoe and Kayak map, available online at mappery.com/map-of/Island-Beach-State-Park-Canoe-and-Kayak-map. Each normally takes about two to three hours to paddle, though they are only 2.5 to 3.0 miles in length. You can combine portions to make a longer route or explore other sections of these beautiful islands.

Marsh Elder Trail

Launch from the little beach at Area 21 into Barnegat Bay. The water is often calm, especially on warm summer mornings. You will be paddling in the conservation zone, where personal watercraft and commercial shell fishing are prohibited (although recreational clamming and fishing are allowed). You will start by paddling

The sandy beach launch at Area 21.

through several deep channels, but once you reach the islands, the water can be just a few inches deep and crystal clear.

To follow Marsh Elder Trail, paddle west (and slightly south) out to the tidal marsh and between the two islands that face the launch. There's a path between the two that leads to an opening called the Horsefoot Slough. This narrow channel is very shallow and can have sandbars at low tide. When you see the sign that says, "Natural Area, No Personal Watercraft," you will be entering the Marsh Elder Thoroughfare (a cut that runs through Main Island on its eastern side). It's best to paddle this section while the tide is incoming to avoid getting stranded on mud flats. When you get to the top of the island, turn right and head southeast (to the left of Dorsett Island) and back to the launch. This loop trail is approximately 2 nautical miles.

Little Bay Trail
To follow Little Bay Trail, head southwest from the launch through the opening at Snake Ditch—which is deep and has plenty of water—and through the marsh channel toward Little Bay. Snake Ditch doesn't really have snakes in it, so don't let that scare you away. When you reach Little Bay you will be treated to a stunning view of Barnegat Lighthouse in the distance. Turn right and paddle through the main channel, called Sea Dog Island Thoroughfare, all the way to Horsefoot Slough. This thoroughfare can be paddled only during high tide. This area is beautiful and is a great place to see many bird species, including osprey, gulls, peregrine falcon, and cormorants. Make an immediate right turn and paddle through the channel directly east to head back to the launch. This loop trail is approximately 3 nautical miles long.

Strong currents are common during new- and full-moon tides, and paddling the area at low tide can be challenging as many sandbars emerge with the receding water. You will likely see people standing in ankle high water, competing with the birds for clams. It's best to check the tide tables before leaving to ensure there will be enough water to paddle. Also, be sure to bring insect repellent and a GPS device.

MORE INFORMATION
Island Beach State Park (www.state.nj.us/dep/parksandforests/parks/island.html; 732-793-0506). Sedge Island Natural Resource Education Center Workshops (nj.gov/dep/fgw/sedge.htm).

11
GREAT BAY

Travel through creeks, marsh, winding tributaries, and open water in this spot along the Atlantic Flyway and see a wide variety of bird species.

Distance ▸ 7.0 or 9.0 nautical miles

Cautions ▸ Strong tidal currents can be found anywhere in Great Bay and the bordering marsh, but the open waters of the bay can be particularly tricky. Make sure your skill level matches the demands of the conditions and if you feel unsure, head back to the launch instead of taking a risk. If you choose to launch from the southern point of the peninsula, at the end of Great Bay Boulevard, be aware that the water here is full of currents since the Atlantic is just off in the distance to the left. Launching from this beach should only be attempted by very skilled kayakers. The water is rough, and there are submerged pilings on the right side as you launch.

Charts and Maps ▸ NOAA Electronic Chart US5NJ20M / Paper Chart #12316

LAUNCHES

First bridge, Tuckerton From the Garden State Parkway, take Exit 58 to CR 539. Go approximately 3.6 miles and turn right onto E Main Street (US 9). Take the third left onto Great Bay Boulevard (CR 601) and follow it to the launch at the first bridge. There is no fee to launch, and there are no restrooms. *GPS coordinates: 39° 33.841' N, 74° 20.540' W.*

Second bridge, Tuckerton Continue on Great Bay Boulevard less than a mile to reach the launch at the second bridge. There is no fee to launch from there either, nor are there restrooms. *GPS coordinates: 39° 33.302' N, 74° 20.262' W.*

Alternative Launch Another launch site is located at the very end of Great Bay Boulevard. You can park in the circular turnaround area and walk your boat down the narrow, sandy path; it's a short distance to the beach. There are no fees to park,

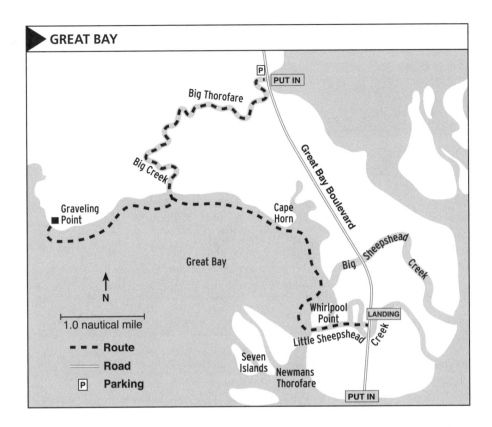

and there are no restrooms. This launch should be used only by advanced paddlers. *GPS coordinates: 39° 30.502' N, 74° 19.214' W.*

ROUTE DESCRIPTION

Great Bay Boulevard Wildlife Management Area is a peninsula of marshland that comprises the eastern side of Great Bay. It is located south of Beach Haven and north of Atlantic City, in an area where there's a break along the barrier islands.

Great Bay is a large circular bay and is considered to be one of the most undisturbed marine wetlands habitats in the northeast. The Mullica River feeds into Great Bay and the two together make up the Mullica River–Great Bay estuary. In Great Bay's southeast corner Little Egg Inlet connects the bay to the Atlantic Ocean.

Great Bay Boulevard runs through the marsh in the Great Bay Boulevard Wildlife Management Area and continues all the way out to the southeastern corner of Great Bay, at the mouth of the Bay, not far from the Atlantic Ocean. This is also the farthest point south on the marsh peninsula.

Driving on Great Bay Boulevard is an interesting experience, to say the least. As you approach Great Bay, the road turns into a narrow, two-lane causeway that traverses the marsh and connects multiple islands. It is virtually the only "solid" land on the whole peninsula. The road was used years ago by large trucks to transport fish when a now abandoned fish processing plant was in operation on a neighboring island. The road surface is hard-packed gravel and sand, but is usually in good condition. It passes over six wooden bridges, and two of the bridges are only one lane wide. Few people make the journey out there except for bird-watchers, anglers, and paddlers. The entire length of the boulevard is beautiful, and there are several very small marinas along it. If you like the feeling of isolation, this is the place for you.

Great Bay is very large and features creeks, marsh, winding tributaries, and open water. As you drive to the end of the road, you will pass two nice public launches on the right side of the road. These put you in the pretty tributaries that lead through tall marsh grass into the eastern portion of Great Bay. The first launch is just after the first bridge. The second launch is just after a tiny marina and two more follow as you make your way to the end of the road. (You will pass another small marina, called Captain Mike's Marina, which rents kayaks.)

I recommend launching at the first put-in along Great Bay Boulevard. This is a protected launch site in the extensive marsh that borders the wide bay. It is located at the first bridge you reach. There is a boat ramp and plenty of parking. There are a couple of nice round-trip routes through the marsh you can paddle from this location or if you have two vehicles, you can do a point-to-point to Little Sheepshead Creek.

First Bridge to Graveling Point

A great out and back paddle begins at the First Bridge launch and goes to Graveling Point on the north side of Great Bay and back. This route offers both the serenity of paddling through the marsh and the open water of Great Bay.

Launch at First Bridge and paddle southwest through the winding creek known as Big Thorofare. Kayaking through the tall marsh grass puts you in the living room of hundreds of species of birds. The area is part of the Atlantic Flyway and is simply spectacular for birding. Massive spring and fall migrations result in thousands of birds visiting the region. Arctic terns and snow geese are just two examples of the type of migratory species found in the refuge. Other favorites, such as rails and ibis, can be seen in this estuary regularly. A downside to this is the accompanying greenhead flies during the warmer months. Come prepared with bug spray.

The route will make an S curve before heading west toward the Mystic Islands area. Mystic Islands is a waterfront development that was built in the 1960s. It originally featured mostly pre-fabricated bungalows and was primarily a vacation community. In recent years, many of the bungalows have been replaced with more modern beach homes. As the creek turns south, you will pass to the east of Mystic Islands and will then be paddling in Big Creek.

Once you pass Mystic Islands, Big Creek continues to meander south until it ends in Great Bay. Once you reach Great Bay, turn right and paddle along the shoreline approximately 1.5 nautical miles to Graveling Point. You will pass Great Bay Marina on your way to the point. There is a small sandy beach near Graveling Point, where you can stretch your legs or have lunch.

The area near Graveling Point supports large beds of eastern oysters. The bay itself is also an active spawning area for blue crab.

Graveling Point is the turnaround on this route. Retrace your route back to the First Bridge launch. The round-trip mileage for this route is a little over 8.5 nautical miles.

First Bridge to Little Sheepshead Creek

A lovely 8.0-mile point-to-point route begins at First Bridge and ends in Little Sheepshead Creek. If you look at a map of Great Bay Boulevard, Little Sheepshead Creek is the creek closest to the end of the road and it runs completely through the peninsula.

Launching at First Bridge, follow the description for the First Bridge to Graveling Point route until you reach the open water of Great Bay. Instead of turning right and heading for Graveling Point, turn left and paddle southeast along the shoreline toward Cape Horn. Cape Horn is the next significant natural landmark and marks the entrance to a wide, marshy inlet.

Continue south past Cape Horn, along the shoreline, and past the entrance to Big Sheepshead Creek. You will then be headed for Whirlpool Point, the next significant

Paddling the marsh at Great Bay.

point of land that marks the entrance to an area known as Newmans Thorofare. As you make your way around Whirlpool Point, you will see the Seven Islands to your southwest. Newmans Thorofare runs between the peninsula and the Seven Islands.

Turn left into Little Sheepshead Creek instead of paddling toward the islands; it's hard to miss the ominous-looking remains of the deserted fish cannery on what is known as Crab Island (some also call it Fish Island). This imposing, empty carcass of a building was once an active fish processing plant that prepared a small oily fish called menhaden for use in fertilizer, fish oil, pet food, and fishmeal. Locally, it's simply known as the "Fish Factory" or more affectionately, the "Stinkhouse," since winds blowing from the south would engulf neighboring towns with the stink of dead fish when the plant was active. The 100-acre island has been abandoned since the early 1970s.

Highly skilled paddlers can head farther out into the bay to paddle around the Seven Islands, but expect the tides, currents, and winds to be very strong on this exposed route, especially on the western side of the islands. Be extremely cautious paddling near the islands due to tidal currents, waves breaking on the shoals, and hidden pilings under the surface of the water. These, however, do not deter playful harbor seals, who can often be seen hanging out in groups on the islands.

Continue paddling into Little Sheepshead Creek and up to the landing off Great Bay Boulevard.

MORE INFORMATION

Great Bay Boulevard Wildlife Management Area, New Jersey Department of Environmental Protection, Division of Fish and Wildlife (njfishandwildlife.com; 866-337-5669).

12
OCEAN CITY

Paddle through a large maze of bays and creeks that naturally lend themselves to kayaking and exploration.

Distance ▶ 3.5, 4.0, or 4.5 nautical miles

Cautions ▶ Ocean City is a popular destination for vacationers and as such many people take their motorized boats into the water. Be wary of them throughout your paddle.

Charts and Maps ▶ NOAA Electronic Chart US5NJ20M / Paper Chart #12316

LAUNCH

Tennessee Avenue, Ocean City I've tried launching at various sites around Ocean City, and I find the best place to launch is at the public ramp at the end of Tennessee Avenue. The launch is $12 for boats using the ramp, but it is free for kayaks. For safety reasons, don't use the ramp, but instead launch from the sandy soft launch. You can park for free, but don't use a trailer spot; instead park in the back row of the lot. There are no restroom facilities. This launch provides access to Blueways Trail. To reach the launch from the Garden State Parkway, take Exit 25 (Ocean City/Marmora). Turn left onto US 9. It will turn into Roosevelt Boulevard (CR 623). Continue over the bridge into Ocean City and turn left on Bay Avenue (to head north). Turn left on Tennessee Avenue, just past 23rd Street and follow to the end. The launch is on the left. *GPS coordinates: 39° 16.248′ N, 74° 36.224′ W.*

ROUTE DESCRIPTION

On paper, bustling Ocean City, New Jersey doesn't look like a top kayaking destination. A quick aerial look on Google Maps shows an organized grid of homes and businesses that cover nearly this entire 7.0-mile barrier island of sand dunes and marsh. Its busy 2.5-mile boardwalk is the centerpiece along this gently curving and highly developed section of the Atlantic coast.

The island is known as a family-oriented vacation destination, and as such, draws a large summer crowd for its beaches, shopping, entertainment, and dining. Ocean City is also a dry city and has been since its founding in 1879.

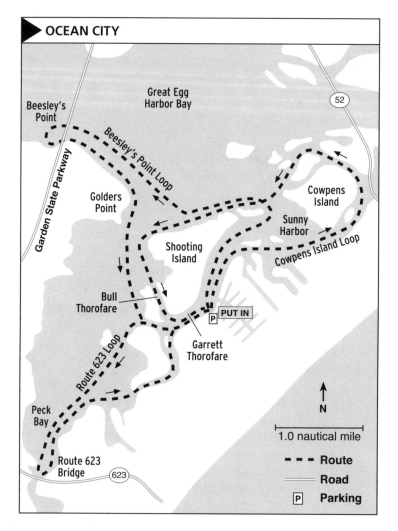

The western side of the island features a large maze of bays and creeks that naturally lend themselves to kayaking and exploration. If you research the history of the island, you will learn that this island has been a destination for human-powered watercraft for centuries. American Indians originally visited the island throughout the summer months because of its superb fishing. They were followed by whalers. The most noted, John Peck (the namesake of Peck Bay), even set up camp on the beaches and used the island as a home base thanks to its easy access and plentiful natural resources.

Today, these waters are still popular for fishing, but they are also an important roadway for recreational use. The Wetlands Institute, an educational institute located at 1075 Stone Harbor Boulevard, is focused on teaching the value of wetlands and coastal ecosystems across the globe. They developed the wonderful Jersey Island

Blueway guide that covers paddling routes in the back bays of Cape May County. This map can be viewed online at the institute's website, wetlandsinstitute.org, but it is best to pick up a printed copy at a local retail location such as Daks Kayak (609-938-1185) and the Cape May Visitor Center (609-391-0240) because the online version is difficult to read.

The map provides an introduction to the back waterways of the South Jersey shore and suggests places to explore and a variety of routes to paddle. The routes were developed by kayakers from different local paddling clubs. It is a good starting point for getting to know the area.

Beesley's Point Loop

Plenty of beautiful scenery can be found in the surrounding waters of Ocean City. The perfect way to become familiar with the back waters of this barrier island is to start with a 4.5-nautical-mile loop to Beesley's Point. Launch from the Tennessee Avenue launch and paddle to the right. The southern side of a low-lying island called Shooting Island is directly in front of you and provides wonderful protection from wind and waves. This lovely stretch of water leads up the eastern side of Shooting Island and is usually calm and easy to navigate. Cross over to the island's shoreline and paddle along its coast. Chances are high that you won't be alone while paddling but instead will have plenty of boat traffic. You will quickly come upon South Harbor (on the right side of the waterway), a large waterfront community of homes with direct water access.

Continue up the Shooting Island shoreline, and you will soon lose direct contact with the busy barrier island shore. As you pass the end of Glenwood Drive, another community called Sunny Harbor will wind around the corner to the right. Continue left, though, as the water opens up at the northeast end of Shooting Island. There will be a cluster of islands visible to the northeast, and as you make the turn around the tip of Shooting Island (to the left), wide open Great Egg Harbor Bay will be visible to the north.

This is the most open part of the route. From the northeast tip of Shooting Island, paddle directly west along its northern shore and make the crossing north to Golders Point. Depending on boat traffic and conditions, that crossing will be anywhere from 0.25 mile to more than 0.5 mile. Either way, set your sights on Golders Point. It sits at the tip of an area known as Beesley's Point. It is located on the mainland but is heavily bordered by marshland to the north. Paddle north up the shoreline to Beesley's Point and Beesley's Point Beach. The beach is a great place to take a break before heading back.

On the return trip, paddle back to Golders Point and cross back over to Shooting Island. This time paddle south along the island's western side. The island has a small split in its southwestern corner called Bull Thorofare. You can either paddle through the split or around the southwestern tip. Either way, after passing the island, turn left into Garret Thorofare to return to the launch.

Cowpens Island Loop

Another short loop that offers a combination of protected shoreline and open views to Great Egg Harbor Bay is the 4.0-nautical-mile loop around Cowpens Island. Launching from the Tennessee Avenue launch, paddle right, as you would for the Beesley's Point Loop. This time, continue paddling on the barrier island shoreline on your right as you pass the communities of South Harbor and Sunny Harbor. You will see the southern end of Cowpens Island, a protected marsh island with several small creeks running through it, in front of you.

When you reach Cowpens Island, you can stick to the left side of the thorofare, along the southeastern shoreline of the island. You will see the NJ 52 Bridge in front of you. Before you reach the bridge, the island curves to the left (north), following the island shore into Little Finger Channel. As you round the top of Cowpens Island, either follow its curve along its western side or make your way around the small neighboring island to its northwest. In either case, you will see Shooting Island to

The boat launch at Ocean City provides a quiet respite from the busy vacation city.

your southwest. Pick a point on Shooting Island, and make the short crossing to the island's northeastern tip.

Continue paddling around Shooting Island, to the west and then south. You can either cut through Bull Thorofare to head back to the launch or go around the tip of Shooting Island.

Route 623 Loop

A pleasant southerly route takes you 3.5 nautical miles round-trip to the CR 623 Bridge and back. Launch from the Tennessee Launch, but this time paddle left through Garrett Thorofare and into Peck Bay. Paddle south as Peck Bay narrows. You will soon see the short bridge for Route 623.

Paddle toward the bridge and the large marina to the right of it, being very careful of boat traffic, and turn around at the bridge. As you head back to the launch, if the tide is high, you can explore some of the small islands near the Municipal Airport. Continue to follow the barrier island shoreline back to the launch.

For a longer route, you can combine any of these loop routes.

MORE INFORMATION

Municipality of Ocean City (ocnj.us; 609-399-6111). The Wetlands Institute, wetlandsinstitute.org.

13
EGG ISLAND–GLADES PADDLING TRAILS

A large salt marsh with countless tidal creeks, Egg Island offers the opportunity to see shorebirds, ducks, hawks, bald eagles, terns, and gulls.

Distance ▸ 2.6, 6.1, 6.7, or 9.1 nautical miles

Cautions ▸ The Glades Wildlife Refuge has deemed each trail appropriate for intermediate to advanced paddlers under calm conditions. The trails are tidal, so water flow can be quite strong with the tide and wind. There are a minimal number of access points to the trails, so once you're out there, you're fairly committed to the entire trail. Be sure to check the weather and tides before you head out. The New Jersey Division of Fish and Wildlife asks that everyone leave a copy of their float plan and expected finish time on the dashboard of their vehicle. They also ask that in an emergency you stay with your boat. It is nearly impossible to walk through the marsh. There are no fees to paddle in the refuge and there are no restroom facilities at the launches.

Charts and Maps ▸ NOAA Electronic Chart US4DE12M / Paper Chart #12304

LAUNCHES

Turkey Point Trail, Downe The launch is from a sandy little beach with a gradual slope. The launch is right next to the bridge on the right side. There is plenty of parking, and you will likely be joined by people fishing and crabbing. To reach the launch from CR 553/Main Street in Downe, take Turkey Point Road until the end of the road. When the street ends turn right to follow the sign for Turkey Point Nature Drive. (This is still Turkey Point Road even though it doesn't seem like it is). Follow the road through the marsh to the end. *GPS coordinates: 39° 14.770′ N, 75° 7.812′ W.*

Oranoaken Creek Trail, Newport The launch is at a private boat rental facility called Beaver Dam Boat Rentals, located off CR 553 at 514 Old Beaver Dam Road, Newport, NJ. *GPS coordinates: 39° 17.044′ N, 75° 8.489′ W.*

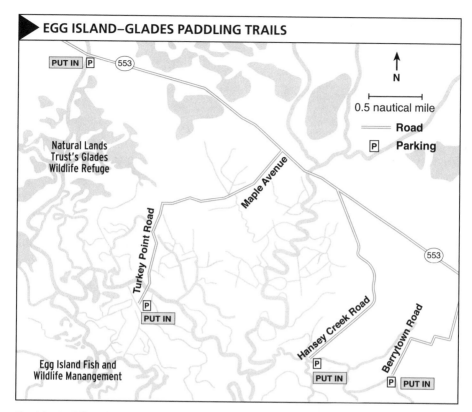

For this trip, follow channel markers and use the more precise maps for your specific trip from njfishandwildlife.com/artpaddletrails.12.htm#maps.

Hansey Creek Trail, Port Norris The launch is at the end of Hansey Creek Road on a free boat ramp. To reach it from Port Norris, take CR 553 north and turn left onto Hansey Creek Road. Sections of the road are not paved. *GPS coordinates: 39° 13.803′ N, 75° 6.036′ W.*

Berrytown Trail, Port Norris This launch area is a little challenging, since it frequently floods at high tide. To reach it from CR 553, turn onto Berrytown Road and take it to the end. Make sure you park on high ground after unloading your boat. *GPS coordinates: 39° 14.443′ N, 75° 4.234′ W.*

ROUTE DESCRIPTION

The Egg Island Wildlife Management Area is a very large salt marsh with countless tidal creeks located near the Delaware Bay shore. The New Jersey Division of Fish and Wildlife manages the area and has developed a system of canoe and kayak trails called Glades Paddling Trails.

The trails go through the Glades Wildlife Refuge, a 7,500-acre landscape of Delaware Bay beaches, tidal marsh, old growth forest, and wooded uplands. The area was once used for agriculture, and remains of old farms can be seen along the trails. The Glades Wildlife Refuge is owned by a non-profit, conservation organization called the Natural Lands Trust.

The trails are incredible for bird-watching, with kayakers often spotting shore-birds, ducks, hawks, bald eagles, terns, gulls, and other birds. Other types of animals, such as fox and deer, live in the area, too. It is also a winter habitat for thousands of snow geese.

There are four paddling trails. Each trail is designed as a loop, or they can be paddled in combination with other trails for a point-to-point trip. The trails are marked with tall poles that are painted at the top, with each trail marked with a different color. Because paddlers can usually see from one pole to the next, they don't get lost.

The refuge has deemed each trail appropriate for intermediate to advanced pad-dlers under calm conditions. The trails are tidal, so water flow can be quite strong with the tide and wind. There are a minimal number of access points to the trails, so once you're out there, you're fairly committed to the entire trail. Be sure to check the weather and tides before you head out.

Following is a description of the four trails, their distances, and access points. Estimated paddling times assume a speed of 2 to 3 MPH, but this can change dra-matically, depending on the wind and tide. The launch sites are remote, so bring a GPS device. A map of the trail put-ins can be found at state.nj.us/dep/fgw/pdf/paddle_trails.pdf.

Trail 1: Turkey Point Trail

Turkey Point Trail is my favorite of the four trails. This is partly due to its scenic launch at the end of Turkey Point Road, next to a stunning foot/fishing bridge, and partly because it is a great distance for a half-day paddle. The trail is marked with green markers and is a 10.5-mile loop. The total paddling time is 3.5 to 7 hours. A map of the trail can be found at www.state.nj.us/dep/fgw/pdf/paddle_turkeypoint.pdf.

At the launch, there is a pretty little footbridge over the water, a parking area, and an observation tower. This is a very scenic and popular spot, where people come to watch the sunset and to hear the songbirds sing in the spring. From August through October, the area is bright with fall wildflower blooms.

There are no restroom facilities.

Trail 2: Oranoaken Creek Trail

This trail begins and ends at Beaver Dam Boat Rentals. It is marked with blue mark-ers and is a 6.1-nautical-mile lollipop loop (an out and back with a loop at the bot-tom). The paddle time is between 2.5 and 5 hours. This route can be shortened to 3.6 nautical miles by paddling one-way to the Turkey Point boat launch. A map of the trail can be found at www.state.nj.us/dep/fgw/pdf/paddle_oranoaken.pdf.

Trail 3: Hansey Creek Trail

Hansey Creek Trail is marked with orange markers. It is a 7.7-mile loop paddle and normally takes between 3 and 5.5 hours. A map of the trail can be found at www.state.nj.us/dep/fgw/pdf/paddle_hanseycreek.pdf.

The Hansey Creek trail is another great trail. It intersects some of the other trails, but you can avoid going off course by following the orange markers. Like the other trails, this loop is mostly tidal marshes and can be challenging to navigate when paddling against the tide. This is a wonderful route for viewing osprey, as several nests are located near the trail. Other birds I've seen from the trail include ibis, egrets, and herons. There is usually a portable toilet at the launch site, but no other facilities.

Trail 4: Berrytown Trail

Berrytown Trail is marked with yellow markers. It is the shortest of the trails and is a 2.6-nautical-mile loop but can lengthened to 5.0 nautical miles by taking a one-way trip to the Hansey Creek boat launch. The paddling time is 1.5 to 3.5 hours. A map of the trail can be found at www.state.nj.us/dep/fgw/pdf/paddle_berrytown.pdf.

Turkey Point Trail launch.

This is a fun, short paddle if you follow the markers. Be aware that many creeks intersect the route, so pay close attention.

One challenge of paddling through the marsh on any of the trails is that the green-head flies can be ferocious in the summer. In this large, widespread, open space, they can gather by the millions and swarm, making things very uncomfortable. Since they are hard-biting flies, the most effective defense against them is to cover your skin, but it's always wise to bring bug spray when paddling the Glade trails between May and October.

MORE INFORMATION

New Jersey Division of Fish and Wildlife (njfishandwildlife.com; 609-292-2965). Egg Island–Glades Paddling Trails (www.state.nj.us/dep/fgw/artpaddletrails12 .htm).

14
CAPE MAY

Choose from a variety of routes to explore this mecca for bird-watchers.

> **Distance** ▶ 2.2, 4.5, 7.0, or 12.5 nautical miles
>
> **Cautions** ▶ Be aware of boats entering and exiting Cape May Canal and as you're paddling on the Atlantic Ocean. Be very careful when paddling on the open water south of Cape Island; only experienced paddlers should attempt it.
>
> **Charts and Maps** ▶ NOAA Electronic Chart US5NJ24M / Paper Chart #12316

LAUNCHES

Cape May Fisherman's Memorial Park, Cape May The best launch is located at Cape May Fisherman's Memorial Park. There are no restroom facilities here, but it is a lovely spot. To reach it from NJ 109 south in Cape May, turn left onto Washington Street, then right onto Texas Avenue, which becomes Pittsburgh Avenue. Turn left onto Missouri Avenue and take it to the end. You can park along Delaware Avenue and launch from there. There is no fee to launch. *GPS coordinates: 38° 56.684′ N, 74° 54.112′ W.*

Douglass Memorial Park, Cape May There is a small park in the southwest corner of Cape May Harbor, but be cautious, as the access to the water is steep and at low tide it can be muddy. To reach it from US 9, exit onto Lincoln Boulevard and turn left onto Beach Drive, taking it to the end. The launch area is west of the parking area and there are portable toilets. There is no fee to launch. *GPS coordinates: 38° 58.076′ N, 74° 57.807′ W.*

ROUTE DESCRIPTION

The city of Cape May, New Jersey, is located at the southern end of the Cape May Peninsula, at the junction of the Delaware Bay and the Atlantic Ocean. It is one of the oldest vacation destinations on the East Coast. The historic district in Cape May is known for its large concentration of historic Victorian buildings, but the area also has beautiful beaches and is a top location for bird-watching.

Water surrounds Cape May and as such, provides endless opportunities for those who have the kayaking bug. To the south and east is the Atlantic Ocean and to the

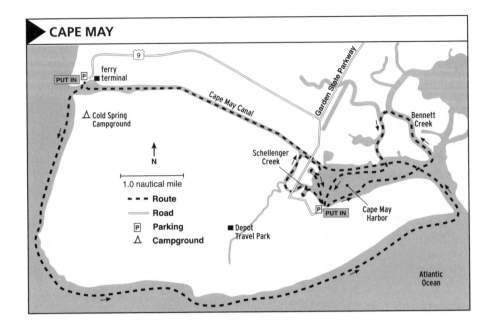

west is the Delaware Bay. In addition to those great bodies of water is the lovely Cape May Harbor and miles of surrounding marshland.

I enjoy paddling from and around the harbor in Cape May the best. The water is mostly protected, interesting creeks adjoin it, there is ample marshland nearby, and the large Cape May Canal flows into it on its west side.

The Cape May Fisherman's Memorial in its namesake park is a moving tribute to local Cape May fisherman who lost their lives at sea between 1897 and 2009. There is a granite monument with 76 names, and for those whose bodies were never recovered, this is the only place of remembrance. Surrounding the monument are flowers, shells, flags, photos, hats, and other items that either belonged to the fisherman or their families. There is also a lovely, but mournful statue of the wife of a fisherman and her two young children facing the bay and the entrance to the harbor, waiting for the return of her husband.

Launching in the southwest section of the harbor puts the entire harbor in front of you and there are endless options for paddling.

Cape May Canal

The opening to the Cape May Canal is between 0.5 mile and 1.0 mile from the Cape May Fisherman's Memorial Park, depending on the route you take. The canal itself connects Cape May Harbor with the Delaware Bay and is approximately 3.3 miles long.

The Cape May Canal was constructed in 1942 as an emergency wartime measure to provide shelter for ships from German U-boats patrolling off Cape May Point during World War II. The canal was built by the United States Army Corps of

Engineers and became part of the Intracoastal Waterway. The creation of the canal resulted in making Cape May an island rather than a true cape. The island is called Cape Island and includes Cape May, Cape May Point, West Cape May, and the southern sections of Lower Township.

Launching from the park, turn left and head up the western shore of the harbor, past the marinas, to the mouth of the canal. Be aware of boats entering and exiting the canal, as this is a very busy area for boat traffic.

Paddle up the canal, staying on the left side. Be careful not to paddle too close to the edge or else you'll hit breaking boat wakes. Three bridges cross the canal, the first coming right away: the NJ 109 bridge. The second is US 162 (Seashore Road), and the third is an old railroad swing bridge. Be careful around the railroad bridge. The current is very strong in this area, and if you throw boat wakes into the mix, you'll be paddling through a washing machine. It's best to keep to the left side since boats aren't really supposed to travel there.

As you approach the end of the canal, the terminal for the Cape May-Lewes Ferry will be on your right. Do not paddle anywhere near a ferryboat. Be extremely careful in the terminal area or turn around before you get there. The last place you want to find yourself is stuck between the side of the canal and a ferry.

Turn around at the end of the canal and paddle back the way you came, to the launch. From the launch to the Delaware Bay and back is approximately 7 nautical miles.

Cape Island Marina Loop

For a quick 2.2-nautical-mile paddle, turn left after launching at the memorial park and paddle along the shoreline, into Schellenger Creek. This is a busy area with many marinas and restaurants, but if you're out in the off-season or early in the morning, it can be a lovely paddle.

The landmass to your right as you enter the creek is a small island around which you'll paddle. Explore the small coves as you make your way up the creek. You'll pass Cold Spring Fish & Supply, the Lobster House Restaurant, and the South Jersey Marina before passing under the US 109 bridge.

After you paddle under the bridge, the creek bends to the right and connects with Cape Island Creek. Stay to the right at the intersection and continue paddling up the western side of the island, passing more marinas and restaurants. Continue to the end of the island and turn right into the Cape May Canal. You will see the second US 109 bridge. Paddle under the bridge and around the point where the large Cape Island Marina is located. Explore the marina cove if it's not too busy and then head back to the launch.

Bennett Creek Loop

The Cape May area is popular and can be very busy. If you're looking for a little more nature and a little less boat traffic, paddle a loop around the harbor and into Bennett Creek.

Starting at the Memorial Park, paddle left, clockwise around the harbor until you reach the entrance to Bennett Creek, on the north side. Paddle north into the creek and you will soon see the bridge for Ocean Drive. Continue under the bridge and to the right into Skunk Sound, which makes a slow curve to the right and then to the left before splitting at Skunk Sound Ditch. Stay to the right at the fork and make another right at the next fork to enter into the eastern arm of Bennett Creek.

The creek offers the opportunity to view beautiful salt marsh and birds such as egrets, herons, and osprey. There are many nooks and crannies you can explore from this route, turning it into a much longer outing.

Follow Bennett Creek south, going under Ocean Drive again, and back out into the harbor. Turn right when you reach the harbor and paddle around the point. If boat traffic allows, make the 1,000-foot crossing near Linger Point to the southern shore of the harbor. Paddle back along the shoreline to the launch. The total distance for this route is approximately 4.5 nautical miles.

Circumnavigation of Cape Island

Paddling around the entire Cape Island is a great trip for experienced paddlers in the summer. The launch for this trip is at Douglass Memorial Park near the Cape May-Lewes Ferry terminal. The park is located at the north side of the mouth of the canal. There is a public beach at the park.

The circumnavigation goes counterclockwise and is approximately 12.5 nautical miles. It should be paddled only on a calm day by experienced kayakers who are comfortable in open water, standing waves up to four feet, and with strong currents.

The best launch time is two hours before low tide at Cape May. This will allow for an "easy" paddle out of Delaware Bay followed by a push from the ebb tide around Cape May Point. This will put you at the Cape May Inlet around low tide. This is a great trip for viewing dolphin in the summertime and even the occasional pilot whale.

After launching, be very careful of boat traffic and fishing lines as you paddle along the north jetty, out of the canal and south into the Delaware Bay. In less than 2.0 nautical miles from the launch, you'll see the concrete shipwreck of the S.S. *Atlantus*, which is in three pieces. The stern is most visible, the bow can be seen at low tide, and the middle is completely submerged. Paddle through the middle of the ship. You can land at Sunset Beach near the wreck if you need a break or to make adjustments.

Be mindful of a series of jetties as you make the slow curve around Cape May Point. Some of the pieces are submerged. Leave ample room between you and the jetties. Your next landmark will be the Cape May Lighthouse, followed by a concrete bunker from World War II. Tough currents and waves can be a challenge anywhere on this route, but there are also days when the water is calm much of the way.

A little more than a mile farther is the Cape May fishing jetty. Be careful near the jetty. There are many sandbars near it, so keep a good distance away from it. The next leg provides some lovely open water. Aim for the western jetty at the Cape May Inlet that sticks out from the United States Coast Guard grounds. There should be two yellow buoys that you can paddle outside of. I've read in several places that these buoys indicate a safe course when the Coast Guard is having shooting practice, but I have not been able to verify this. It's best to just paddle outside of them to be safe.

Paddling through the inlet can be the most challenging. This trip is best during the week when there is less boat traffic, and this is an especially high traffic area. There are no good rest points or beach landings along the Atlantic, but you can take a break once safely in the harbor just past the Coast Guard installation (located on the south side of the inlet). As the flood tide starts, the water will push west up the harbor.

Once in the harbor, make the crossing to Linger Point and follow the north shore of the harbor to the Cape May Canal. At this point, you are a little more than 2.5 nautical miles from completing the trip. Paddle up the canal and back to the launch.

MORE INFORMATION

City of Cape May (capemaycity.org; 609-884-9525).

The Cape May Fisherman's Memorial features 76 names of local fishermen who have died at sea since 1897 and a statue of a fisherman's wife and her children looking out to the sheltering waters of Cape May.

THE CAPE MAY DIAMONDS

If you are strolling on the beaches of Cape May and your eye catches a glimpse of something shimmering along the tide line, it's most likely a "Cape May Diamond." Don't plan to pay for your next kayak with the proceeds from your find, since unfortunately, these "diamonds" are merely pieces of pure quartz that have had their coatings removed by the force of the surf. But they are nonetheless a local treasure and are very pretty little stones.

People have beach combed for these quartz crystals since the early 1800s. The most likely source of these sparkly little "gems" are either the larger rocks in the Delaware River or gravel deposits left from the Pleistocene (around the time of the last glacial period). As pieces of rock break off and wash down the river, they get pounded against other rocks along the way and then finally, the surf of the bay and the Atlantic Ocean. This constant rubbing wears them down and makes them smooth and round. The journey to the beach can take many years.

The average "diamond" is a small, smooth stone. Once polished, they greatly resemble diamonds. Although the stones don't yield a high return on the market (the largest ever found weighed in at three pounds, 14 ounces and sold for $500), hunting for them is a sort of local sport.

One of the best places to find these little beauties is on Sunset Beach, on the Delaware Bay. Some people believe that a sunken ship (visible as a chunk of concrete sticking out of the water) forces the pretty stones to wash ashore in this location as the water rushes around it. The beach consists mostly of small stones and pebbles (which actually aren't that nice for walking on), but it is a prime spot for finding the diamonds. Simply grab a handful of sand and sift through it.

The diamonds are clear quartz stones. Samples are on display at the Cape May Courthouse Museum. Several local books show photos of the stones as well and they are sold in local shops as souvenirs. If you want to turn your stones into jewelry or another type of keepsake, a local jeweler can polish them for you.

Even if you don't find any of these pretty little stones, Cape May is known for having beautiful sunsets, so there is always something special to look forward to on an evening beach walk.

DELAWARE

Delaware is small in area but big in coastline. Despite its tiny size (just over 2,000 square miles), it is dominated by water and has approximately 117 miles of coastline along the Atlantic Ocean and Delaware Bay. Most of the state is located on the Atlantic coastal plain.

Delaware offers a string of lovely beaches along 28 miles of the Atlantic Ocean. Popular vacation spots such as Bethany Beach, Rehoboth Beach, and Lewes draw thousands of visitors each summer and have become year-round destinations for many in recent decades. Kayaking has become an integral part of the atmosphere along the coast, with opportunities for launching, rentals, and guided tours.

Delaware has many state parks, and most offer lovely facilities for kayaking. Some even offer guided kayaking trips. Information about this can be found at destateparks.com.

Hundreds of acres of tidal marsh have been set aside in Delaware as wildlife habitat. Refuges near the Delaware Bay include Prime Hook National Wildlife Refuge (see Trip 15), Bombay Hook National Wildlife Refuge, and the Great Marsh Reserve. These reserves are known for attracting large numbers of migratory birds each year, and bird-watchers come from all over the East Coast to observe the yearly spectacle.

For the most part, launch areas in Delaware are well marked and include parking. Many do not have launch or parking fees but as a result are also primitive, with no amenities. The exception is Cape Henlopen State Park (Trip 16), which charges a fee but also has many amenities such as restrooms, changing facilities, and concessions.

15
BROADKILL RIVER

*Take a relaxing one-way trip down a river
steeped in history and featuring rare plants
and many birds.*

> **Distance** ▶ 11.0 nautical miles
>
> **Cautions** ▶ This can be a challenging paddle if you choose to travel against the tide and current.
>
> **Charts and Maps** ▶ NOAA Electronic Chart US5DE10M / Paper Chart #12216

LAUNCHES
Memorial Park, Milton From DE 1 North, turn left on Beach Highway (16). Turn left onto DE 5 South (to Union Street) and turn left on Chandler Street. Take the first right into the parking area. There is no fee to launch. *GPS coordinates: 38° 46.746' N, 75° 18.640' W.*

Lewes Public Boat Ramp, Lewes From Lewes, take Pilottown Road north to the end. There are portable restrooms, and there is no fee to launch. *GPS coordinates: 38° 47.498' N, 75° 10.152' W.*

ROUTE DESCRIPTION
The Broadkill River flows between the small village of Milton and the Delaware Bay, not far from the coastal town of Lewes. A paddle down this tranquil river provides a nice respite from the hustle and bustle of the Delaware beaches and an opportunity to view wildlife such as osprey, blue herons, migratory shorebirds, and otter.

The river's source is Wagamons Pond in the center of town and the river runs east. It rambles in a series of twists and turns through wetlands, salt marsh, and the Prime Hook National Wildlife Refuge, before turning sharply south and paralleling the Delaware Bay for its final 2.0 miles. The river ends by entering the bay at Roosevelt Inlet. The mouth of the river meets the Lewes and Rehoboth Canal, part of the Atlantic Intracoastal Waterway, a 3,000-mile inland water route that runs along the Atlantic and Gulf coasts.

It's hard to believe that the small village of Milton was once the hub of a thriving shipbuilding industry. For centuries, the 13.3-mile Broadkill River was used to

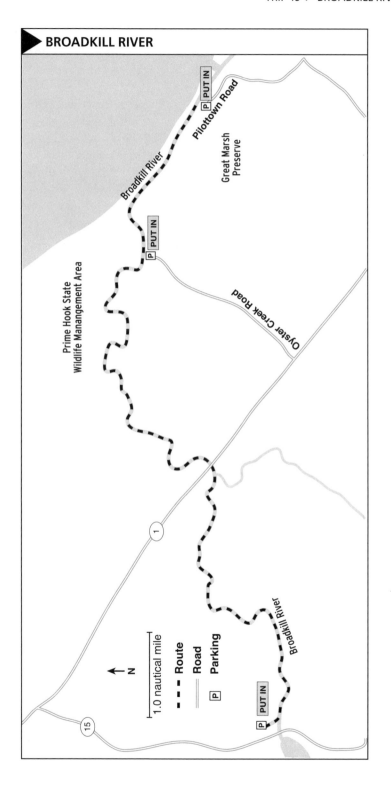

BROADKILL RIVER

Pilottown Road

PUT IN

Broadkill River

Great Marsh Preserve

PUT IN

Prime Hook State Wildlife Manangement Area

Oyster Creek Road

1

Broadkill River

PUT IN

N

1.0 nautical mile

- - - Route
—— Road
P Parking

15

transport local resources, such as grain and wood, between Milton and Roosevelt Inlet. The river provided reliable access to the inland forests that furnished the timber from which craftsmen built small ships, which in turn carried local goods to market downstream.

Settlement expansion continued throughout the seventeenth and eighteenth centuries, resulting in the building of larger and larger vessels that could reach increasingly distant ports. As the number of ships increased on the river, so did the reputation of the Milton shipbuilders. By the nineteenth century, Milton was the key ship supplier in the region and even produced ships for use in coastal and trans-Atlantic trade. The industry, however, rapidly declined during the 1890s as steamboats became more popular and the lack of quality timber in the region became an issue. Today Milton is best known as the home of Dogfish Head's production brewery.

The Broadkill is tidal, so it is possible to kayak in either direction on the river or time a round-trip excursion with the tides.

Following is a description of a one-way route from Milton to the Lewes Public Boat Ramp. From the launch in Milton, the first 2.0 nautical miles of your trip are on what is known as Broadkill River Canoe Trail. The shoreline starts out mostly forested and links Milton to the Edward H. McCabe Preserve, a 143-acre preserve that is maintained by The Nature Conservancy. As you near it, freshwater marshland forms a boundary between the river and the shore and then spills into mostly pastoral land. Several rare plants are found in the preserve, such as the seaside alder, bluejoint reedgrass, and saltmarsh bulrush.

There's a dock on the south side of the river in the preserve, where visitors are welcome to tie up their boats so that they can go exploring.

Continuing downstream, you'll paddle through meandering wetland and under DE 1. Be aware of an old submerged fishing pier near the bridge. The area is known for its abundance of shorebirds and other wildlife, so it's a good idea to bring binoculars.

About 1.0 mile past the bridge is the Steamboat Landing Campground, a seasonal establishment that's open May 1 to October 15. There are two boat ramps at the campground and a 70-slip marina.

The number of shorebirds generally increases as you approach the coast. During the spring migration, the waterfowl flocks can reach epic proportions. Bird-watchers from all over the mid-Atlantic region visit this area in late May to observe the spectacle.

The river continues to twist and turn through wetland and marshes and borders the Prime Hook National Wildlife Refuge. The refuge is a 10,000-acre sanctuary for migrating birds and was formed in 1963. The refuge is a mix of salt marsh, freshwater, forest, and grasslands. It is home to 267 species of birds, including bald eagles. Prime Hook offers a number of planned activities throughout the year and has launched many conservation efforts. One such effort includes prescribed burnings, which entails the planned burning of dozens of acres of successional field habitat. It returns succession to its early stages in order to curtail the growth of undesired plant species, remove hazardous fuels, and benefit grassland dwelling birds.

A number of canals meander off the main river into the marsh, and there are several communities of seasonal homes. It is helpful to bring a GPS device with you to reduce the likelihood of making a wrong turn into a canal. Duck blinds become more numerous in this area, a reminder of the enormous flocks of waterfowl that pass through the area on their annual migrations.

About 8.5 nautical miles into your trip, you'll pass a small boat launch area called Oyster Rocks (located at the end of Oyster Rocks Road). This is the start line of the annual Broadkill River Canoe and Kayak Race, an 8.5-nautical-mile race that runs upriver to Milton. The race takes place near the end of August and is one of the most well-respected and well-known flatwater races on the Delmarva Peninsula. Nearly 100 paddlers enter each year and battle it out for medals and prizes. If you're thinking of trying a race, this is a great one to start with.

As you continue toward the Delaware Bay, the river makes an abrupt right turn to the south and then parallels the shoreline for its final 2.0 nautical miles. You will likely see an increase in boat traffic in this part of the river, as you get closer to the bay.

The boat launch in Milton.

Approximately 1 mile northwest of Lewes, the river flows into the bay at Roosevelt Inlet. There is a United States Coast Guard station near the mouth of the river. Take out at the Lewes Public Boat Ramp, at the end of Pilottown Road, just prior to the inlet. There is parking at the ramp and portable toilets.

The trip down the Broadkill River is distinctly coastal, yet protected, and offers a remote feel. Under normal water conditions, it can be a great trip for novice paddlers, but is interesting enough for experienced kayakers.

Working with the tide, the entire trip between Milton and Roosevelt Inlet takes approximately 3 to 3.5 hours. It's wise to consult a current tide chart before launching in either direction.

MORE INFORMATION
Town of Milton (milton.delaware.gov; 302-684-4110). Prime Hook National Wildlife Refuge (fws.gov/refuge/prime_hook; 302-684-8419).

16
CAPE HENLOPEN STATE PARK

Check out two historic lighthouses and possibly dolphins on this paddle through potentially challenging waters.

Distance ▶ 1.5 or 4.0 nautical miles

Cautions ▶ The waters surrounding Cape Henlopen differ from day to day and are very unpredictable. Some days are calm, but other times paddlers must grapple with standing waves and whirlpools. These hazards stretch around the cape and also out to the Harbor of Refuge Light. It is best to time this trip with slack tide. The mouth of Delaware Bay is a major thoroughfare for cargo ships making trips to and from Wilmington and Philadelphia, so be wary of boat traffic.

Charts and Maps ▶ NOAA Electronic Chart US5DE10M / Paper Chart #12216

LAUNCH

Cape Henlopen State Park, Lewes The kayak launch area is on the Delaware Bay side of the park, on the beach near the fishing pier. When you enter the park ($10 entrance fee for non-Delaware residents and a $5 fee for Delaware residents), pick up a map and follow the signs to the pier. You'll find a large parking lot, restrooms, showers, a kayak rental facility, concessions, and a pavilion. Because this is a popular spot, you may have difficulty finding a parking space on a nice summer day. Once you've parked, unload your boat and take the sandy path down to the beach. To reach the launch from DE 1 south in Delaware, take US 9 east all the way to the Cape Henlopen State Park entrance. From the park entrance, follow the signs to the fishing pier, making two left turns and then one right turn. *GPS coordinates: 38° 47.163' N, 75° 6.097' W.*

ROUTE DESCRIPTION

Cape Henlopen State Park is located in Lewes, Delaware, at the point where the Delaware Bay meets the Atlantic Ocean. The beautiful 5,193-acre park consists of shoreline along the bay, wide ocean beaches, a large interior pond/saltwater

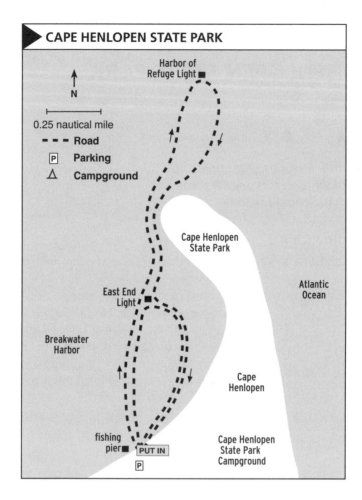

CAPE HENLOPEN STATE PARK

N

0.25 nautical mile

- - - Road

P   Parking

△   Campground

Harbor of Refuge Light

Cape Henlopen State Park

Atlantic Ocean

East End Light

Breakwater Harbor

Cape Henlopen

fishing pier   PUT IN

P

Cape Henlopen State Park Campground

impoundment, abundant wildlife, salt marsh, pine forest, and large sand dunes. The diversity of habitats within the park boundaries make it a wonderful place to view a variety of bird species, reptiles, and mammals. The park is also a prime nesting area for piping plovers, a threatened species of shorebird.

Since Cape Henlopen is strategically located at the mouth of the Delaware Bay, it has a significant military and commercial shipping industry history. The U.S. Army built a military base at the cape in 1941, placing gun emplacements in the dunes and observation towers along the coast. In 1964 the military declared the area surplus property and the park was established.

At low tide, you'll have to portage over sandbars to reach water deep enough to float your boat. The beach is wide, sandy, and gradually slopes to the water. As you can see on the park map, a stone breakwater and lighthouse is off the beach, to the north. You can see the lighthouse from the beach. This is also a swimming beach, so be considerate of others when you launch.

The first Cape Henlopen Lighthouse was the first built in Delaware, and the sixth one built in colonial America. Constructed in 1767 on the north side of what is known as Great Dune (an 80-foot-high dune), the lighthouse guided ships from the Atlantic Ocean into Delaware Bay for more than 150 years before beach erosion led to its collapse into the ocean in 1926. Today, there are two lighthouses on the bay side of the park: the Harbor of Refuge Light and the Delaware Breakwater East End Light.

For the hundreds of miles between Cape Charles, Virginia and Sandy Hook, New Jersey, there are no natural harbors to protect ships during storms. The Delaware Bay sits in the middle of this stretch of coastline, but its large size precludes it from providing protection from rough seas. In the early 1800s, mariners along the seaboard called for a breakwater to be built inside Cape Henlopen. Construction began in

Low tide at the Cape Henlopen beach launch.

1828 and was completed in 1869, and the Delaware Breakwater East End Light was built on the breakwater.

As shipbuilding progressed, the safe harbor could not handle the deep keels of newer and larger Navy ships, so a second, outer breakwater was built in 1892, just 1.25 miles north of the original breakwater. The new, safe harbor was named the Harbor of Refuge. The Harbor of Refuge Light was built on the breakwater and is still an active navigational aid today. The Delaware Breakwater East End Light was officially discontinued as a navigational aid in 1996, but it has been preserved and tours of it are given during the summer.

The Delaware Breakwater East End Light is the one you can easily see from the launch at the fishing pier. Fog is often an issue at Cape Henlopen. In fact, records show that in 1905 the fog horn at the Delaware Breakwater East End Light blared for a record 645 consecutive hours.

After launching from the beach, you will be in Breakwater Harbor. Be careful of fishing lines coming off the pier. A great short, easy-to-moderate paddle is a trip to the Inner Breakwater to see the East End Light. This is a great area to ride small swells and to see schools of fish and horseshoe crabs.

As you paddle toward East End Light, be aware that the area between the pier and the light is prime for dolphin viewing. Thousands of dolphins make their way to the Delaware Coast each year, and in the summer they can be very numerous—so keep an eye out for these playful visitors. A round-trip route out to the East End Light and back is approximately 1.5 nautical miles.

Another good option on a calm day, or for experienced paddlers when the waters are choppy, is to continue past the East End Light and the point of the cape. From there, continue toward the Harbor of Refuge Light. The cape is a sandy hook that separates the Atlantic Ocean from the Delaware Bay. Because the waters can be difficult to navigate in this area, it is best to time this trip with slack tide.

You can sight first off of the East End Light, then off the cape point, and finally the Harbor of Refuge Light. The currents around the point will likely be the strongest you'll encounter on this route and they can differ significantly, depending on the wind and tide. Keep in mind that the Atlantic Ocean is on the other side of the cape. Be sure to evaluate the water conditions and your ability to handle it; staying close to shore can often provide the best protection.

As you pass the cape you can see an area called Hen and Chicken Shoal off to the east. There is a large buoy marker along the shoal. This is a particularly dangerous area for ships since the water is shallow; you can see waves breaking along it. But it's also another great place for viewing dolphins. Be very careful of boat traffic between the point and the Harbor of Refuge.

The mouth of the bay is a major thoroughfare for cargo ships making trips to and from Wilmington and Philadelphia. Be on the lookout for pilot boats that meet cargo and tanker ships coming into Delaware Bay. They have large sharks' teeth painted on their bows and can be a danger to kayakers. You may also see the Cape May–Lewes Ferry making one of its daily trips between Cape May, New Jersey and

Lewes, Delaware. The ferry ships are very large, so plan on only seeing them from a distance.

Much of the beach along Cape Henlopen is closed during spring and early summer so that the piping plovers can nest undisturbed. During this time you are not allowed to land your kayak between the last fishing pier and around the hook of the cape. Rangers patrol the area. When the beach is open, it's a popular spot for anglers, so during that time, be mindful of fishing lines.

A round-trip route from the launch past the East End Light, past the tip of the cape, out to the Harbor of Refuge Light, and back is approximately 4 nautical miles.

Cape Henlopen is a beautiful spot to paddle as long as you pay attention to water conditions and take the challenges of the open water seriously. Many people enjoy the area regularly, but there have been deadly accidents over the years. Like any coastal area, take precautions and turn around if conditions become too much for your skill or comfort level.

If you have extra time after your paddle, it's worth exploring the nearby town of Lewes. The Dutch established this little gem in 1631 as a whaling station. It is a charming town with many shops, restaurants, a fantastic gift store for dogs, and, of course, ice cream.

MORE INFORMATION

Cape Henlopen State Park (destateparks.com/park/cape-henlopen; 302-645-8983).

HORSESHOE CRABS: NATURE'S SUCCESS STORY

The Delaware Bay is an ancient breeding ground for the largest population of American horseshoe crabs. These "crabs," which were originally named "horse foot crab" for their resemblance to a horse's hoof, are not really crabs at all, but instead are more closely related to spiders, ticks, and scorpions.

Horseshoe crabs have changed little over the past 400 million years. Nearly unrivaled in longevity, this species has weathered multiple ice ages, changes in sea levels, and even asteroid impacts. They have few predators in the wild due to their tough shells, they can withstand a wide range of temperatures, and they can go nearly a year without eating. Horseshoe crabs can live more than 20 years.

Horseshoe crab.

They also have had a hand in modern medicine. An entire industry evolved just to harvest their blood, a copper-based substance that has a unique property that causes it to turn to jelly and create a barrier when bacteria are present. It is used in the medical industry to ensure that injectable drugs do not contain endotoxins. Up to one third of a horseshoe crab's blood can be harvested without killing the animal. Once the blood is extracted, the crabs are returned to the wild. Horseshoe crab blood was also used to clean the surfaces of the space shuttle to make sure no bacteria was present.

Each year in late May and early June, hundreds of thousands of horseshoe crabs come ashore along the Delaware Bay to lay their eggs. They are most numerous during high tide and at times of low surf. Each female can produce up to 10,000 eggs in one season.

During their mating ritual, male crabs, which are about a third smaller than their female counterparts, gather along the edge of the surf to wait for the females. Upon their arrival, the male grabs onto the female's shell with a long glove-like claw. The female then drags her mate up the beach to the high tide line, pausing every few feet to dig a nest hole and lay thousands of small eggs. As she drags the male over the nest, he fertilizes the eggs. The crabs then return to the sea, leaving the nest to be washed over with sand.

During this time, thousands of crabs can be seen at one time on a single beach. They are usually shadowed by huge flocks of shorebirds who stop during their spring migration to eat the eggs.

17
DELAWARE SEASHORE STATE PARK

Paddle through marshes, into creeks, and around islands to catch glimpses of gulls, great blue herons, terns, osprey, egrets, oystercatchers, and diamondback terrapins.

Distance ▶ 3.5 and 4.0 nautical miles

Cautions ▶ Wind, tides, and weather conditions should always be heeded before heading out. The open waters of both Rehoboth Bay and Indian River Bay can be rough at times. There are also very strong tidal currents in the Indian River Inlet. This area should be avoided.

Charts and Maps ▶ NOAA Electronic Chart US5DE10M / Paper Chart #12216

LAUNCH

Savages Ditch Road, Bethany Beach There are several launch sites in the park, but my favorite is off of Savages Ditch Road, behind the barrier beach of the park, between Rehoboth Bay and Indian River Bay. There is a small group of islands that separates the two bays and provides the best jump off spot for exploration. It's open every day year-round from 8 A.M. to sunset; between May 1 and October 31 there is a $10 fee for non-Delaware residents and a $5 fee for Delaware residents. There is plenty of parking at this launch site, a portable toilet, and a covered pavilion with picnic tables and a grill. To reach it from DE 1, traveling south past Dewey Beach, turn right on Savages Ditch Road. If you reach the Indian River Inlet Bridge, you've gone too far. There is a sign for Savages Ditch Road and the Kayak Launch on DE 1. *GPS coordinates: 38° 37.677' N, 75° 4.200' W.*

ROUTE DESCRIPTION

Delaware Seashore State Park is a narrow, 2,825-acre barrier island sandwiched between the Atlantic Ocean to the east and Rehoboth Bay and Indian River Bay to the west. Compared to the neighboring developed resort areas the park is a wonderful oasis of natural beauty. It is 6.0 miles long and was established in 1965.

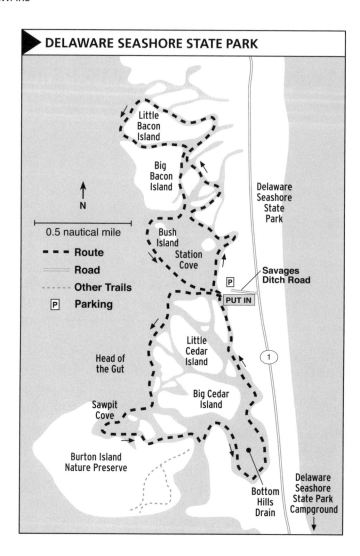

DELAWARE SEASHORE STATE PARK

Little Bacon Island

Big Bacon Island

Delaware Seashore State Park

N

0.5 nautical mile

Bush Island

Station Cove

Savages Ditch Road

PUT IN

Route

Road

Other Trails

Parking

Head of the Gut

Little Cedar Island

1

Sawpit Cove

Big Cedar Island

Burton Island Nature Preserve

Bottom Hills Drain

Delaware Seashore State Park Campground

There is a large campground with RV and tent sites that faces the Indian River Inlet. The park is known for its great fishing and is one of the most popular destinations in Delaware.

There is a short sandy path that leads down to the launch. You will see the entrance to the path on the left when you drive in on Savages Ditch Road. It is 60 steps from the pavement of the parking lot to the beach launch. At low tide the launch area has very little water. Low tide exposes mussels on the shoreline, but it's best to paddle at high tide; otherwise, you may have to portage through low, muddy water. It's a short paddle down a scenic little creek to the bay. This is a beautiful spot.

Delaware Seashore State Park is located on a barrier island that changes frequently with the forces of tide, wind, and storm. The area was actually largely inaccessible until two steel and stone jetties were built in 1939 to stabilize the Indian River Inlet. As such, there are many potential routes to enjoy in this pristine area of marsh islands. Pack a GPS device, and take as much time as you have to explore. Following are two routes I enjoy, but feel free to paddle anywhere that looks appealing to you.

Northern Route

To paddle a nice 3.5-nautical-mile route to the islands just north of the launch, put in at high tide and turn right out of the launch inlet, into the marshes of Rehoboth Bay. Paddle north along the marsh and into the first tidal creek on the right. You should be able to see a bit of the Indian River Life-Saving Station. This fully restored station looks just as it did back in 1905. Originally built in 1876, it was created to respond to the high number of shipwrecks that occurred along the Atlantic coastline. The building is actually 400 feet farther from the ocean today than when it was built. A sand dune began to naturally form around it as soon as it was built, so it was relocated in 1877. The building is listed in the National Register of Historic Places. If you're interested in a tour after your paddle, it's open to the public. The park's nature center is also located in the station.

Paddle back out of the creek, into Station Cove, and continue northwest along the marsh. You can take one of the next two narrow paths on your right that lead through the marsh. Either one will take you near Old Inlet Bait & Tackle. Continue to wind your way west to the next big tidal inlet and then make your way north again until you reach the east side of Big Bacon Island.

Big Bacon Island is the first large island you'll reach when paddling north toward Rehoboth Bay. On this route, you'll just "touch" the east side of the island before paddling northeast around Little Bacon Island (the second large island). This area is the nesting ground for many types of shorebirds. At certain times of the year, the islands seem overrun with gulls, herons, terns, osprey, egrets, and oystercatchers. You can also see pelicans in this area, especially when winds off the Atlantic make it difficult for them to fly along the coast. You will also likely see horseshoe crabs (especially in the spring) and turtles.

You will then circumnavigate Little Bacon Island. The western side of the island faces the open water of Rehoboth Bay and is the least protected part of the route. Once you complete the circumnavigation of Little Bacon Island, return by going down the entire length of Big Bacon Island on its east side.

Once you return to Station Cove, you can paddle around Bush Island and then return to the Savages Ditch launch site.

Southern Route

Another pleasant 4.0-nautical-mile paddle south of the launch area puts you immediately in the Cedar Islands.

Turn left once you exit the launch creek and head south through the narrow marsh trail. Little Cedar Island will be to your right, past the marsh. As you emerge into a larger but still protected area, stay between Big Cedar Island and the parkland to your left. Continue south into Bottom Hills Drain. You will likely see heavier boat traffic in this area from the local marina. Explore the Drain and continue out of the bay on its west side. You will be paddling around Indian River Marina.

Just west of the marina is the Burton Island Nature Preserve. Located on the largest of the islands, the preserve is an important nesting habitat for the diamondback terrapin. You are also likely to see fiddler crabs, muskrat, shorebirds, osprey, egrets, and great blue herons on the island.

On the east end of the island is an easy 1.5-mile interpretive hiking trail. The loop trail starts at the north end of Indian River Marina and is connected to the island by a causeway. The trail travels over sand and elevated boardwalks that pass over tidal creeks. It offers nice views of Indian River Bay and Rehoboth Bay. Unfortunately, there is no official kayak launch on the island, but you can park at the park

A calm river provides the perfect boat launch at Savages Ditch.

office and marina off Route 1 (south of the launch site) after your paddle to explore the island.

Continue paddling along the northern side of Burton Island and into Sawpit Cove. After exploring the cove, head out of its northern end, into the open waters of the Head of the Gut (which leads into Indian River Bay), and then paddle north along the western shore of the Cedar Islands.

You can easily take time to pass through the many creeks and channels that run through the Cedar Islands. When you've had enough or are out of time, continue north around the top of the island and turn east to head back to the launch.

For a great 7.5-mile paddle, combine both the northern and southern routes.

MORE INFORMATION

Delaware Seashore State Park (destateparks.com/park/delaware-seashore; 302-227-2800). Indian River Life-Saving Station (destateparks.com/attractions/life-saving-station; 302-227-6991).

18
ASSAWOMAN CANAL

Take a ride down a lush, serene canal that was originally built in the late nineteenth century.

Distance ▶ 5.5 nautical miles

Cautions ▶ Boat traffic can be heavy on the canal during the summer months. Stay to one side of the canal to allow larger boats access to the deepest water.

Charts and Maps ▶ NOAA Electronic Chart US5DE10M / Paper Chart #12216

LAUNCH

Kent Avenue, South Bethany My favorite place to launch is from a small, hidden, sandy ramp right by the Jefferson Bridge off Kent Avenue. The launch is technically on Guy Street, but Guy Street is a small, unmarked dirt road. You will likely share the small parking area by the launch with other kayakers, jet skiers, and small boats under 20 feet. This is a very primitive launch site with no amenities, but there is no fee to launch and park. To reach it from DE 1 South, travel through Bethany Beach to the Sea Colony area, and turn right onto Westway Drive. You will drive through the Sea Colony community. Turn left at the traffic light onto Kent Avenue (Road 361). There is no street sign at the intersection. As you round the curve and approach the bridge that runs over the canal, there is a very small dirt road on your left with no street sign. This is Guy Street, although it doesn't look like a real road. Follow it down to the sandy launch. *GPS coordinates: 38° 31.340' N, 75° 4.111' W.*

ROUTE DESCRIPTION

The presence of the Assawoman Canal escapes most vacationers to the Delaware beaches. The scenic, straight, more than 3.0-mile canal connects the Indian River Bay via White Creek, to the north, with the Little Assawoman Bay via Jefferson Creek, to the south. Jefferson Creek adjoins the 3,100-acre Assawoman Wildlife Area.

The Assawoman Canal was originally dug by hand in the 1890s and was financed by the United States Army Corps of Engineers. It was dredged in the 1950s to allow boat traffic to continue to travel through it. The canal was once part of the Intracoastal Waterway and provided a great opportunity for farmers to transport produce

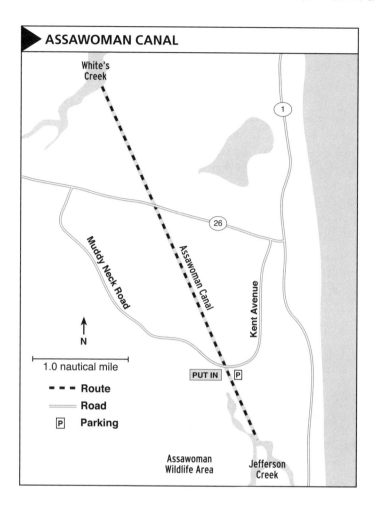

to summer resorts on the coast. However, after decades of neglect following the initial dredge in the 1950s, it became too shallow for motorboat traffic.

A plan was then created to maintain the waterway as a navigational boat route. After several years of dredging, the canal was reopened to motorboat traffic in 2010, creating a way for boaters on the northern end of the canal to reach popular restaurants and recreation on Fenwick Island and in Ocean City. The center depth of the canal is 3 feet below mean low water and it has a base width of 35 feet. Special attention was given to maintaining environmental and ecological buffers on either side of the canal.

Although it is bordered by Bethany Beach and South Bethany to the east and Ocean View to the west, many sections of the canal have a lovely tree canopy that make it feel remote. Even though the canal was dredged, there are still hazards to be aware of. To preserve valuable wildlife habitat, buffers were left untouched on either side of the canal. This means that approximately 10 feet of water on both sides has undisturbed vegetation and submerged logs. In addition, swift currents can reach four to five knots, making the waterway a challenge for kayakers. Luckily, the entire canal is a no-wake zone, so that helps. Another plus is that the canal is very sheltered from the wind, so on days when the bays are too rough to paddle, it provides a good alternative for kayakers.

The paddle through the canal is just beautiful. It is green and serene, and in many places the tree canopy makes a complete arch over the canal. Kayakers can feel as though they're paddling through a green tunnel, and the trees provide nice shade on hot, humid days. Three bridges cross the canal: Road 357 (near the northern end), Atlantic Avenue (near the middle of the canal), and Road 361 (Jefferson Bridge) at the southern end. A second canal enters the Assawoman Canal near the Atlantic Avenue Bridge, and because it comes in at nearly a right angle, it's easy to stay on course.

Since the launch is located near the southern end of the canal, I normally paddle north toward White's Creek and then pass the launch on my way back to cover the entire canal. This round-trip is just less than 7.0 nautical miles. The Ocean View

Assawoman Canal at Guy Street launch.

Marina is situated at the north end of the canal and it is a good place to stop and stretch and maybe have some ice cream or another snack if you so desire.

The tide will make paddling in one direction significantly more difficult than the other, so take this into consideration. If it feels as if you're flying up the canal when you start out, you're probably riding the current.

You will likely encounter boat traffic on the canal, but many are courteous to kayakers, and some even cut their engines back further than required to fulfill the no-wake requirement. Pontoon boats are common in the canal since it's a nice place to cruise up and down slowly.

Be mindful of the tree stumps and debris along the sides of the canal. Stay to the center if there is no boat traffic, but allow larger boats to use the center of the canal where the depth is 3.0 to 7.0 feet in most areas.

At the southern end of the canal is a small, marshy island in Jefferson Creek that is interesting to paddle around before making your way back up the canal. This is a good place to view shorebirds. The state puts out markers during the summer season to help with navigation. The Assawoman Wildlife Area sits just to the southwest of the end of the canal and contains a mix of loblolly pine forest and food crops for wildlife.

If you are paddling into the canal from White Creek on the north end, the canal entrance is just past marker 13 and sits between Canal Street and Elliot Avenue, by the private Sunset Harbor community. There's a large pool at the end of Canal Street that you can use as a marker for the entrance. If you're facing the pool, the entrance is the waterway to the right, then go right again immediately past the entrance at the fork.

MORE INFORMATION

Assawoman Canal (destateparks.com/park/holts-landing/assawoman-canal.asp; 302-227-2800).

MARYLAND

Maryland is a kayaker's dream. Although it's a small state, it contains more than three percent of the country's coastline. Exactly how many miles of coastline it includes seems to be up for debate. Official estimates range between 3,190 miles and 7,719 miles. The vast range is likely due to differences in the definition of coastline since the portion of tributaries included can vary greatly. Whatever the exact number, one thing is certain: Maryland has more than enough miles of coastline to keep a paddler busy for many years.

One of the most prominent features in eastern Maryland is the mighty Chesapeake Bay. The Bay is a 200-mile long estuary that separates the mainland from the Delmarva Peninsula. It is a major feature in the state, from both an economic and recreational standpoint. The Chesapeake Bay allows for worldwide trade to pass through the busy Port of Baltimore and also provides a traditional waterman life for many local fishermen throughout the quiet Eastern Shore.

Maryland offers many choices for sea kayakers. They can paddle around the historic capital city of Annapolis (see Trip 20), through the busy industrial harbor of Baltimore (Trip 21), or in serene settings such as Wye Island (Trip 27), Blackwater National Wildlife Refuge (Trip 23), or Assateague Island (Trip 28).

There are many public launch sites in Maryland. Most can be accessed without a fee or parking permit. Some are located inside state or local parks that do require fees or via public boat ramps that impose minimal launch fees. For the most part, fees are readily posted and parking is relatively safe, although always lock your car and do not leave valuables inside.

19
POINT LOOKOUT

Explore the Chesapeake Bay, Potomac River, a creek, and a lake at this gorgeous haven for birds.

> **Distance** ▶ 1.5, 3.0, and 4.6 nautical miles
>
> **Cautions** ▶ Rough water can be present along the exposed shoreline of Lighthouse Trail.
>
> **Charts and Maps** ▶ NOAA Electronic Chart US5VA27M / Paper Chart #12233

LAUNCH

Point Lookout State Park, Scotland From Interstate 495 in Maryland, take the exit for MD 4 (Pennsylvania Avenue) south to Upper Marlboro. Continue on MD 4 until you cross the Solomons Island Bridge. After the bridge, turn left at the first traffic light onto MD 235 South. Continue to MD 5 and turn left (south). Follow MD 5 to the park and follow signs to the launch. Admission to the park is $7 and the ramp fee is $12. There are restrooms in the park. *GPS coordinates: 38° 3.127′ N, 76° 19.630′ W.*

ROUTE DESCRIPTION

Point Lookout State Park is a paddler's paradise that is located on a peninsula at the confluence of the Chesapeake Bay and the Potomac River. Located at the southern tip of St. Mary's County, it covers 1,042 acres and is managed by the Maryland Department of Natural Resources.

The park's name comes from its function as a lookout post during the War of 1812, when it was used to track the movement of British war ships. Point Lookout was also the base for a secret pony express organization that brought intelligence reports to Washington, D.C. under the cover of darkness.

Point Lookout Light guards the entrance to the Potomac River and sits at the southernmost point on the western shore of the Chesapeake Bay. The well-known lighthouse operated from 1830 to 1966 and is rumored to be the most haunted lighthouse in the country. The subject of numerous paranormal investigations, it has been featured in television shows such as *Mystery Hunters*, *Haunted Lighthouses*, and *Weird Travels*.

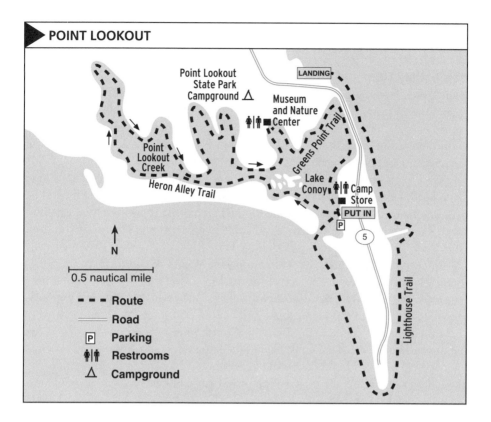

The park features several boat launch areas, canoe rentals, fishing, hiking, picnic areas, beaches, a playground, a museum and nature center, and camp store. Three waterways in the park are excellent for paddling: the lower Potomac River, the Chesapeake Bay, and Point Lookout Creek, which flows into Lake Conoy.

A water trail map is available at the store that shows three wonderful point-to-point paddling routes. The trails are Greens Point Trail (in Lake Conoy), Lighthouse Trail (in the Chesapeake Bay and Potomac River), and Heron Alley Trail (in Point Lookout Creek). They average 2.3 nautical miles in length.

Greens Point Trail
Greens Point Trail is a short, 1.5-nautical-mile trail that's great for novice kayakers. It begins near the boat ramp in Lake Conoy and follows the eastern shore of the lake. It offers views of shore birds, crustaceans, and a pine forest. It is a great place to see bald eagles. The trail ends at the museum and nature center.

Lighthouse Trail
Lighthouse Trail starts at the Pet Beach on the Chesapeake Bay and travels about 3 nautical miles south around the Point Lookout Lighthouse and into the Potomac

River. This is a challenging paddle and has strong currents, open water, boat traffic, and wind. The trail ends at Lake Conoy.

Heron Alley Trail

Heron Alley Trail is the longest of the three trails (4.6 nautical miles) and is another great route for novice paddlers since it flows through protected tidal marsh areas on Point Lookout Creek. The trail winds through a group of small islands and is terrific for bird-watching. It starts near the Lake Conoy boat ramp, heads west, and ends at the museum and nature center.

One of my most memorable paddles at Point Lookout was on a hot day in June when I paddled with a friend on both Greens Point Trail and Heron Alley Trail. The park was the location of the finish line for the Potomac River Swim for the Environment. The event is a very challenging 7.5-mile swim across the Potomac River from Hull Neck, Virginia to Point Lookout State Park. My husband was providing kayaking support to supply food, water, encouragement, and navigation assistance to a friend who entered the race. Meanwhile, my friend Andy and I were training for a 90-mile kayak race and seized the opportunity to squeeze in an early morning workout while the bulk of the swimming event occurred offshore. We then planned to cheer the swimmers as they approached the finish line.

After parking near Lake Conoy, paying the launch fee, and stuffing my keys into my dry bag, Andy said, "There's a snake over here." I looked at the rocks piled up along the shoreline, next to the boat ramp, and saw a rather thick but pleasant looking brown snake stretched out.

"Is it a water moccasin?" I asked.

A park ranger nearby answered, "No, we don't have those here. These will give you a nasty infection if they bite, but they aren't poisonous. This is a little one."

"Yeah, nothing like old Oscar," said a second ranger approaching.

"Who's Oscar?" I asked, shifting my kayak into the water and rolling up my paddling pants.

"He's a really old grumpy one who lives over there around the end dock," he said, pointing to a dock a few yards away. "They're pretty tame on land, but once they get in the water, they can get aggressive."

I quickly dropped into my kayak and paddled away from shore, yelling to Andy over my shoulder that he could paddle out to meet me.

The boat ramp puts you on Lake Conoy, in a large protected area between the Potomac River and a causeway that separates the lake from the Chesapeake Bay. It was a beautiful calm morning and the water was still. Sitting there, waiting for Andy, I looked up into a large dead tree at the edge of the water; there sat a gorgeous bald eagle. He was breathtaking. Wishing I had a more powerful camera with me, I managed to snap a few photos before he flew off.

"Well, that was worth the trip already," I said as Andy paddled up. We headed out to explore.

Point Lookout is a haven for birds. I know I say that about every trip, but let's face it: we're not looking for whales or caribou in the mid-Atlantic, so we usually have to rely on large raptors for wildlife excitement. This place, however, is truly loaded with birds. There were juvenile eagles calling in their rather delicate voices, more blue herons than I've seen in one location, and numerous osprey (my personal favorite).

We took our time exploring the grassy shoreline. We completely forgot that we weren't really there to sightsee, but to prepare for our race with a good workout. But the tranquility of the lake and the abundant wildlife made it difficult to remember our goal. We explored every nook and cranny, moving very slowly. We even got a good look at a few snapping turtle heads before they scurried underwater.

On return trips to the park, I've enjoyed challenging paddles through incoming waves on the Potomac side of the park, as well as more tranquil paddles on both the Potomac and Chesapeake sides. With the lake, river, and bay right at your fingertips,

Kayakers waiting to support swimmers in a race near Point Lookout.

the park offers an interesting diversity of conditions. The park itself is also lovely. It has wonderful picnic areas and ample beach to explore.

During the summer, the park occasionally reaches capacity on the weekends. When this occurs, cars are turned away at the front gate. It is best to paddle during the week in the summer or any time in the spring and fall, when the crowds have died down and there is less boat traffic. The park is open year-round.

Point Lookout has an extensive Civil War history. The Civil War Museum and Marshland Nature Center is located in the park campground and offers nature and historical programs. Lighthouse tours are also available.

MORE INFORMATION

Point Lookout State Park (dnr2.maryland.gov/publiclands/Pages/southern/pointlookout.aspx; 301-872-5688).

THE HAUNTED POINT

Point Lookout has a morbid chapter in its long history. It was the location of a large prison camp where many soldiers perished during the Civil War. Although the land on the point was used by the Union army as a hospital facility, it later became the largest Confederate prison camp and held more than 52,000 soldiers throughout the war.

The camp was primarily for enlisted men and it was known for having horrendous conditions. Prisoners lived in torn canvas tents with inadequate supplies, spoiled food, and contaminated water. Summers were hot and insect-infested and many prisoners froze to death over the winter months. Smallpox also ran rampant in the camp and forced the development of an infectious disease unit. Those who were lucky enough to survive lived in utter filth. Between 3,000 and 8,000 soldiers died at Point Lookout and were buried in a mass grave.

Whether or not you believe in ghosts, the numerous unexplained incidents and claims of encounters with spirits of those who passed at Point Lookout are interesting.

Many so-called supernatural events have been experienced and documented by park rangers at Point Lookout over the years. Some include conversations with unusual visitors looking for gravesites that have been gone for more than a century, while others include sightings of one particular "soldier" running as if fleeing in the same exact spot on multiple days. In addition, fishermen have reported hearing cries for help on the water when no one was there.

The lighthouse itself is often referred to as the most haunted lighthouse in America. For decades, paranormal activity has been reported there and the site has been scrutinized and investigated by many ghost hunters. More than 24 voices (some singing) have allegedly been recorded in the lighthouse, including those from both males and females; one particular female voice is said to be the wife of the first lighthouse keeper.

Rotten smells, chilly air, and spectral visions have also been recorded in the lighthouse and images of people from another era have shown up in the background of modern photographs taken inside.

Buildings from the prison camp are long gone and some of the land they stood on is now underwater. The lighthouse is open on select days to the public and occasionally hosts special events.

An interesting note to mention is that the "ghosts" reported have never threatened those who claim to see them. In fact, several past park rangers felt that they were being looked out for in some form or another during their time in the park.

20
ANNAPOLIS

Experience the fun intimacy of Maryland's capital city and the tranquility of its nearby creeks.

Distance ▶ 11.0 nautical miles (longer routes are possible)

Cautions ▶ Be alert when exiting Spa Creek and entering Annapolis Harbor, since the water can be choppy with boat traffic flowing into the harbor from both the Chesapeake Bay and the Severn River. Throughout the paddle, be prepared for changing tide, wind, and weather conditions.

Charts and Maps ▶ NOAA Electronic Chart US5MD32M / Paper Chart #12283

LAUNCH
Truxtun Park, Annapolis The most convenient place to launch is at the Truxtun Park boat ramp. Public launch sites are particularly sparse in this water-lovers' paradise, and Truxtun Park provides easy access to Spa Creek and allows for a short paddle to the Annapolis waterfront. There are two concrete ramps and finger piers at the end of Truxtun Park Road. Daily launch permits for launching and parking are available at the park for $8. The park is open sunrise to sunset. To reach the launch from MD 301 East in Maryland, take the exit for MD 665 East. Drive for approximately 4 miles and turn left onto Hilltop Lane. After approximately 1 mile, turn left onto Primrose Road. Stay left at the fork and continue on Truxtun Park Road until the end, where the launch is located. There are no restrooms. *GPS coordinates: 38° 58.108' N, 76° 29.915' W.*

ROUTE DESCRIPTION
Annapolis, Maryland is a picture-perfect seaport that sits at the intersection of the Severn River and the Chesapeake Bay. It is the capital of Maryland and temporarily served as the United States Capital in 1783 and 1784. Annapolis is home to the United States Naval Academy, world-famous blue crabs, and more eighteenth century buildings than any other city in the country.

From the beginning, Annapolis welcomed visitors from around the globe and due in part to its prime location, quickly became a playground for the wealthy. The

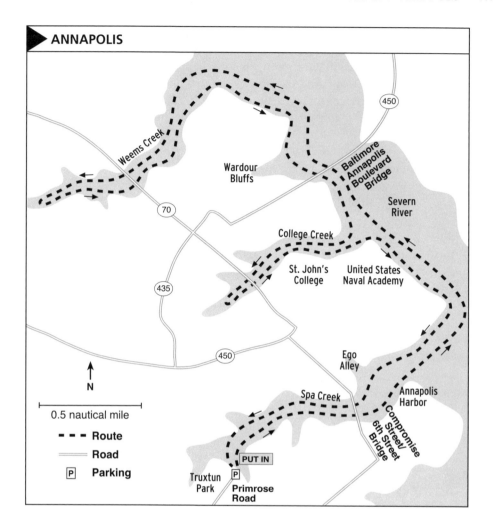

ANNAPOLIS

Weems Creek

Wardour
Bluffs

Baltimore
Annapolis
Boulevard
Bridge

Severn
River

College Creek

St. John's
College

United States
Naval Academy

Ego
Alley

Spa Creek

Annapolis
Harbor

Compromise
Street/
6th Street
Bridge

PUT IN

Truxtun
Park

Primrose
Road

N

0.5 nautical mile

- - - Route
═══ Road
P   Parking

city is known as the "sailing capital of the world," but it also makes a mighty fine place to paddle.

Before you set out with your kayak, paddle, and an appetite for seafood, here's a quick orientation lesson to help get you started (but won't replace a GPS device). Annapolis is surrounded by water on three sides: Spa Creek to the south, the Severn River to the east, and College Creek to the north. Spa Creek spills into the Chesapeake Bay, so it appears that Annapolis is on the Bay; most people think it is, but we won't split hairs about this.

Numerous additional creeks flow from the Severn River; there are eight just on the western side of the river that are located within 4.0 miles of Annapolis. In short, there is no deficit of fantastic places to explore by kayak.

Spa Creek is home to the bustling historic waterfront area and Annapolis Harbor. I highly recommend checking out the waterfront before or after your trip, and if you're a seafood lover, indulging in some blue crabs. The area is vibrant yet quaint, has many shops and restaurants, and hosts an international crowd.

Most of the shoreline along the usually calm Spa Creek is privately owned. I enjoy paddling past the well-maintained properties and ogling the beautiful homes that sit at the waters' edge. There are also numerous old oyster and crabbing boats tied up at the many private docks. From the creek, you can get a nice view of our nation's oldest state house, a reminder of the long history of Annapolis.

About 1.0 mile from the launch, depending on how many nooks and crannies you explore, is the Annapolis City Dock in Annapolis Harbor. You'll see it just after you pass under the bridge on Compromise Street. The Annapolis Yacht Club will be on your left, and boat traffic will increase dramatically, especially in the summer.

Annapolis Harbor is a sharp contrast to the busy industrial harbor in nearby Baltimore. Although Annapolis is packed with small marinas and city boat slips, it retains an intimate feel. Granted, you will be keeping company with some of the most beautiful and luxurious sailing yachts in the world and may wonder how this can feel comfortable, let alone intimate. The truth is, it's the people on board (not all, but most) who give Annapolis its own fun feel. I have found most of the sailing crowd in Annapolis to be very welcoming to kayakers. I've been on both sides of the railing (so to speak), as both a kayaker and a sailor and have engaged in many friendly exchanges.

Be careful as you paddle into the harbor, and wear bright clothing since it can be very difficult to be seen in such a congested area. Although the boaters may be nice, it won't stop them from running you over if they can't see you.

The historic, colonial-style waterfront is packed with seafood restaurants, bars, and shops, and the Naval Academy gives it a patriotic feel. You won't have any trouble identifying the famous Ego Alley, where for decades boaters have cruised up and down to show off their pride and joy.

Be alert when exiting Spa Creek. The water can be choppy, due to boat traffic flowing into the harbor from both the Chesapeake Bay and the Severn River. Paddle out of the harbor and into the mouth of the Severn River, to the left. To your right, you can see into the Chesapeake Bay, which on a nice day will be littered with white sails.

As you round the bend and head up the Severn River, the United States Naval Academy will be on your left. A large seawall around the academy compound throws wakes back at you as you paddle by, letting you enjoy crazy waves not once, but twice. Sometimes this area of the river has rollers that can be fun to surf on, but when it's really busy, the waves create more of a washing machine effect.

I prefer to paddle along the left shoreline instead of crossing the busy river. The first creek you will come to is College Creek. This pretty tributary passes by the Naval Academy's boating facilities and St. John's College (the third oldest college in the country, founded in 1696). The creek shoreline is less developed than the Spa Creek shoreline, and you'll paddle under three small bridges to explore the backwater. The creek offers a nice, sheltered route in comparison to the open water of the Severn.

Paddling into the Severn River again, continue upstream, under the Baltimore Annapolis Boulevard Bridge (MD 450), around Wardour Bluffs, and into Weems Creek, which flows past beautiful waterfront properties. Like College Creek, Weems Creek is normally calm and offers the opportunity for relaxing exploration. It is also known for its pickerel fishing.

If you return to Spa Creek after exploring Weems Creek, your trip distance will be approximately 11 nautical miles. If you continue your journey up the Severn, you can paddle into Luce Creek, past Martin's Pond Archeological Site (a historical site from the Middle-Late Woodland period), and up Saltworks Creek. The list of creeks along the Severn River goes on and on, and you could easily spend a full day or more exploring this area.

When you've had enough paddling and the crab houses and pubs are calling your name, head back down the Severn River toward Spa Creek. No matter how long you

Ego Alley, a narrow waterway that leads to the heart of Annapolis, got its name from the boats and yachts that sail down the dead end canal, usually only to see and be seen. See the essay on page 115.

plan to paddle, be prepared for changing tide, wind, and weather conditions. Your trip down the Severn River will likely be different from your trip upstream. In addition to boats of all sizes, be on the lookout for the Naval Academy's crew team—they move like lightning through the water.

MORE INFORMATION
Truxtun Park boat launch (annapolis.gov/government/city-departments/harbormaster/facilities/boat-ramps; 410-263-7973). City of Annapolis Department of Parks and Recreation (annapolis.gov/government/city-departments/recreation-and-parks; 410-263-7997).

EGO ALLEY

"See and be seen." That could be the slogan of downtown Annapolis's central gathering point. Known by all and loved by most who live and visit the city, "Ego Alley" is a slim strip of water that dead ends off Spa Creek, right on the Annapolis waterfront.

It's called Ego Alley for a reason. For wealthy boaters, it's the place to show off their pride and joy and also check out others' pride and joy. Annapolis has a long history as a wealthy seaport town (it boasts more original eighteenth century buildings than any other city in the country). Boats of all sizes, makes, and shapes from all corners of the world gather in this boater's dream town.

On the weekends and weekday evenings, a steady parade of yachts floats down Ego Alley, passing by the waterfront. They reach the end of the channel, turn around right at the bottom of Main Street, and then float back out.

The show is never the same. There are souped-up racing boats with flashy graphics and one-of-a-kind wooden sailboats. Some owners try to look as cool as possible with shades and nods, while others give a ceremonial wave as if they were the pope. There are ladies in long dresses holding wine glasses and others wearing bikinis shooting tequila. The spectators on shore are equally diverse. Most watch the ongoing show with interest, giving captains a thumbs-up or a wave, while some hold up a less friendly finger if they sense an attitude.

The show occasionally gets exciting as yachts too big to make the narrow turnaround get stuck front and center. It is tricky business maneuvering a large boat through the tight turn and many first-timers don't realize the skill involved in safely executing it with no room for error.

Ego Alley is within steps of countless shops and restaurants. Musicians often play outside in impromptu jam sessions and sometimes there are even people dancing. The city dock is also very dog-friendly. Every breed of canine friend can be seen strolling the waterfront and sometimes steal the show away from those cruising the alley.

If you're in the neighborhood around the holidays, don't miss the Eastport Yacht Club Parade of Lights. This community celebration is a highlight of the season and an annual holiday tradition on the waterfront. Boat owners show off elaborate holiday decorations and celebrate in style with a unique evening parade. Highlights from past parades include Santa's full sleigh and reindeer, an "A Christmas Story" themed boat complete with a 10-foot tall leg lamp, and a tropical Christmas theme with palm trees and Santa. The best places to watch the parade are at the Eastport Bridge and Annapolis City Dock. The Naval Academy also offers a good vantage point.

21
BALTIMORE'S INNER HARBOR

The fun vibe of Baltimore's Inner Harbor
makes for an enjoyable trip around this
historic body of water.

> **Distance** ▶ 4.5 nautical miles (longer routes are possible)
> **Cautions** ▶ Because of the abundant number of boats, be wary of wakes coming from every direction. Be prepared to contend with large yachts and huge freighters.
> **Charts and Maps** ▶ NOAA Electronic Chart US5MD11M / Paper Chart #12281

LAUNCH

Canton Waterfront, Baltimore I normally launch my kayak from the Canton Waterfront, into Northwest Harbor. A well-positioned jump-off point to the Inner Harbor, it's free to park and launch, but there are no real amenities except for seasonal portable toilets. The boat ramp places kayakers right into the thick of things and is approximately 2.5 nautical miles from the Inner Harbor by water. To reach the launch from I-95, take Exit 57 for Boston Street. Turn left off the ramp onto Boston Street and continue over the railroad tracks. Turn left onto S East Avenue and into Canton Waterfront Park. You will see the launch next to the parking lot. Parking is free. *GPS coordinates: 39° 16.614' N, 76° 34.356' W.*

ROUTE DESCRIPTION

Now a major tourist destination in the mid-Atlantic, the city of Baltimore sprouted out of a tough industrial port that dates back to the 1700s. Nicked-named "Charm City" for its hidden charm, Baltimore has greatly benefited from a series of urban renewal projects that helped rebrand the city as a spot for art, sports, fine dining, and luxury hotels.

Most people think Baltimore is located on the Chesapeake Bay, but the harbor is actually located at the mouth of the Patapsco River. East of the city, the river flows into the Chesapeake Bay, which is why this sheltered, yet deep-water harbor has been so popular for ships for so many years.

Baltimore's Inner Harbor and the surrounding area boast a constant bustle of activity. The harbor is the main tourist destination in the city and it is flanked with

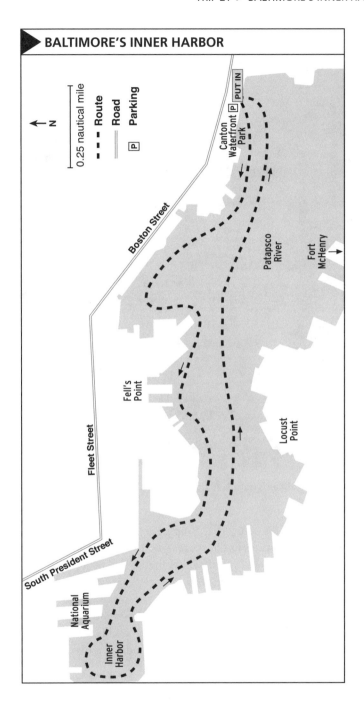

BALTIMORE'S INNER HARBOR

N

0.25 nautical mile

- - - Route
=== Road
Ⓟ Parking

Canton Waterfront Park Ⓟ PUT IN

Boston Street

Patapsco River

Fort McHenry

Fell's Point

Locust Point

Fleet Street

South President Street

National Aquarium

Inner Harbor

A kayaker approaches Baltimore's Inner Harbor. Photograph by Peter Gaaserud.

hotels, markets, and restaurants. The shipping industry still has a firm hold on the harbor, but Baltimore now has its fair share of wealthy residents and visiting yachters of both the sailing and power variety. This makes for a very busy, but interesting harbor, and it is certainly worth a look by kayak.

The harbor is blanketed nearly end-to-end with marinas and private boat docks. Within just a few minutes of paddling, you will come across everything from the local weekend sailor to multimillion-dollar cruising yachts. Paddle to your right after you launch for a direct route to the Inner Harbor, and you will pass hundreds of boats tucked into their slips. On my last trip out I was even greeted by a small replica of the Statue of Liberty.

As you can imagine, boat traffic in the harbor is substantial. In fact, it is one of the busiest locations featured in this book, which is to be expected, given its urban environment. For the most part, the boats will keep to the channel in the middle of the harbor, but watch out for those entering or exiting the marinas. There is also a very active water taxi service that appears from around every bend. They do not hesitate to get close to kayakers, but fortunately, the ones I've encountered don't draw big wakes. Speaking of wakes–expect them all the time from every direction.

As you paddle past the nooks and crannies formed by the marinas, you will soon make your way to the historic waterfront community of Fell's Point. It is one of the oldest neighborhoods in Baltimore and has many historic buildings and trendy restaurants. Admire the nice shops and eateries from the water, but return to the neighborhood after your paddle to stroll the cobblestone streets, have lunch, rent a bike, or take a walking tour. The town was first established in 1763 and most of the businesses are still locally owned.

You can paddle around the City Pier and see some of the Baltimore tugboats on the other side as you approach the Broadway Pier. If you pass the Bond Street Wharf (off Thames Street) in Fell's Point, you will likely see one of the Canton Kayak Club's busiest docks.

The Canton Kayak Club is worth mentioning because of its unique and friendly set-up. Club members pay an annual fee in exchange for free training and the use of more than 80 club kayaks and their gear. The club has six docks in and around the Baltimore area that have kayaks, paddles, and life vests. Members use the kayaks for commuting and recreation, and the club also offers organized outings. The Canton Kayak Club was first organized in 1999 with just 10 boats and 30 members, but now has more than 500 members. It's a fantastic way to help people conveniently enjoy the harbor.

As you continue paddling toward the Inner Harbor, the size and grandeur of the power yachts and equally beautiful sailboats will seem to increase. Spend some time exploring. You can literally paddle under the city streets if you so desire, although I can't vouch for the cleanliness of the water. Unfortunately, garbage does seem to be a problem on the water. Little blue boats actually cruise the perimeter of the shore to gather trash.

Despite the congestion, it is hard to not appreciate the view of the Baltimore skyline as you paddle into the Inner Harbor. So much work has been put into the beautification and development of the area that it is easy to get swept up in its fun vibe. The Inner Harbor has long been the center of activity in this large port city and most of the beauty shots of Baltimore are taken here.

For centuries people have arrived in this port in all kinds of vessels, and it was a thriving destination for visitors even during the steamboat era. As you paddle around the harbor, you'll notice several of Baltimore's Historic Ships and also the National Aquarium. Be on the lookout for pirate ships in the summer. They will be full of laughing tourists and yelling pirates. You might even be the target of a water cannon.

Heading back out of the harbor, you will have a great view of the Domino's sugar refinery and its iconic red neon sign. The refinery has been in business for more than 90 years. Just recently, large solar panels were installed on the rooftop to illuminate the sign, which has lit up the Baltimore sky for more than 60 years, as part of Domino's efforts to be more environmentally conscious. Giant freighters from across the globe can often be seen docked nearby.

You can return to the boat launch the way you came, or paddle along the opposite shore, past the industrial area of Locust Point, and to Fort McHenry, or continue exploring the outer reaches of the harbor.

No matter how frequently you explore the Inner Harbor and Northwest Harbors, no two days will be the same. You may share the water with cargo freighters from exotic places or paddle by some of the world's most elaborate yachts. One thing is for sure: As the years go by, more and more kayaks can be found in the harbor, exploring the shoreline, peeking under the city streets, and transporting Baltimore residents to work.

MORE INFORMATION

Canton Waterfront Park (bcrp.baltimorecity.gov/ParksTrails/CantonWaterfrontPark .aspx). City of Baltimore, Department of Recreation and Parks (bcrp.baltimorecity .gov; 410-396-7900).

BALTIMORE'S HISTORIC SHIPS

Amidst the hustle and bustle of busy Baltimore Harbor is one of the finest collections of historic military ships in the world. The collection makes up a unique museum called "Historic Ships in Baltimore" that includes four ships, a lighthouse, thousands of photographs, and personal items that relate to the ships.

All of the ships and the lighthouse are stationed around Baltimore Harbor and are within walking distance of each other.

The first, the *USS Constellation*, is located at Pier 1. This was a "sloop of war" ship from 1854 until 1955 and was the last all-sail ship constructed by the United States Navy. Visitors begin their tour in the museum gallery located at the pier and from there can take an audio tour aboard the ship. A plan for the day will be posted with a list of activities taking place onboard that day. If you're lucky, you may be onboard during the firing of the Parrott rifle. Uniformed crew will also be available to answer questions.

Your second stop will likely be at Pier 3 to visit the submarine *USS Torsk*. This is the most exciting ship in the collection, as it was one of only 10 Tench class submarines to serve in World War II. Visitors are able to tour the entire submarine including the torpedo room, navigation station, engine room, operation station, and the cramped crew quarters. It is difficult to comprehend how 80 crewmembers could live aboard this impressive vessel at one time.

The third stop is also on Pier 3. It is the lightship *Chesapeake*. A lightship is a ship that is designed to be moored and has a beacon mounted to it. It functions like a mobile lighthouse and is often stationed in one spot for long periods of time. Manning a lightship meant long days sitting in one place on the water and often scary times riding out storms. The lightship *Chesapeake* was built in 1930.

The fourth ship, located on Pier 5, is the USCG cutter *Taney*. Cutters are defined as Coast Guard ships that are more than 65 feet in length and can accommodate a live-aboard crew. It was built in 1935 and decommissioned in 1986.

The Knoll Lighthouse is the final stop on the Historic Ship tour and is located on Pier 5. It is 40 feet tall and is one of the Chesapeake Bay's oldest lighthouses, having been erected in 1856. It originally stood at the mouth of the Patapsco River and is also known as the Seven Foot Knoll Lighthouse since it stood on a shallow shoal known as the Seven Foot Knoll.

Museum staff maintain the historic ship collection and oversee restoration efforts. Additional information can be found at historicships.org.

USS Constellation

22
SOLOMONS ISLAND

This kayakers' paradise offers a paddle on a river and through the nooks and crannies of a creek.

> **Distance** ▶ 5.0 or 9.5 nautical miles
> **Cautions** ▶ Be prepared for difficult conditions on the Patuxent River if you attempt to cross it at Point Patience.
> **Charts and Maps** ▶ NOAA Electronic Chart US5MD31M / Paper Chart #12284

LAUNCHES

Patuxent River, Solomons The first of two great launches on Solomons Island is on the Patuxent River, near the MD 4 bridge (Thomas Johnson Bridge). The launch is a little hard to identify unless you know where it is. The beautiful boardwalk along this portion of the waterfront was built in recent years, and just before it is what remains of the beach that once ran along the entire waterfront. To reach the launch from MD 4 South, take MD 2 (Solomons Island Road South) to bypass the bridge. You will soon see a field with a wooden fence along the road. Parallel park along the fence and look for the small public beach next to the boats. You can take your boat through an opening at the end of the fence and carry it down to the beach. There is also a large public parking lot a little farther down the road, but parking along the fence will provide the closest access. A popular place for people to take their dogs to swim, it is a lovely, gradual, sandy launch. There is a public bathroom near the boardwalk. Look for the gazebo; there is a large public restroom facility across the street from it. There is no fee to launch. *GPS coordinates: 38° 19.494′ N, 76° 27.711′ W.*

Back Creek, Solomons The second launch is on beautiful Back Creek, a protected harbor "around the point" from the Patuxent River that is thick with marinas, homes, and docks for boats of all sizes. The harbor offers miles of scenic and well-protected water for paddlers. To reach this hidden launch, follow the directions above and continue past the boardwalk on Solomons Island Road South. When it splits, stay to the left on Charles Street. When you see the sign for Williams Street on the right, turn left. The small road that looks like a driveway is actually a continuation of Williams Street. The road ends at an unmarked, sandy public launch, although you will need to park your car back up near Charles Street (or near the Tiki Bar). There

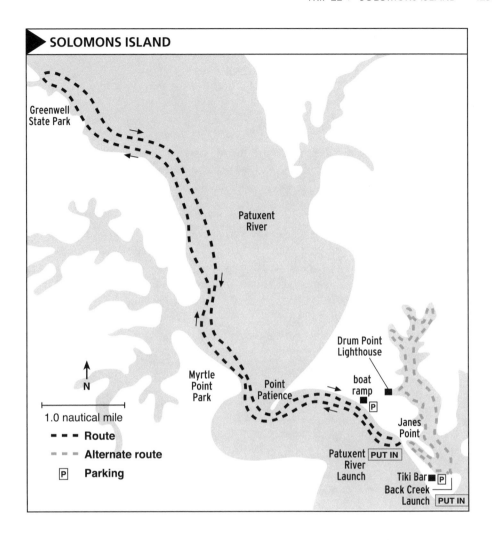

SOLOMONS ISLAND

Greenwell
State Park

Patuxent
River

N

1.0 nautical mile

- - - **Route**
- - - **Alternate route**
P **Parking**

Drum Point
Lighthouse

Myrtle
Point
Park

Point
Patience

boat
ramp
P

Janes
Point

Patuxent PUT IN
River
Launch

Tiki Bar ■ P
Back Creek
Launch PUT IN

are no facilities near the Williams Street launch, and there is no launch fee. *GPS coordinates: 38° 19.216' N, 76° 27.206' W.*

Alternative launch There is also a public boat ramp for the Patuxent River under the MD 4 bridge. You can reach it from the exit ramp to MD 4 South. This ramp is very heavily used but is an option if there is no parking near the little beach. *GPS coordinates: 38° 19.738' N, 76° 28.086' W.*

ROUTE DESCRIPTION

Solomons Island is one of the gems in Maryland. It's not exactly a beach setting, and I wouldn't put it in the same category as the glamorous nautical city of Annapolis, but Solomons Island is definitely a sailors' and kayakers' paradise. The island is more of a peninsula, located on the point where the Patuxent River flows into the Chesapeake Bay, and its comfortable ambiance can be described as hip with a family flair.

The main street (Patuxent Street) loops around the point where the Patuxent river mouth opens toward the Chesapeake Bay. It's lined with restaurants, shops, and a world-famous Tiki Bar appropriately named "Tiki Bar," that's worth all the hype it receives.

I find Solomons Island to be very relaxing and easy to get around, although it can be quite busy in the summertime. I recommend kayaking early in the morning or in the off-season to avoid some of the heavy boat traffic, but even on a cloudy day in June, I've found uninterrupted solitude while paddling off the banks of the Patuxent.

Patuxent River

Launching from the small beach on the Patuxent River, you can paddle in either direction along the shoreline. Because the river is very wide, especially south from the launch toward its mouth, the water can be choppy and the currents can be strong.

If you paddle north, you can kayak under the Thomas Johnson Bridge (MD 4) and along the shoreline to Point Patience. Point Patience dangles into the river like a tail and the water near it reaches 120 feet deep. The point is owned by the Navy (so don't land there) and was named because the river juts to the left and then turns sharply right, forcing sailors to exercise patience while waiting to catch the wind and tide at the right moment in order to make it past the point.

If conditions allow, you can cross the river after the point and paddle past Myrtle Point Park and continue upstream to Greenwell State Park. Greenwell State Park is a good turnaround point to paddle a round-trip route of 9.5 nautical miles.

If you paddle south from the launch, you can go to the tip of Solomons Island and look out toward the Chesapeake Bay. A lot of military aircraft fly nearby and over this area since the Naval Air Station Patuxent River is nearby.

Back Creek

Once you launch on Back Creek, you will find countless protected areas to explore. You will also have plenty of company since the shoreline is thick with private docks and marinas. Despite the crowds, it is still a very enjoyable place to paddle and often has calm water, so both novices and experienced paddlers can enjoy it.

A pleasant 5.5-mile paddle will take you up Back Creek. Begin by immediately turning left after the launch and paddle through the lower end of Back Creek. You will avoid the open waters of the mouth of the Patuxent River. You will see Solomons Island Yacht Club on your left as you paddle up the western arm of Back Creek. This will take you behind the shops and restaurants that line Solomons Island Road South. Paddle to the end of the creek, turn around, and paddle out. When you reach the opening to the beginning of the creek (not far from where you launched), turn left and paddle around Janes Point.

Continue along the left shore and head north into the main part of Back Creek. There are many nooks and crannies to explore as you head up the creek, but make

The Drum Point Lighthouse.

sure to paddle into the bay that houses the Calvert Marine Museum and the Drum Point Lighthouse.

The Drum Point Lighthouse is a "screw-pile" lighthouse, which is a lighthouse that stands on pilings that are screwed into the sand or mud. It is one of only three that remain from the 45 similar lights that served the Chesapeake Bay at the beginning of the twentieth century. It was originally located at the mouth of the Patuxent River at Drum Point, but was relocated to its current position in 1975 after being decommissioned in 1962. The lighthouse has been beautifully restored and is a landmark that has been placed on the National Register of Historic places; visitors can tour the lighthouse for a fee.

Continue past the lighthouse up the creek and explore each of the three, short, northern branches of the creek, then return down the creek to your starting point.

MORE INFORMATION

Myrtle Point State Park (www.co.saint-marys.md.us/recreate/myrtlepointpark.asp; 301-475-4200, ext. 1800). Greenwell State Park (dnr2.maryland.gov/publiclands/Pages/southern/greenwell.aspx; 301-872-5688). Calvert Marine Museum and Drum Point Lighthouse (calvertmarinemuseum.com; 410-326-2042).

CALVERT CLIFFS

A premier attraction in Calvert County is Calvert Cliffs State Park, located approximately 7 miles north of Solomons Island, on the Chesapeake Bay. Although there is a sandy beach, playground, fishing, 13.0 miles of hiking trails, and pristine marshland, the main attraction in the park is fossil hunting on the beach.

The huge cliffs are the primary feature along the shore of the Chesapeake Bay for nearly 24 miles. They were formed 10 to 20 million years ago at a time when a shallow ocean covered southern Maryland. As the sea slowly receded, the massive cliffs became exposed and slowly started to erode. Today the cliffs continue this erosion process and as such unveil remains of prehistoric animals including sharks, rays, whales, barnacles, and giant seabirds.

The sediment layers in Calvert Cliffs are slightly inclined to the south. This means that progressively younger layers are exposed from north to south (so the oldest beds are at the northern end).

To access the cliffs, follow Red Trail (1.8 miles from the parking lot) to the open 0.25-mile beach area. A map of the park trail system can be downloaded at dnr2.maryland.gov/publiclands/Pages/southern/calvertcliffs.aspx.

Once you arrive, feel free to start combing the shoreline for ancient remains. More than 600 species of fossils left behind during the Miocene Era have been found and identified in the park. The most likely finds will be fossilized shark teeth and oyster shells. The shark teeth are the most famous of the fossils in the park because they are so plentiful and because some have been found from the giants Megalodon and Carcharocles.

It is fine to use sieves and shovels for your search while sifting through the sand, but be aware that areas at the base of the cliffs are closed due to the potential for landslides. Climbing on or walking under the cliffs is prohibited and it is illegal to search for fossils beneath the cliffs.

It is best to fossil hunt after a storm, when shells and fossils are uncovered in the surf and the beach is "replenished" so to speak. Low tide is also a good time to search for fossils since the beach is most exposed at that time.

Swimming offshore of the beach is allowed at your own risk. There are no lifeguards on duty. The park is open sunrise to sunset between March and mid-November. Admission is $5. Pets are allowed.

Driving Directions: Take MD 2 and MD 4 south from Prince Frederick for approximately 14 miles. Exit onto H.G. Truman Road. The park entrance is immediately ahead. *GPS coordinates: 38° 23.719' N, 76° 26.214' W.*

23
BLACKWATER NATIONAL WILDLIFE REFUGE

Meander through marshy streams and across open water to experience solitude and silence in a lovely refuge that features 250 bird species.

Distance ▶ 6.6, 7.0, or 8.0 nautical miles

Cautions ▶ Purple Trail is about one-third marsh and the rest open water. Much of the water is very shallow, so it's important to stay on the trail to avoid getting stuck in the mud. Check the wind direction and speed before deciding which way to paddle on the trail. Paddling against the wind will make for slow progress on this route since the open water is shallow and waves can kick up with just a stiff breeze. Winds coming from the northwest make for the most difficult paddling in the refuge.

Charts and Maps ▶ NOAA Electronic Charts US5MD23M and US4MD80M / Paper Charts #12261 and #12263

LAUNCHES

MD 335 (Purple and Green Trails), Church Creek From US 50 South in Cambridge, turn right onto MD 16 (Church Creek Road). Continue approximately 7 miles and turn left onto MD 335 (Golden Hill Road). The launch site and parking is just before the first bridge. There is no fee to launch, and there are no restrooms. *GPS coordinates: 38° 26.376′ N, 76° 8.708′ W.*

Shorter's Wharf (Purple and Orange Trails), Crapo Follow the directions above and turn left onto Key Wallace Drive from MD 335, about 4 miles from the junction with MD 16. Pass the visitor center, on the right, taking the road until the end, and then turn right onto Maple Dam Road. Travel approximately 4 miles until you reach Shorter's Wharf. The launch is on the right side of the road. There is no fee to launch, and there are no restrooms. *GPS coordinates: 38° 22.893′ N, 76° 4.043′ W.*

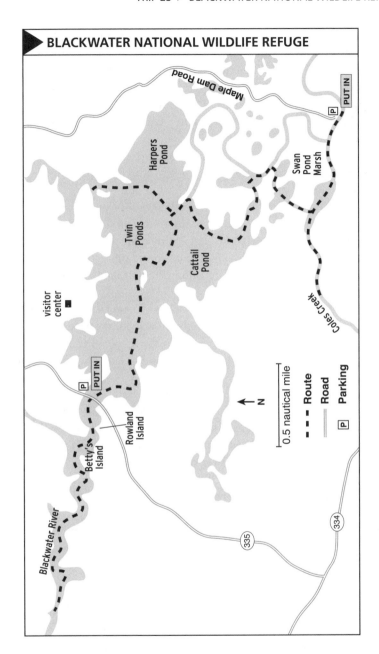

ROUTE DESCRIPTION

"Solitude and silence" could be the slogan for the Blackwater National Wildlife Refuge, located near Cambridge, Maryland, on the Eastern Shore. That's what popped into my mind as I glided through the shallow marshes of the refuge on a delightfully cool summer morning.

It was Saturday—a rare Saturday in July with temperatures in the 70s, overcast skies, and low humidity. Although it was a paddler's dream day, there were only a small handful of kayakers in the refuge and plenty of parking. Jackpot.

The Blackwater National Wildlife Refuge was established in 1933 and is managed by the U.S. Fish and Wildlife Service. Primarily known as a rest stop for migrating birds, the refuge encompasses 27,000 acres. In October and November, approximately 50,000 waterfowl refuel at the refuge on their journey up the Atlantic coast. More than 250 bird species, including 20 types of ducks, have been identified in the refuge.

It's no surprise that the Blackwater River is the primary feature in the refuge. The river is so named for its dark color, a result of the tannic acid released by decomposing leaves in the surrounding forests. The acid is then washed into the river by rainwater.

Currently, approximately 7,000 acres of the refuge are forested, with mixed evergreen and deciduous trees, and the rest is freshwater, brackish water, and tidal marsh. As water levels in the Chesapeake Bay rise, more and more forested acres are lost to the water. Snags (dead trees) can be seen along the marsh edges and serve as perches for resident birds.

The best way to explore the area is by kayak. Paddlers get the best seat in the house since the shallow trails at times contain only a few inches of water and make motor boat passage impossible. The brackish ponds in the refuge offer a great opportunity for viewing bald eagles, terns, turkey vulture, barred owl, and osprey, all of whom are regular inhabitants of the refuge.

The biggest decision you'll need to make is which trail to paddle, or which trail to paddle first. The Purple, Green, and Orange paddling trails feature easy-to-read markers that guide paddlers through the wetlands and across long, shallow stretches. A group called Friends of Blackwater carefully mapped the trails and each provides a unique experience and its own level of difficulty.

Before heading out, you'll want to pick up a waterproof trail map from the Blackwater National Wildlife Refuge Visitor Center for $4 or purchase one ahead of time online for $5 (friendsofblackwater.org/store.html). The visitor center is open Monday through Friday from 8:00 a.m.–4:00 p.m. and weekends from 9:00 a.m.–5:00 p.m. It is closed Thanksgiving Day and Christmas Day. There are restrooms at the visitor center.

Purple Trail

The longest water trail is Purple Trail. It is a 9.0-mile, point-to-point route that follows the Blackwater River. It will take most paddlers between 3 and 4.5 hours to complete. A one-way paddle will require leaving a second vehicle at your take-out spot.

Purple Trail is the most difficult to navigate. It requires the use of a trail map and/ or GPS device since large stretches of open water can make sighting difficult.

The trail is about one-third marsh and the rest open water. Much of the water is very shallow, so it's important to stay on the trail to avoid getting stuck in the mud.

Check the wind direction and speed before deciding which way to paddle on the trail. Paddling against the wind will make for slow progress on this route since the open water is shallow and waves can kick up with just a stiff breeze. Winds coming from the northwest make for the most difficult paddling in the refuge.

This trip traverses open water on Purple Trail. Photograph by Peter Gaaserud.

Marked by black arrows and orange buoys, this is one of my favorite trails on the Delmarva Peninsula. It feels like you're paddling in open water, yet marsh and islands full of loblolly pine surround you. If you're an osprey fan, this is your route. The trail runs under more than a dozen nests.

Purple Spur Trail is a nice detour off the primary Purple Trail and runs north. The spur is a 2.4-nautical-mile out-and-back. It ends at a wooded landing and is the only place in the trail system with restrooms. (Walk to the right of the landing on the paved trail.)

Purple Trail is closed October 1 through March 31 so that paddlers don't interact with migratory waterfowl. The refuge hosts managed hunts for turkey, deer, and waterfowl, so the closure also protects paddlers during hunting season.

Green Trail

Green and Orange trails are open all year, although hunting takes place on private land near the Green Trail in the fall and winter. Green Trail is better suited for beginner paddlers than the Orange and Purple trails and follows a narrow portion of the Blackwater River. It's marked with black arrows.

From the launch for Green Trail at the bridge on MD 335, paddle away from the bridge, toward Betty's Island. The trail is 7.0 nautical miles round-trip and typically takes between 2.5 and 4 hours to complete.

Look for eagle nests to your left, on Rowland Island. On a recent paddle I was delighted to see two giant juvenile eagles perched high in a tree, and a huge nest was nestled in a treetop nearby. Wood duck houses can also be seen along the trail. They look like backyard birdhouses on steroids. Because freshwater creeks feed into the Blackwater River along Green Trail, the water is less brackish here. Stunning narrow-leaved cattails grow along the shore, and water lily can be seen blanketing the surface of the water in the summer.

On that brilliant day in July, I paddled the Purple and Green trails and only saw four other kayaks. My bald eagle count was five. I always consider it a good day when eagles outnumber people.

On the same trip I was reminded that cell phone service is spotty in the refuge, but one can provide some level of safety. I witnessed a rescue by the Department of Natural Resources when a couple paddling an inflatable kayak on Green Trail became stranded when a hole was torn in their inflatable boat. Fortunately, they were able to call the visitor center and seek help, but this is not a reliable safety plan in the refuge, especially given their equipment and their route through shallow water where submerged branches are not uncommon. Plan ahead for all circumstances, and if that includes carrying a patch kit and pump, then it's worth the extra effort.

Orange Trail

The launch for Orange Trail is off Maple Dam Road. Marked by black arrows, it is 6.6 nautical miles round-trip (there is no parking at the turnaround point at Loblolly Landing) and is best suited for intermediate paddlers with navigational experience. Roughly one-third of the trail is through the open water of the Swan Pond Marsh and the rest is through the more narrow Coles Creek. The creek is bordered by marsh grass that leads into forest.

Orange Trail can be tricky to navigate and is best covered with the help of a GPS device or compass. Allow about 2.5 to 4 hours for the trip.

From late July through August, the shore of Orange Trail is dotted with the white and pink blooms of the marsh hibiscus. Animal life throughout the refuge includes the sika deer (a small brown elk with white spots), the endangered Delmarva fox squirrel, muskrat, nutria, and the northern diamondback terrapin. There are no poisonous snakes in the refuge, although the Northern water snake looks similar to the water moccasin.

Since the water is brackish, it can be difficult to know its depth. If you capsize and get stuck in the thick marsh mud, use your paddle to push yourself out. The same is true if your boat gets stuck; do not exit your boat, but instead use your paddle to maneuver your boat into deeper water.

MORE INFORMATION

Blackwater National Wildlife Refuge (fws.gov/refuge/Blackwater/;410-228-2677). The Friends of Blackwater (friendsofblackwater.org; 410-228-2677).

24
TILGHMAN ISLAND

Paddle along long stretches of shoreline, past a bird sanctuary and a site where some of the oldest ancient artifacts in Maryland were discovered.

Distance ▶ 8.7 nautical miles (shorter routes are possible)

Cautions ▶ Depending on conditions, paddling in the open water around the island can be too challenging for a novice paddler. The western shoreline of the island can be very choppy and doesn't offer many places to land in the event of a summer storm or sudden winds since all the riprap (rock used to protect the shoreline) makes landing difficult.

Charts and Maps ▶ NOAA Electronic Chart US5MD16M / Paper Chart #12266

LAUNCH

Dogwood Harbor, Tilghman Island Launch at the public ramp in Dogwood Harbor, on the east side of the island, about 0.5 mile from the bridge. This is a busy harbor with a working fleet of fishing boats, so leave your car in a single car space that doesn't block access to the fleet. There is no fee to launch. To reach the launch from US 50 East, turn right onto Easton Parkway (MD 322) and then right again on Saint Michaels Road (MD 33). Follow Saint Michaels Road for about 23 miles until you reach the Knapp Narrows Drawbridge, which connects the mainland to Tilghman Island. After the drawbridge, continue on 33 and turn left onto Dogwood Harbor Road. There are portable toilets at the harbor. *GPS coordinates: 38° 42.786′ N, 76° 20.092′ W.*

ROUTE DESCRIPTION

Tilghman Island is a charming little Eastern Shore community located at the end of a peninsula, 11.0 miles southwest of the popular tourist town of Saint Michaels. About an hour's drive from the Bay Bridge, Tilghman Island is bordered by the Chesapeake Bay on the west and the Choptank River on the east.

The island is approximately 3 miles long, 1 mile wide, and was settled in 1659. It is also home to one of the last waterman communities in the United States.

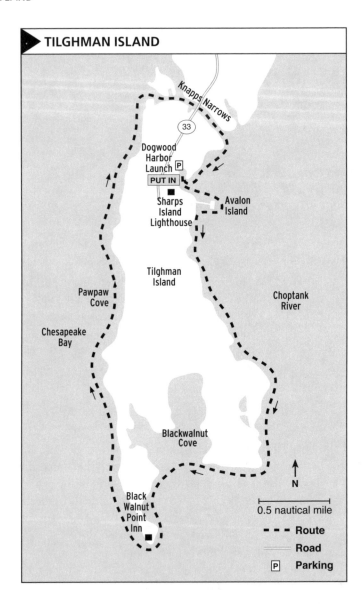

TILGHMAN ISLAND

Knapps Narrows

33

Dogwood
Harbor
Launch P
PUT IN

Sharps
Island
Lighthouse

Avalon
Island

Tilghman
Island

Choptank
River

Pawpaw
Cove

Chesapeake
Bay

Blackwalnut
Cove

N

0.5 nautical mile

- - - Route
——— Road
P   Parking

Black
Walnut
Point
Inn

Watermen are men and women who make a living fishing. They work independently and sell their catch to wholesale seafood houses. The term *waterman* dates back to eleventh century England, when smugglers used tiny boats to move stolen goods across waterways. When the English colonized the Chesapeake Bay, the name was used to describe those in the fishing industry. Watermen normally own their own boats and work all year to harvest fish, crab, and oysters.

When steamboat routes were established at the end of the 1800s, it became more convenient to distribute oysters to Washington and Baltimore. As a result, during the twentieth century, seafood processing plants were built on the island and the hospitality industry soon followed. Tilghman Island became a popular summer getaway for mid-Atlantic city dwellers and guesthouses sprang up to accommodate the demand. Today the island is still a vacation destination and although the seafood industry is not what it used to be, many local residents still make a living off the water. Oyster-shucking, crab-picking, and boat-docking contests are held every October on Tilghman Day.

A circumnavigation of the island is possible by kayak and consists of mostly shoreline and open-water paddling. Depending on conditions, this can be too challenging for a novice paddler. At times, however, a favorable current can make the paddle extremely pleasant, and you can even ride the tidal flow through Knapps Narrows. A full circumnavigation without paddling into protected Blackwalnut Cove (at the southern end) is approximately 8.3 nautical miles. If you add the cove to your trip, it's about 8.7 nautical miles.

Dogwood Harbor is known as the home of the only commercial sailing fleet in the country, the Chesapeake Bay Skipjacks. A skipjack is a wooden oyster-dredging boat that was developed specifically for use in the Chesapeake Bay and is Maryland's state boat. It is entirely wind-driven. The oldest skipjack in Dogwood Harbor, built in 1886, is named the *Rebecca T. Ruark* and is a national historic landmark. Although more than 100 skipjacks worked in the Chesapeake Bay during their peak, only a handful remain today. Tours of the *Rebecca T. Ruark* are available from April to December.

If you launch into Dogwood Harbor early in the morning, you will likely be accompanied by many fishing boats leaving for work. You will also pass Harrison's Chesapeake House—a legendary marina, inn, restaurant, and boat charter company known across the Chesapeake Bay region for its seafood.

I have heard of people paddling both directions around the island, but on a recent trip I chose to go clockwise, turning south out of the harbor into the lower Choptank River. Paddle south around Avalon Island and down the eastern side of the island. You'll see the natural beauty of the island, wetlands, and many types of birds.

It is approximately 3.5 miles south to the protected Blackwalnut Cove, where you'll find wetlands. As you round the point at the southern tip of the island, the Sharps Island Lighthouse is visible approximately 4 miles to the southwest. Constructed in 1881 and 1882, it was built to warn ships of the shallow shoals near Tilghman Island. The lighthouse's trademark is its 15-degree tilt to the south, which is a result of severe ice flows in the winter of 1976–1977.

In early summer, porpoises often swim off the island's point, near the Black Walnut Point Inn, which is located in a 52-acre bird sanctuary. As anyone who has paddled near porpoise will confirm, they can turn any kayaking trip into a memorable excursion. In the fall, hordes of monarch butterflies can be found near the point, and tundra swans can be seen anytime.

Heading up the western coast of the island, you'll pass the Naval Research Laboratory (NRL) Tilghman Island Field Site. The site was originally 81 acres and was acquired by NRL in 1944 for research during World War II. It currently sits on 2

The *Rebecca T. Ruark* skipjack is the oldest in the Chesapeake Bay fleet.

acres, but the 75-foot observation tower and several other buildings are still actively used for research.

Near the laboratory, you may see clusters of posts poking out of the water. Keep a healthy distance away from these, as they hold pound netting. Tilghman Island is one of the last places on the Chesapeake Bay to use pound netting, which is basically a series of nets that trap fish. Local watermen take the fish they want and release the rest back into the bay.

Soon you'll pass through Pawpaw Cove. In the cove is an overgrown piece of land about the size of one city block where Paleoindian artifacts have been found. The artifacts date back about 13,000 years, before the Chesapeake Bay was created and the climate there was similar to that of modern day Alaska. The beach at the cove was an ancient bluff that rose high above the distant Susquehanna River. The artifacts found here are primarily very rare and ancient spearheads that were used to hunt mammoths nearly 12,500 years before Captain John Smith explored the Chesapeake Bay, which formed after glaciers melted to flood the lower Susquehanna and formed the bay. The artifacts are among the oldest ever found in Maryland.

Continue up the western coast of the island and into Knapps Narrows. Remains of once thriving seafood processing plants can still be seen; today the narrows offers marinas and lively waterfront restaurants. Continue under the drawbridge and go south, back to Dogwood Harbor.

MORE INFORMATION
Tilghman Island information (tilghmanisland.com).

25
JANES ISLAND

Choose from among six trails to travel through and around an island that features bald eagles, turtles, white-tailed deer, red fox, otters, and muskrats.

Distance ▶ 1.0 to 11.0 nautical miles

Cautions ▶ Much of the trail system is protected from wind and currents, so Janes Island is good for kayakers of all skill levels. When the wind kicks up, the outer trails can be challenging, so keep this in mind when planning your route. Be aware that greenhead flies can be a huge pain during much of the summer. They thrive in the salt marshes and are vicious when they attack in large numbers. Other bugs in the area include horseflies, mosquitoes, and "no-see-ums."

Charts and Maps ▶ NOAA Electronic Charts US5VA16M and US5VA21M / Paper Chart #12231

LAUNCH
Alfred J. Lawson Drive, Crisfield This is a beautiful launch area with plenty of parking, restrooms, multiple piers, a boat ramp, and a floating dock for kayaks. There is no fee to launch a kayak as long as you do so from the floating dock. They also rent kayaks for $10 an hour and have a camp store in the launch area. To reach it from MD 413 south in Crisfield, turn right onto Plantation Road, then turn right again by the park sign onto Alfred J. Lawson Drive. Follow the signs to the park entrance and the boat launch. *GPS coordinates: 38° 0.524' N, 75° 50.872' W.*

ROUTE DESCRIPTION
If I were to create the perfect kayaking park, it would be modeled after Janes Island State Park in Crisfield, Maryland. The island is located in the southwest corner of the Eastern Shore in Maryland, on Tangier Sound. Crisfield is known for being the Maryland launching point for those wishing to visit Tangier Island.

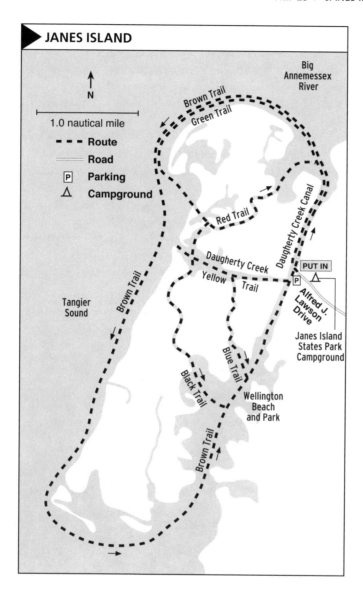

JANES ISLAND

N

1.0 nautical mile

- - - Route
——— Road
P   Parking
Δ   Campground

Big
Annemessex
River

Brown Trail
Green Trail

Daugherty Creek Canal

Red Trail

Daugherty Creek

Yellow   Trail

PUT IN

Alfred J.
Lawson
Drive

Janes Island
States Park
Campground

Tangier
Sound

Brown Trail

Blue Trail

Black Trail

Wellington
Beach
and Park

Brown Trail

Janes Island is a gorgeous 2,900-acre island consisting of marsh, beach, and highland. The eastern portion of the park is located on the mainland, across the Daugherty Creek Canal from the island. The mainland portion is a large camping resort with 104 campsites, three heated restrooms with hot showers, a conference center, a dump station, four full-service waterfront cabins, and five waterfront camper cabins.

The park is well maintained, friendly, and very kayak-oriented, with six designated kayak trails. At the camp store you can pick up a free map and brochure called the *Self-Guided Water Trail Tour*. It discusses points of interest along each trail and provides the distance between markers. Each trail is marked by large signs with symbols, such as a square, circle, or triangle, and are colored to correspond with the name of the trail. In 2005, the trails were included on the American Canoe Association's inaugural list of best paddling trails in North America and remain there today.

Janes Island is traversed by creeks and marsh trails. The trails, each designated by a different color, intersect one another and can be combined to make a longer trip. The total distance of all the trails combined is between 22 and 26 nautical miles.

Dougherty Creek Canal flows past the launch area, dividing the mainland from the island. Dougherty Creek flows into the canal and cuts Janes Island into two main sections. The launch is at this intersection, giving you three directions to paddle.

The island features abundant wildlife. Within five minutes of arriving at the launch, I saw two bald eagles (one was the largest I have ever seen), a turtle, and a small water snake. Other residents include white-tailed deer, red fox, otters, and muskrats.

Crabbing boat near Janes Island launch.

The hardest decision to make is where to paddle first. If you look at the *Self-Guided Water Trail Tour*, you will see that some of the trails are complete loops, such as Brown Trail, which runs the entire circumference around the island, and some are one-way; all can be accessed from the launch on Alfred J. Lawson drive. I couldn't find official distances for each trail, but I used my GPS device to approximate distances.

The Janes Island area is known for its great crabbing. So don't be surprised if you end up sharing the waterways with local crabbing boats.

Although all the trails are marked, they aren't always easily seen. It helps to bring binoculars with you so you can look for the markers, or a GPS device. Don't take all the trail descriptions you can find online at face value; many have inaccurate descriptions and mileages. Just know that all the trails are lovely, and you can expect a great day on the water in this beautiful park.

Brown Trail

Brown Trail circumnavigates the entire island. This is the longest trail (approximately 11 nautical miles) and it is primarily an open-water route that can have tidal currents and wind. This is the most challenging of the six trails. It includes the Big Annemessex River, at the northern end of the island. This river is 2.0 miles wide and a little over 15.0 miles long. From there you will pass into the beautiful Tangier Sound, along the western side of the island, which is known throughout the region for having spectacular sunsets. Finally, as you return up the eastern side to the launch, you go into Daugherty Creek. There are some lovely stretches of beach on the western side of the island, and you will pass the remains of an old fertilizer company that burned down in 1932.

Yellow Trail

Yellow Trail runs approximately 1.3 nautical miles, directly west from the launch. On both sides of Daugherty Creek you can see eastern red cedar, eastern white cedar, and Virginia pine trees. Be on the lookout for osprey and bald eagles along this trail, often nesting near the treetops. On a recent trip to the island, I saw a pair of giant bald eagles being chased by some smaller birds near the beginning of the trail. At the end of the creek is access to a great little beach.

Blue Trail

The starting point of Blue Trail is at about the midway point of Yellow Trail and meanders south into Daugherty Creek. The trail is a little more than 1.0 nautical mile long. Depending on the season, you could see Virginia glasswort, a saltwater plant that has red or purple stems in the fall. Glasswort was used in the past for glassmaking and the treatment of arthritis, rheumatism, and other aches and pains. At the end of the trail, where it empties into the creek, is a swimming beach on the mainland called Wellington Beach. Turn left to head back to the launch area.

Black Trail

Black Trail starts near the end of Yellow Trail and winds its way southeast, through the island, and joins Brown Trail up through Daugherty Creek Canal to the launch. The trail is approximately 2 nautical miles long. Look for diamondback terrapin (the state reptile of Maryland) in this section. It is the only turtle species in North America that lives in brackish water. The great egret and American bittern (a stocky heron) also live in this area of the island.

Red Trail

Red Trail starts at the end of Yellow Trail and winds through the northeast side of the island before returning to the launch. Some wildlife you are likely to see on this trail include black ducks, cattle egrets, fiddler crabs, greater yellowlegs (a large slender shorebird with yellow legs), jellyfish, otters, hooded mergansers, and osprey. The trail is approximately 3 nautical miles in length.

Green Trail

Green Trail starts at the end of Yellow Trail and runs north to Tangier Sound. It then circles clockwise around the northern part of the island and returns to the launch. This route is mostly through open water along the outer shore of the island. It is approximately 4.3 nautical miles long.

MORE INFORMATION

Janes Island State Park (dnr2.maryland.gov/publiclands/Pages/eastern/janesisland .aspx; 410-968-1565).

26
CHOPTANK RIVER

Take either a long journey or a brief paddle on a windy river to see rural, undeveloped shoreline thick with forest or farmland.

Distance ▶ 7.0, 14.0, or 30.0 nautical miles

Cautions ▶ If you choose to travel the 35.0 miles between Denton and Cambridge, be sure you're physically fit, ready for that type of challenge, and time the tides correctly.

Charts and Maps ▶ NOAA Electronic Chart US5MD19M / Paper Chart #12268

LAUNCH

Steamboat Wharf, Denton The best place to launch at the wharf is to the right of the building near the sunken skipjack. There is a small soft landing there that can be a bit muddy when the tide is low. To reach the launch from the Bay Bridge, take US 50 East toward Ocean City and turn left onto MD 404 (Queen Anne Highway). Continue approximately 12 miles and turn right on to MD 404 Business (Meeting House Road). Turn right onto 328 and then left onto River Landing Road. Continue to the Caroline Office of Tourism. There is no fee to launch, and there are restrooms at the tourism office. *GPS coordinates: 38° 53.306' N, 75° 50.374' W.*

Crouse Park, Denton The other place to launch is across the river from the wharf, at the Daniel Crouse Memorial Park. There is a fee to launch boats off the ramp in the park, but kayaks can launch for free on the sandy beach located on the opposite side of the bridge from the ramp. To reach the launch, follow MD 404 toward the Historic District. Follow signs to Crouse Park. *GPS coordinates: 38° 53.289' N, 75° 50.267' W.*

ROUTE DESCRIPTION

The Choptank River is the largest river on the Delmarva Peninsula. It starts in Kent County and ends 71.0 miles later in the Chesapeake Bay. The river is navigable from the town of Denton down to the Chesapeake Bay (approximately 45 miles) and used to be dredged regularly to allow for large boat passage.

Denton is a great place to paddle from. The town was an important shipping port for agricultural products after the Civil War, and as steamboat transportation

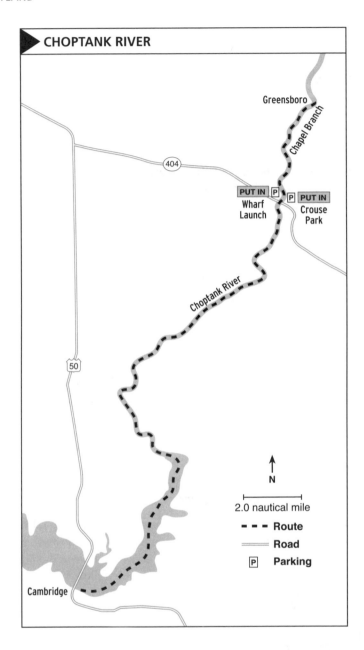

became more popular on the Chesapeake Bay, it turned into a busy port-of-call for steamboats based in Baltimore.

Steamboat Wharf is a replication of the Maryland Steamboat Company's Denton wharf as it existed in 1883. This terminal was called Joppa Wharf and was the pick-up place for passengers making overnight trips to Baltimore. It's a pretty little property on the river that includes a re-created main terminal (with a passenger waiting room, steamboat agent office, and warehouse), wharf platforms (docks), and the preserved *F.C. Lewis, Jr.*, an original 1907 Chesapeake Bay skipjack.

A 39-foot-long, two-sail bateau, with a V-bottomed centerboard sloop, the *F.C. Lewis, Jr.*, is one of less than 50 traditional Chesapeake Bay skipjacks still around today. It was part of the last commercial sailing fleet in the country. Today, visitors can see how the ship's crew lived aboard the ship.

From Denton you can paddle upriver or downriver. The Choptank River is tidal, so regardless of which way you go, check the tide table to time your trip to take advantage of the tide.

Denton to Cambridge

If you are adventurous and very fit, you can do a one-way, 30-plus-nautical-mile trip down to Cambridge, Maryland. I don't recommend doing such a long route in one day unless you're looking for an endurance challenge and have trips of similar length under your belt. Also, with tides of up to 4.0 feet, timing your trip is critical. I would also only attempt this during the summer when there's the most daylight.

If you feel like spending the night in luxury after such an undertaking, land at the Hyatt Regency Chesapeake Bay Golf Resort (just before the US 50 bridge) and spend the night. Just be sure to leave a pick-up car there before heading to Denton to launch.

The trip down the river toward Cambridge is very curvy as the river winds its way southwest, toward the Chesapeake Bay, and becomes wider and wider the farther south you travel. In Cambridge, near the MD 50 bridge, the river is more than 1.5 miles wide. This results in more and more boat traffic as you proceed downstream. You will pass just a handful of small towns on this route, but the majority of the trip passes farmland.

Many segments of this trip feel remote and very far removed from the Chesapeake Bay. You could potentially paddle for miles without seeing anyone else. Be prepared to be self-sufficient on this long route and again, only attempt it if you are accustomed to doing paddles of similar length.

Denton to Greensboro

A nice day paddle from Denton is upstream to the town of Greensboro. Greensboro is approximately 7 nautical miles from Denton. This trip can be completed as a point-to-point or round-trip. If you are doing a point-to-point, your takeout will be at the public boat ramp located at 222 East Sunset Avenue in Greensboro. It is located off Route 314 between Mill Street and the Route 313 Intersection.

The route between Denton and Greensboro is well-travelled by kayaks. In fact, it is the course for the annual Caroline County Paddlefest that features kayaks, canoes, and paddleboards. The Paddlefest course is one-way, from Greensboro to Denton, and normally has more than 300 participants.

The route is rural and pleasant and is usually easy to navigate. Much of the time, the river is suitable for beginner paddlers if they're traveling with the tide. The scenery harkens back to a time before modern development, and much of the shoreline remains as it has been for centuries, thick with native vegetation.

Paddling upstream from the launch, you will pass most of the town of Denton, on the right shore. Once you pass under the MD 404 bridge, the shoreline becomes rural and natural with short stretches of residential homes interspersed.

The Choptank River is very twisty and turn-y, so be mindful to stick to the main part of the river. Many small creeks and not-so-small creeks run into the Choptank. The first tributary that can be confusing is located after the second bend in the river, where the Chapel Branch meets the river on the right side. Stay to the left to remain on the Choptank. There will likely be other boats traveling the same way you are.

After you pass the Chapel Branch, you will see the Caroline Career and Technology Center along the left bank. The river makes a sharp right turn there, and then shortly after that, it makes a sharp left turn and narrows considerably. The left shoreline in this section is natural, and there is sparse residential development on the right shore, which will soon be part of an area known as Choptank Overlook. This is

The Choptank River from the Hyatt Regency Chesapeake Bay Golf Resort.

roughly the halfway mark between Denton and Greensboro. Much of the shoreline on the second half of the trip is forested and is a buffer between the riverbanks and the farmland beyond.

As you approach Greensboro, the river makes a right turn and then turns left again as you approach the boat landing. This is the end point for a one-way trip, or you can turn around and paddle back downstream to Denton for a 14.0-nautical-mile trip.

MORE INFORMATION

Town of Denton (dentonmaryland.com; 410-479-2050). City of Cambridge (chooseambridge.com; 410-228-4020). Caroline Office of Tourism (tourcaroline .com; 410-479-0655).

27
WYE ISLAND

This leisurely journey around an island along the Eastern Shore presents the opportunity to see bald eagles, osprey, blue herons, and turtles.

Distance ▶ 11.7 nautical miles

Cautions ▶ Boat traffic and wind can make conditions challenging.

Charts and Maps ▶ NOAA Electronic Chart US5MD17M / Paper Chart #12270

LAUNCH

Wye Landing, Wye Mills There is a public boat launch in Wye Mills on the Wye East River. It is primarily used by local fisherman and crabbers and is adjacent to a tiny marina. The facility is public and car-top boats are allowed to launch for free from a very tiny beach to the right of the ramp. A permit is required to use the ramp. For permit information, contact the Queen Anne County Parks and Recreation Office (qac.org). To reach the launch from the Bay Bridge, take US 50 East toward Ocean City. Take a slight right onto MD 662 (Wye Mills Road). Stay to the right on Old Wye Mills Road, where it intersects with Route 213. Turn right onto Wye Landing Lane, and follow it to Wye Mills Public Landing. There are portable restrooms at the launch. *GPS coordinates: 38° 53.527' N, 76° 6.187' W.*

ROUTE DESCRIPTION

For years I've wanted to do the Wye Island Regatta, a 13.1-mile race around the beautiful Wye Island. Wye Island is located off Maryland's Eastern Shore and is made up primarily of the Wye Island Natural Resources Management Area. Finally, after several years of schedule conflicts on race weekend, I decided to just go ahead and not do the race, instead circumnavigating the island with my husband.

Wye Island is located about 25 minutes south of the Bay Bridge, near Wye Mills. A counterclockwise circumnavigation will take you around the island, on the Wye Narrows, Wye River, and Wye East River. If you take the most direct route around the island (skipping most of the coves), you will paddle approximately 11.4 nautical miles.

It was a warm July Saturday and I heard that parking at the Wye Mills Public Landing could be a nightmare during the summer, especially on the weekends.

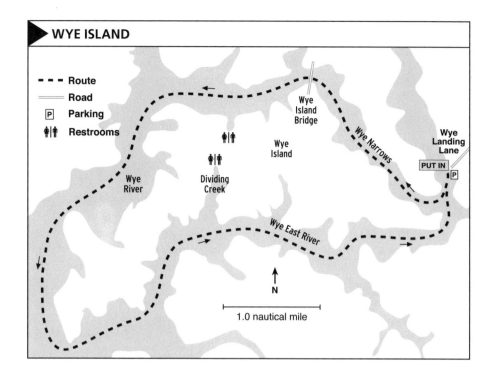

When I neared the ramp, there was a half-mile-long line of boats and trailers parked on the side of the road. Not deterred, I pulled into the launch area and *voila!* There was one parking space open that was specifically for cars without trailers. Clearly, it was my lucky day.

It was 9:30 A.M. and many fishing boats were coming off the water with their morning catch. The sky was overcast and the wind was calm. I launched into the Wye East River and was immediately happy that I brought my GPS device. The island looks similar to the rest of the Eastern Shore, with lots of twists, turns, and inlets.

For a counterclockwise circumnavigation (which is the same direction the race runs), head south from the landing and make your first right into Wye Narrows. The red boathouse you see in the distance is on Wye Island, and for the rest of your trip, be sure to keep the island on your left.

The rivers are tidal, so taking a look at the current tide charts can be beneficial. I tried to time my paddle to benefit from a tidal push during the last few miles of the trip.

Wye Island is mostly natural, with 2,450 of its 2,800 acres managed by Maryland's Department of Natural Resources. One of their goals is to provide inviting habitat for migrating waterfowl and native wildlife, and it seemed to me that they are highly successful. During the first half mile, I saw a bald eagle, half a dozen osprey, several blue herons, and a large turtle. I figured it wouldn't get any better than that, and joked about turning back and calling it a day. But then I would have missed one of the most "memorable" encounters I've had on the water (more on that later).

The first couple miles were peaceful and very relaxing. The wind was still and a rain cloud opened up for a short time, bouncing large drops off the river's surface. A few houses dot the shoreline opposite the island, but the only other boats on the water were small crabbing boats.

About 2.9 nautical miles into the route, there is a small inlet (the third of three) on the island, where there is a no-frills kayak landing and a short walk to restroom facilities. Neither of us needed a pit stop, so we kept pushing forward. Near mile 3.5, you'll paddle around a bend in the island and into the Wye River (where the Wye Narrows meet the Wye River). The opposite shore is noticeably more developed at this point, and you will likely pick up additional powerboat company.

For more than 300 years, Wye Island was under private ownership and was mostly used for agriculture. Tobacco and wheat were the primary crops on the island. The third governor of Maryland, William Paca, whose signature also appears on the Declaration of Independence, owned half of the island in the late 1700s and died there in 1799. The other prominent owner was Charles Bordley, a distinguished attorney who left his law career and made the island completely self-sufficient. Under his direction, Wye Island had vineyards, orchards, a brewery, and brickyard and even produced its own textiles. Today there are still a few privately owned parcels of land on Wye Island, but most of it is owned by the state of Maryland.

A kayaker passes by on the Wye East River.

Between miles 4.0 and 5.0, the most direct route is actually along the shore opposite the island. Head for the large duck blind, and then set your sights on the obvious
point of land ahead on the island. You will have to cross the river twice, but there are
areas where that distance isn't too great. If you have ample time or need a lunch
break, there are some great beaches along Wye Island on this stretch, and you may
see some impressive sailboats moored off the island shore. To take advantage of these
nice break areas, stay close to the Wye Island shoreline.

We experienced the heaviest boat traffic between miles 5.2 and 6.5. Unfortunately, the boats are not always courteous, so be aware of large wakes. The route
around the island turns directly south until about mile 6.5, when you'll make a
90-degree left turn into the Wye East River. You may see a lighthouse in the distance marking the opening to the Chesapeake Bay. If you go toward the lighthouse
you'll be completely off course, but it makes a nice side trip if you want to add a
couple of miles.

Where the Wye River and the Wye East River meet is the closest point on the
route to the Chesapeake Bay. This is key because as we headed up the Wye East
River (around mile 8.0), I experienced something that had never happened to me in
my 20-plus years of kayaking.

I was paddling steadily; by this time the sun had come out and it had turned into
a beautiful summer day. The winds were still light, and there was just one small boat
within sight of us. I paddled slightly ahead of my husband, who was behind me, to
my left.

Suddenly, out of nowhere, a chill ran down my spine and I felt what I can only
describe as a primal rush of fear. I instinctively stopped paddling and looked at the
water ahead of me just as a large fin broke the surface. I immediately knew this was
no "fish." It skimmed the top of the water in a sort of skidding motion, and I could
see that it was at least six feet long.

As quickly as it came up, it dived back under water and out of sight. I turned to my
husband and gasped, "Did you see that?"

"Yes," was all he said.

"Was it . . . ?"

"Yes."

I've paddled in remote areas of Alaska and Canada many times and often have
been just feet from humpback and orca whales. Those experiences are some of the
most incredible memories of my life. However, coming face-to-face with a shark was
a totally different experience. The only way I can describe it is a complete feeling of
being alone.

Now, I didn't include this part of my experience to scare you from paddling around
Wye Island. The truth is that there are twelve known types of sharks that frequent the
Chesapeake Bay waters, and most of them are harmless. The area is not known for
shark encounters, and nobody that I know of has ever been attacked in the Chesapeake
Bay. I do not know what kind of shark I saw, and I realize that my encounter was the

exception, and it was thankfully rather uneventful. I think sometimes we forget how awesome nature can be, and these encounters serve as good reminders. After all, isn't that one of the reasons we kayak in the first place—to experience nature?

We continued without speaking about the encounter. The day was beautiful, and we had timed our trip up the Wye East River so that we'd receive a pleasant push from the incoming tide.

At about mile 8.3 there is another restroom on the island, about a third of a mile into an inlet called Dividing Creek. It is located on the left, near the end of the inlet.

Several stunning sailboats were moored in the inlet, as it is a popular spot for pleasure boats. Access to the shore of the island is allowed as long as boaters are mindful of where they land and don't destroy the shoreline. Legend has it that pirates used the protected coves of the island to hide, which seems likely, given the history of pirating on the bay—even Blackbeard was said to have roamed the waters.

We had packed a lunch and planned to picnic on the shore, but when the sun came out the temperature rapidly rose. So we decided to push on and eat after we returned to the launch.

The remaining several miles were calm and relaxing. The river is widely used by sailboats, and we kept company with some beautiful vessels as they glided silently past us.

It is helpful to have a GPS device in this section, as there are many inlets on both sides of the river that can make it difficult to sight which way the river actually goes. I've heard that at times there are many stinging nettles (small jellyfish) in the river, but we saw only one the entire day. Interestingly enough, we saw no other kayakers, which I found strange given the popularity of the area and the annual kayak race.

The boat launch was a welcome sight for two kayakers who had been paddling for 3.5 hours straight and the portable toilets were an even better sight. Our GPS read 13.5 miles (11.7 nautical miles).

The parking area had cleared out a bit, since many of the local fishing boats had returned with their catch. We spoke briefly with a few pleasure boaters who were coming in off the water, and after packing up our kayaks, turned on the air conditioning in the car and ate our egg salad sandwiches.

Another great kayaking spot to add to my list and certainly one that will remain in my memory for years to come.

MORE INFORMATION

Wye Island NRMA (dnr2.maryland.gov/publiclands/Pages/eastern/wyeisland.aspx; 410-827-7577).

28
ASSATEAGUE ISLAND

Explore the nooks, crannies, and coves of Assateague State Park to find wild ponies, sika deer, pelicans, and osprey. This is also a great area for bird-watching.

Distance ▶ 4.0 or 9.0 nautical miles

Cautions ▶ Wind could pose a challenge when crossing from South Point to Great Egging Island. Coastal storms can spring up suddenly any time of the year, but particularly during the summer. Check the forecast before you head out and keep an eye to the sky, especially on hot, humid afternoons.

Charts and Maps ▶ NOAA Electronic Chart US4VA50M / Paper Chart #12211

LAUNCHES

Assateague Island Maryland State Park Boat Ramp, Berlin There are two good launch sites. The first is located just before the Verrazano Bridge, where there is plenty of parking. There is a fee to use the boat ramp, but you can launch for free from the sandy beach in front of the parking lot. (You will still need to pay the park entrance fee, which is $4 for Maryland residents and $6 for non-residents.) To reach the launch, take US 50 West from Ocean City and turn left onto MD 611/Stephen Decatur Highway. Follow the road for just over 7.0 miles. The launch site is located just before the Verrazano Bridge, on the left side of the road. There are restrooms at the launch. *GPS coordinates: 38° 14.860' N, 75° 9.092' W.*

I recommend stopping at the visitor center across the street. They have maps available of the park and the entire island. Since part of the island is run by the state of Maryland and part is National Park, there are different fee structures and rules for each area.

Ferry Landing, Berlin The second launch site is on the island. Follow the directions above and cross the bridge. Turn right onto Bayberry Drive and then go right onto Ferry Landing Road and drive to the end. *GPS coordinates: 38° 12.011' N, 75° 9.743' W.*

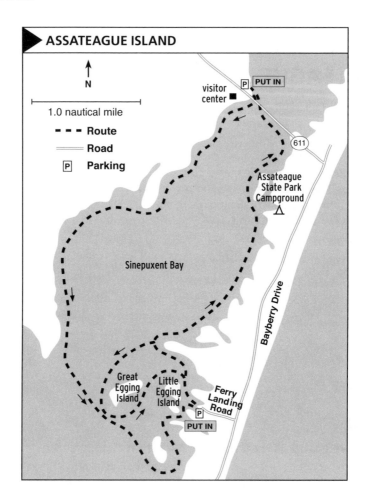

ROUTE DESCRIPTION

Assateague Island National Seashore is one of the few natural stretches of barrier island that remain on the east coast. The 35-mile-long, undeveloped seashore (two-thirds in Maryland and the rest in Virginia) is within sight of bustling Ocean City but is reserved for hiking, camping, kayaking, and other outdoor recreation.

The barrier islands along the Atlantic coast are familiar to most people who live in the eastern part of the country, but they are actually not that common. Barrier islands are found on only roughly 13 percent of coastlines worldwide. Since they are formed by the accumulation of sand caused by tides and wind, they are considered temporary features. It is believed that numerous barrier islands were deposited before the formation of Assateague Island, and that they may have stretched much farther out to sea. This might help explain the numerous shipwrecks that have historically occurred off its shore.

Assateague Island is located north and east of Chincoteague Island in Virginia (see Trip 34). A plan to develop it into a resort town similar to Ocean City, Maryland, was once in place. Although some houses were built, a tremendous storm hit the island in 1962 and the forceful surge of the Atlantic, which completely enveloped the island in several places, destroyed everything that was built, including the roads. Federal intervention to safeguard the island from future storms was denied, and the National Seashore designation was made in 1965. There are still some private properties on the island, so if you see a sign that indicates this, be considerate.

Miles of paddling real estate surround Assateague Island, which houses Assateague State Park. It has 2.0 miles of Atlantic beaches and the bay side is a wonderful venue for kayaking.

Kayaking is allowed everywhere in the Sinepuxent Bay. Paddling along the Atlantic coast is an option, but the salt marshes, countless coves, wildlife, and open water of the Sinepuxent Bay offer diversity and beauty that is hard to find elsewhere on the East Coast.

From the Verrazano Bridge launch, you can look across the inlet and see Ocean City in the distance, 9.0 miles away. This is a great location for the start of a round-trip day paddle, with a mix of open water crossings and marsh exploration. Beginning paddlers may wish to start from the Ferry Landing Road launch and explore some of the sheltered marsh, since that has less potential for strong winds and waves. There are also four backcountry camp sites (permit required) that are easier to reach from the Ferry Landing Road launch.

Be aware that the bugs in this area can be brutal. As a rule, May is the worst month, but they can be a problem all summer. The greenhead flies and no-see-ums are a threat but pale in comparison to the mosquitoes in this area. When the wind kicks up, it can provide relief from the little bloodsuckers, but the tradeoff is a more challenging paddle.

The Assateague Island wild ponies are a huge attraction in the park. If you spend a day along the National Seashore, you can bet you'll see these adorable furry ponies. Although the ponies get the greatest amount of attention, sika deer also roam the island. These small deer are originally from Japan and were introduced to the island in the 1920s. They are often called Asian elk, for the elk-like behavior they exhibit, including the way males physically challenge each other during mating season and the loud sounds they make.

I hesitate to proclaim one specific paddling route in this beautiful park as the best. Really, you can choose where to paddle based on the wind direction, its strength, and the amount of time you have. You may also vary your route to observe wildlife or if you're camping, to reach a specific campsite. Following are two routes I've enjoyed in the past.

Sinepuxent Bay Loop

This beautiful 9.0-mile loop runs along the western shoreline of Sinepuxent Bay before crossing to the eastern side of the bay along the barrier island parkland.

Launch from the state park and paddle under the Verrazano Bridge. Paddle down the shoreline for approximately 3.5 nautical miles until you are opposite Great Egging Island.

Make the crossing from around South Point to Great Egging Island. The bay is tidal, although the tidal pull isn't typically that strong and doesn't make paddling difficult. Low tide can expose muddy areas in the shallow water, but regardless of the tide, there are plenty of places to paddle. Wind will likely pose the biggest challenge during the crossing.

Paddle around the south end of Great Egging Island and turn north to head up the eastern side of the bay along the backside of the barrier island. This is a lovely stretch of protected land, where you are likely to see the wild ponies and other wildlife. You will soon pass the Ferry Landing Road launch site. Take the opportunity for a break if you need one.

Continue paddling north along the jagged shoreline until you reach the eastern side of the Verrazano Bridge. Make the final crossing back to your launch.

Assateague State Park boat launch by the Verrazano Bridge.

Ferry Landing Loop

This fun, 4.5-mile loop starts from the Ferry Landing Road launch and lassos three small marsh islands. It is a great place to see wildlife and to take some time to become acquainted with the bayside of the barrier island.

After launching, paddle northwest to the eastern side of Little Egging Island. Paddle to the northern tip of the island and then duck into the marsh on the right for a little exploration, before setting your sights on the point at the end of Bayside Drive. Even if you're not a bird-watcher, you may consider bringing a field guide with you. This is a tremendous place for viewing birds.

Paddle northwest to the point and then make a sharp left turn to start paddling southwest and aim for the back side of Great Egging Island. Paddle along the western edge of the island and then past the southern tip. Continue southeast, crossing the open water to Lumber Marsh Island. Paddle around the southern end of the island and back to the western shore of the barrier island. Explore the nooks, crannies, and coves as you make your way back up to the launch. Look for ponies, pelicans, deer, and osprey.

You can lengthen this trip by circumnavigating all three islands.

MORE INFORMATION

Assateague State Park (dnr2.maryland.gov/publiclands/Pages/eastern/assateague .aspx; 410-641-2918). Assateague Island National Seashore (nps.gov/asis/index.htm; 410-641-1441).

THE WILD PONIES OF ASSATEAGUE ISLAND

The beautiful herds of wild ponies that roam the beaches, forest, and salt marshes on Assateague Island are no newcomers. Their ancestors have lived on the island since the 1600s. The tale of their arrival is one of adventure, danger, and survival. It goes something like this: A large Spanish sailing ship with multiple decks called a galleon (possibly named the *La Galga*) sank offshore in 1750. The ship was carrying a cargo of horses and when it went down the strongest ones escaped and were able to swim to shore and survive on the island.

Although the theory of how the ponies arrived has not been proven, strong evidence exists to suggest that this is how it happened, since ships traveling to the colonies often carried ponies. And it is known that the *La Galga* wrecked in the area around that time.

Shipwrecks in those days were common. Ships navigated by the stars with the help of lighthouses, which were often cloaked in fog or rain. When a ship ran aground on a sandbar, its wooden structure would often be split apart by the force of the waves beating against it. If the cargo area of the *La Galga* was destroyed, this would allow for the ponies to swim free.

There was also a terrible storm in 1749 that is said to have killed all the livestock on Assateague Island prior to the shipwreck. This negates the second most popular theory for how the ponies arrived—that they were released by early settlers. A Spanish shipwreck was also found off the island's shore that helps support the *La Galga* theory.

Regardless of how the ponies first got to their home on Assateague Island, one thing is clear, these shaggy little horses are hardy and have adapted extremely well to island life. They eat wild grass that grows on the dunes and in the marsh and are able to find fresh water in the island's ponds.

It is easy to assume that these adorable little guys are friendly and tame, but they remain wild. Visitors are strongly urged to not pet, interact, and especially feed the ponies.

There are two herds of wild horses on the island. They are divided by a fence along the Maryland and Virginia border. The National Park Service manages the herd located in Maryland and the Chincoteague Volunteer Fire Company owns the herd in Virginia. The two herds combined have approximately 300 ponies.

VIRGINIA

Virginia is one of the largest states in the mid-Atlantic region. It has approximately 132 miles of coast along the Atlantic Ocean and more than 7,000 miles of tidal bay coastline.

Kayaking in Virginia is excellent. In addition to paddling options near the Atlantic, there is also the Chesapeake Bay, and several major tributaries, including the Rappahannock, Potomac, York, and James rivers. As such, paddlers can enjoy a variety of scenery ranging from launches in the historic Jamestown area (see Trip 29) to the crowded beaches of the Atlantic to the pristine Eastern Shore.

Virginia's Eastern Shore (see Trip 38) is located at the southern end of the Delmarva Peninsula. It is 70.0 miles long and separates the Chesapeake Bay from the Atlantic Ocean. There is a line of barrier islands that border the Atlantic that have been widely protected as conservation areas by the state. This line of islands makes up the longest undeveloped stretch of coastline on the eastern seaboard.

Virginia Seaside Water Trail (see Trip 37) is a playground of 37 day-paddling routes that are located on the Atlantic between the barrier islands and mainland. It runs the length of Virginia's Eastern Shore. The trail offers miles of undeveloped coastline for exploration and also goes by small villages and farmland.

Launch sites vary in Virginia in terms of accessibility and amenities. Generally speaking, most do not have launch or parking fees, and amenities such as restrooms are not a given but are available in many places. Most of the sites are generally safe for leaving a vehicle, but as with any launch, do not leave valuables inside your car.

29
JAMESTOWN ISLAND

Paddle past one of the country's foremost historic sites and see trees like oak, pine, and cypress and a thriving wildlife community with shorebirds, songbirds, turtles, otter, raccoons, and deer.

Distance ▶ 8.5 nautical miles

Cautions ▶ The James River can be rough in windy conditions. The lower section of the island is the most exposed and has the highest potential for rough water. The currents in the Thorofare can be strong, and the channel connecting Sandy Bay with the James River can have one of the fiercest rips in the region. You will need to be very aggressive and confident as you paddle through its currents and whirlpools.

Charts and Maps ▶ NOAA Electronic Chart US5VA25M / Paper Chart #12248

LAUNCH

Jamestown Beach Event Park, Williamsburg A kayaking trip around Jamestown Island is best started from Jamestown Beach Event Park. It is located north of the island and is a gorgeous little park with four scenic beach areas on the river. To reach the launch from the Colonial National Historic Parkway, take VA 31 South. Follow the signs for the Jamestown Settlement. Pass the entrance to the settlement (on the left) and continue to the end of the road. Turn left to stay on VA 31. The park entrances are on the right. On weekends, take the first entrance into the park. Follow the road to the end right by the fourth beach. You can unload your kayak and park right there. *GPS coordinates: 37° 13.637' N, 76° 47.036' W.*

During the week this entrance is closed, so you should enter at the second entrance (by the ferry terminal) and park in the grassy parking lot on the right. You will need to walk your boat down to the water. The first and second beaches are located closest to the lot. There is a small snack bar and restrooms, and it is free to park and launch. *GPS coordinates: 37° 13.550' N, 76° 47.148' W.*

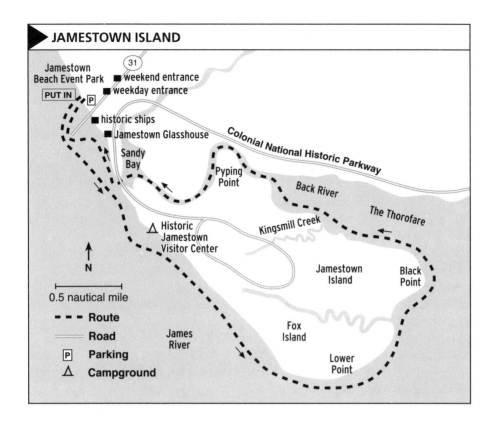

JAMESTOWN ISLAND

Jamestown
Beach Event Park   ■ weekend entrance
PUT IN   P   ■ weekday entrance
■ historic ships
■ Jamestown Glasshouse
Sandy
Bay
Pyping
Point
Colonial National Historic Parkway
Back River
The Thorofare
△ Historic
Jamestown
Visitor Center
Kingsmill Creek
N
0.5 nautical mile
Jamestown
Island
Black
Point
- - - Route
——— Road
P   Parking
△   Campground
James
River
Fox
Island
Lower
Point

ROUTE DESCRIPTION

Jamestown is one of the most historic locations in the entire country. It is the site of the first permanent English settlement in the new world and as such, it was the first British colony. The colony was established in 1607 and was the first capital of the colonies, from 1616 to 1699.

Today's Jamestown includes two tourism sites that are related to the original town and fort. One is Historic Jamestowne, located at the original settlement site on Jamestown Island. The second is nearby Jamestown Settlement, a living-history park and museum located a little over a mile away from the original site and adjacent to the island.

Jamestown Island is 1,561 acres and is surrounded by the James River and Back River. Most of the island is made up of marshland and is part of Colonial National Historical Park.

After launching, head south (left) down the shoreline. You will immediately pass the Jamestown–Scotland Ferry, a free ferry between Williamsburg and Surry, Virginia. (The Jamestown sites are technically located in Williamsburg.) Be very careful of the ferry when you pass this section of the shoreline.

Continuing south, you will soon see re-creations of the historic ships docked at Jamestown Settlement. Take a minute to consider the small size of the wooden ships and how incredible it is that they could carry the colonists on a four-and-a-half month journey across the Atlantic to Virginia. Be aware that they shoot cannons off the ships for the tourists and that they are very loud. The ships are docked at the Jamestown Settlement and are open to the public.

Continue past the ships and down the shoreline, toward Jamestown Island. You will pass the Jamestown Glasshouse, the first industrial manufacturer in the new world.

Jamestown Island is just barely an island. It is separated from the mainland by a tiny causeway over which is a small bridge. Continue on the James River, past the opening, to circumnavigate the island counterclockwise.

The James River can be rough in windy conditions, and normally the best time for calm winds is early in the day. Much of the western side of the island has rip-rap, but there are beautiful trees at the water's edge that often serve as perches for bald eagles.

As you continue along the island's shore, you will pass the archeological dig site located at Historic Jamestowne. You will likely see interpreters speaking to tourists about the site of the original settlement. It is an active dig site and is also the location of the ruins of a historic church and a statue of John Smith.

Be extremely careful while paddling this section of the island. There are old submerged pilings just offshore that can be mostly seen at low tide. A deep boat channel is located a few hundred yards offshore.

As you approach the southern end of the island, it turns very wild. The lower third is separated from Jamestown Island by marshy creeks and is called Fox Island. Exploring some of the inner island channels is possible, so if you wish to extend your trip you can paddle through the narrow marsh. I recommend bringing a GPS device if you decide to do so, in case you get disoriented in the marsh.

The landscape of marsh, oak, pine, and cypress creates the conditions for a thriving wildlife community with shorebirds, songbirds, turtles, otter, raccoons, and deer. Low tide exposes deserted sandy beaches in some areas, while in others the marsh seems to melt into open water. Since the lower section of the island is the most exposed, it has the highest potential for rough water.

Lower Point is the southern tip of the island. Once you round the tip, you can sight off of Black Point, the easternmost point on the island. As you round Black Point, you will paddle into an area called the Thorofare. This body of water separates Jamestown Island from the mainland and is also the mouth of the Back River. The currents in the Thorofare can be strong, so stay alert and keep to the left side of the shoreline since your destination is Back River straight ahead.

On the left you will pass Kingsmill Creek. It is the largest creek on this part of the shoreline. You can explore it if you'd like to extend your time on the water, but since the creek doesn't lead anywhere, you will need to turn around and paddle back out to the Thorofare.

From the Thorofare, paddle straight into Back River and wind your way around Pyping Point, the northernmost point on Jamestown Island. The river is fairly narrow in this section, and you will make several turns before reaching Sandy Bay. Remains of old wooden ships can be seen along this stretch. This area features boat traffic on most days, so be aware.

Cross the bottom of Sandy Bay and head for the causeway, paddling under the bridge that connects the mainland to the island to return to the James River. If the tide is against you, the channel will have one of the fiercest rips in the region. You will need to be very aggressive and confident as you paddle through the currents and whirlpools. The good news is, this section is short—just about 100 feet or so, so the challenge is brief.

Once you're back on the James River, paddle north and back up to the beautiful Jamestown Beach Event Park.

MORE INFORMATION

Historic Jamestowne (nps.gov/jame/index.htm; 757-856-1200). Jamestown Settlement (historyisfun.org/jamestown-settlement; 757-253-5299). Jamestown Beach Event Park (jamescitycountyva.gov/Facilities/Facility/Details/Jamestown-Beach -Event-Park-15; 757-259-5360).

The Jamestown Beach Event Park offers visitors a beautiful view as well as amenities such as charcoal grills and picnic areas.

THE HISTORIC TRIANGLE

Virginia has done a fantastic job of preserving many of its historic treasures.

The Historic Triangle is the name given to three colonial communities located on the Virginia Peninsula: Jamestown, Colonial Williamsburg, and Yorktown.

Jamestown was the first permanent settlement in the new world and was established in 1607. Visitors can enjoy two heritage sites, the Jamestown Settlement and the Jamestown National Historic Site. The settlement is a living history museum operated by the Commonwealth of Virginia. It is a re-creation of the original settlement and transports visitors back to the 1600s. There are costumed guides and wonderful replicas of the three English ships that sailed there from England. The Jamestown National Historic Site is the actual site of the original settlement and has historical remains, a burial ground, and an active excavation site from the original James Fort.

Colonial Williamsburg is the largest living history museum in the country and one of the most visited tourist destinations in the world. This amazing colonial town is run by the Colonial Williamsburg Foundation and is the restored eighteenth century colonial capital city of Virginia. The museum features the real city streets and buildings from the colonial period and costumed interpreters make visitors feel absorbed in colonial life. Historic shops, taverns, and inns help add to this one-of-a-kind experience. Eat, drink, sleep, and shop like the colonists did in this unique and elaborately historic town.

Yorktown is a quaint waterfront town that is best known as the site of the historic Revolutionary War victory in 1781 where General Cornwallis surrendered to George Washington.

Capitol building in Colonial Williamsburg.

The Yorktown National Battlefield is a major attraction in the town, but there are also good opportunities for shopping, dining, and outdoor sports.

All three communities in the Historic Triangle are linked by the Colonial Parkway. The parkway is run by the National Park Service and is a scenic road with views of water and other natural areas. The parkway is intended to help tourists travel between the communities with views much as they were in colonial times. The route begins in Yorktown, goes through Colonial Williamsburg, and ends in Jamestown.

30
REEDVILLE

Take a paddle in a thriving fishing community and enjoy calm protected bays, open water, and beautiful scenery.

Distance ▶ 6.0 and 8.0 nautical miles

Cautions ▶ Use caution when crossing the Great Wicomico River. Heavy boat traffic can be a danger, especially on summer weekends.

Charts and Maps ▶ NOAA Electronic Chart US5VA41M / Paper Chart #12235

LAUNCH

VA 692, Reedville There is a perfect launch site located on the east side of town, off Fleeton Road. It sits on a scenic, sheltered, picturesque bay off Cockrell Creek and has plenty of parking, two cement ramps, and two docks. There are no restroom facilities and there is no fee to launch. The launch area is notably well maintained and clean. In fact, the water is also very clean and clear. Even if there is nobody else using the launch area when you're there, you won't be alone, as this pretty little bay is home to a surprising number of osprey. There are often multiple nests within eyesight of the ramp. To reach the launch from US 360 East, turn slightly left onto VA 657, which becomes Fleeton Road. Just after passing Bayberry Lane, on the left, turn right onto VA 692. There is a small sign for the launch on VA 657. Follow VA 692 to the end (it is a short road). *GPS coordinates: 37° 49.469′ N, 76° 16.298′ W.*

ROUTE DESCRIPTION

On a large scale, Reedville, Virginia is located on a spit of land that separates the mouth of the Potomac River from the mouth of the Rappahannock River, where each run into the Chesapeake Bay. On a localized level, Reedville is a town in a rural area of Virginia known as the Northern Neck.

When you arrive in Reedville, after driving past mile after mile of farmland, you'll find a charming, yet quiet little town nestled in a protected creek (Cockrell Creek) by the mouth of the Wicomico River. What makes its location so appealing is that although its port is protected, it is also strategically located just around the corner from the mighty Chesapeake Bay.

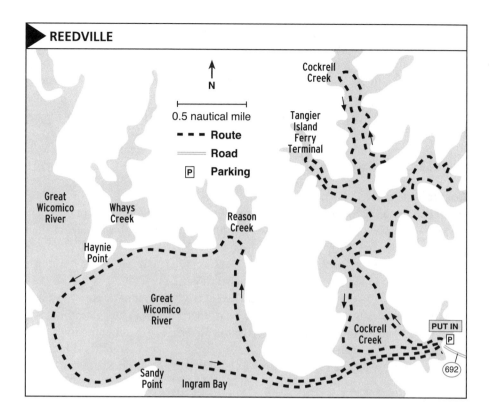

Partly due to this prime location and partly due to its namesake, Captain Elijah Reed, Reedville left its mark on history and continues to thrive today. Founded in 1867, it was a very young town when Captain Reed moved his menhaden fishing industry from Maine to the Northern Neck, bringing with him an experienced team of watermen. Your next question is likely, "What are menhaden?" This was mine as well.

Menhaden are a small, soft, oily fish (usually no longer than 15 inches long) that are native to the mid-Atlantic. At one time their oil was used for lighting, but today they are primarily processed into fishmeal, fish oil, and bait. Menhaden aren't normally directly consumed, but they are a vital ingredient for some food products, cosmetics, and animal feed.

By the late 1800s, Reedville was an established fishing port, primarily for the harvesting and processing of these little, soft-skinned fish. By the early twentieth century, although the town had just 500 residents, Reedville's per capita wealth was higher than it was in any other city. Millionaire's Row, a string of pretty Victorian mansions along its waterfront, is evidence of this wealth.

Today, Reedville still enjoys a thriving fishing industry, remains dependent on the menhaden, and is one of the top five fishing ports in the country. More commercial fish are hauled in Reedville annually than any other port on the eastern seaboard. Omega Protein, a fish processing company, is the largest local employer.

So aside from a small, oily fish that you can't really eat, what makes Reedville special? Kayaking, of course. Reedville is a paddler's paradise, with much more to see from the cockpit of a kayak than from a car. The town itself can be driven in just a few minutes, even at a snail's pace. For kayakers, it has a lot to offer: calm protected bays, open water, and beautiful scenery.

There are plenty of paddling options once you launch. You can paddle up Cockrell's Creek, into the mouth of the Wicomico River, or out to the Chesapeake Bay.

Cockrell's Creek

If you paddle to the left after launching and then head to the right out of the small bay, into Cockrell's Creek, you will see the local Reedville Fishing Fleet at their home base at Omega Protein. Paddling up Cockrell's Creek, past the fish plant and through many of the creek's arms, nooks, and crannies, can be a very rewarding paddle and is suitable for novice kayakers in calm weather.

Although the shoreline has a lot of residential development, the area still has a pleasant, quiet feel. Boat traffic is the biggest hazard, but in my experience, this is one area where boaters are normally courteous to kayakers. There are many impressive homes built on the water in Reedville. As you paddle in and out of the numerous inlets, you will see a large variety of pleasure craft tied to private docks and out on the

A paddler enjoying the scenery of Cockrell's Creek.

water. In some places the banks are high, and the landscape overall is quite beautiful.

A circular route along the right shoreline of Cockrell Creek, taking time to go into many of the bays, is an approximately 8-nautical-mile paddle. Of course, how far into each twist and turn you go will impact your mileage.

It is worth noting that Reedville is the jumping off point to Tangier Island. The Chesapeake Breeze passenger ferry runs between Reedville and Tangier Island daily during the summer (leaving at 10:00 A.M. and returning at 4:15 P.M.) and docks at Buzzard's Point Marina, located on the western arm of Cockrell Creek. Tangier Island is a popular tourist attraction and kayaking spot in the middle of the Chesapeake Bay.

If you are paddling in mid-June, be aware that the Reedville Bluefish Derby, a large fishing tournament, is held annually. This is a very popular event since it offers large cash prizes.

Great Wicomico River

Another great route for more experienced paddlers is to head south out of Cockrell Creek, around the corner to the right, and into Ingram Bay. Ingram Bay is wide and has some lovely unspoiled shoreline. It sits at the mouth of the Great Wicomico River and has exposed beaches, especially at low tide.

A pleasant, circular paddle takes you around Cockrell Point, up the shoreline to Reason Creek, and then west along the shoreline by Whays Creek and Haynie Point. At Haynie Point, make the short crossing of the Great Wicomico River and head south to Sandy Point, a large spit of land that sticks out into the river and Ingram Bay. From Sandy Point, cross the mouth of the river back to Cockrell Point and head back to the launch. The total mileage from the launch site is approximately 6 nautical miles and does require two open water crossings, but each are less than 1.0 mile. There are many shorebirds along this route, including osprey, herons, and even bald eagles.

The Chesapeake Bay

If your skill set is such that you'd like to paddle into the open water of the Chesapeake Bay, you can kayak south out of Cockrell Creek and around Fleeton Point (left) into the Chesapeake Bay. This is only for advanced kayakers who enjoy the challenge of open-water paddles. The shoreline is interspersed with bays and long stretches of beaches with moderate development. Taskmakers Creek is about 1.5 nautical miles from Fleeton Point. There are three smaller creeks between it and the point, but after Taskmakers Creek is a long stretch of uninterrupted shoreline, rimmed in part by a long sandy beach.

MORE INFORMATION

Town of Reedville (virginia.org/Cities/Reedville).

THE STEAMBOAT ERA

In 1760 a Scottish inventor developed an engine powered by steam for the purpose of removing water from mines. By 1787, the idea of using steam as power was applied to boats and completely revolutionized water transport. Flatboats that were used on the Ohio and Mississippi rivers previously floated down river in approximately six weeks, but the return trip required four or five months of hard labor. The steam engine drastically cut this time and their popularity exploded.

Steamboats burst onto the Chesapeake Bay scene in the early 1800s and quickly became an important link between coastal cities along the Bay. Much like the railroad was to the rest of the country, by the mid-1800s, steamboats were used for transporting passengers, goods, and even mail.

By the turn of the twentieth century, there were nearly 600 steamboats plowing the bay waters. They carried thousands of passengers to cities such as Norfolk, Baltimore, and nearly every port in between. Steamboat excursions became extremely popular with those who could afford it, and commerce flourished.

In the years that followed, steamboat travel became synonymous with leisure, gambling, and a romantic culture of travelers. The potential for the distribution of goods also rapidly expanded and local farms and canneries were established near the shore. Suddenly, rural communities were connected to large cities and local goods could be distributed globally. At one point, 85 percent of the world's oysters came from the Chesapeake Bay and their journey from the bay started by steamboat.

Steamboat races and accidents were documented, as were the daily lives of some of the crews. This engineering marvel opened new frontiers, sparked new economic growth and helped carve new trade routes. More importantly, it led to the development of the steam locomotive.

The twentieth century brought a new invention called the automobile. As cars grew in popularity and became more affordable, passenger traffic on the steamboats began to dwindle. Thus, the slow demise of the steamboat began.

Steamboats continued to be used for commerce until the 1930s, when a hurricane destroyed many of the wharfs on the Chesapeake Bay. The last excursion of a famous steamboat named the *Anne Arundel* was completed on September 14, 1937. The date is still known in some parts of Virginia as "Steamboat Era Day." A Steamboat Era Museum can be visited in Irvington, Virginia (steamboateramuseum.org).

31
FLEETS ISLAND

Tackle the challenge of open water to enjoy a lovely paddle around this tranquil and beautiful island.

> **Distance** ▶ 8.0 nautical miles
>
> **Cautions** ▶ The open water of the Chesapeake Bay produces wind and waves on the eastern side of the island, and the Rappahannock River to the west produces challenging water as well.
>
> **Charts and Maps** ▶ NOAA Electronic Chart US5VA41M / Paper Chart #12235

LAUNCHES

Windmill Point Road, White Stone There is a designated kayak launch area near the end of Windmill Point Road. There is a portable toilet at the launch site, a small floating dock, a bench on a higher dock, and a grassy put-in. There is no fee to launch. To reach the launch from White Stone, Virginia, take VA 695 South (Chesapeake Drive). After Chesapeake Drive turns into Windmill Point Road, you will pass over a very small bridge onto Fleets Island. Follow Windmill Point Road almost to the end. Just before you reach the small public beach at the end of the road, you will see a sign for the kayak launch, next to a grassy parking lot. Turn right into the lot. In the back, right corner of the parking area is a sign for the kayak launch. If the conditions aren't too wet, you can drive down to the launch on the small, muddy, one-lane trail (four-wheel drive is best). There is just enough room for one car to turn around. Another option is to park in the lot and carry your kayak to the launch. If you drive down to unload, be sure to park back up into the parking lot so that others can use the launch area. *GPS coordinates: 37° 37.146′ N, 76° 17.544′ W.*

Alternative Launch At the very end of the road is a second viable launch, in the form of a very small public beach (Westland Public Swimming Beach) and a small parking area. A private community borders both sides of the beach, so be mindful that their part of the beach is not open to the public. It is possible to launch from here, but the launch area is exposed and can be very challenging. The safest place to launch is at the designated kayak launch. *GPS coordinates: 37° 36.945′ N, 76° 17.617′ W.*

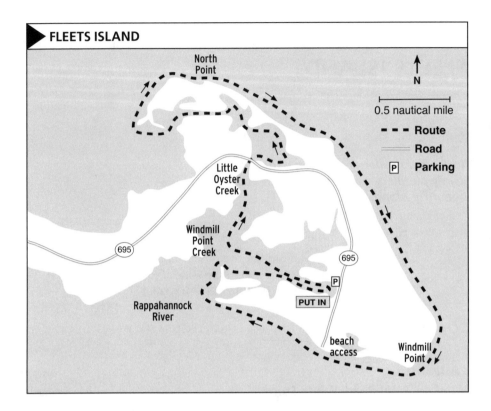

FLEETS ISLAND

North
Point

N

0.5 nautical mile

- - - Route
——— Road
P Parking

Little
Oyster
Creek

Windmill
Point
Creek

695

695

P

PUT IN

Rappahannock
River

beach
access

Windmill
Point

ROUTE DESCRIPTION

Fleets Island is a beautiful and remote island located at the southern tip of an area known as the Northern Neck, the most northern of three peninsulas along the western shore of the Chesapeake Bay (the other two are called the Middle Peninsula and the Virginia Peninsula). The Northern Neck borders the Potomac River to the north, the Rappahannock River to the south, and the Chesapeake Bay to the east.

The first European known to have visited it was Captain John Smith, who traveled as a prisoner of the Powhatan up the Rappahannock River during the winter of 1607. Early development on the peninsula was mainly near the navigable waters at its end, which led to the establishment of tobacco plantations up and down it. Because of these plantations, the Northern Neck was a wealthy area during the colonial period and was sometimes called the "Athens of the New World." Many of the country's founding fathers were born and lived there, including George Washington, James Madison, and James Monroe.

By the mid-1800s, the Northern Neck became famous as a prosperous location for farms and fishing. Local oysters from the Chesapeake Bay were exported globally for their large size and excellent flavor. Watermen enjoyed a good life during this time, as new harvesting techniques were being developed. Farming was still the number one profession in the area, as livestock and potatoes made their way into the local economy.

Fleets Island sits at the mouth of the Rappahannock River and the Chesapeake Bay. On a map it looks more like a peninsula, but if you look closely you can see where VA 695 (Windmill Point Road) connects the island to the mainland.

The island is named for Captain Henry Fleet, who lived in Jamestown and first set foot on the island around 1622, hoping to trade with the native people. During one of his trading trips, Fleet was captured by the Anacostan and held prisoner for five years. After a ransom was paid and he was released, Fleet, who had learned the Anacostan language and had become more of a friend than foe, became a trade negotiator. He ended up serving on both the Virginia and Maryland General Assemblies, before settling permanently in Fleets Bay. He is buried on Fleets Island, near Windmill Point.

A circumnavigation of this rural island is a rewarding and scenic trip, but should only be attempted by expert paddlers. The open water of the Chesapeake Bay produces wind and waves on the eastern side of the island, and the Rappahannock River to the west produces big water as well.

The designated launch area puts you on Windmill Point Creek, which flows into Little Oyster Creek. Paddle left out of the small inlet into Windmill Point Creek and then turn right as it meets Little Oyster Creek. This is the most protected part

A secluded bridge adds rustic charm to this designated kayak launch.

of the paddle and a good way to warm up before hitting the open water of the Chesapeake Bay.

The first part of the route, although protected, requires some concentration in order to find your way. It's best to bring a GPS device to avoid getting lost, as the twists and turns can be confusing. Since Little Oyster Creek has a wide, shallow mouth, its depth allows only small boats to enter the creek at low tide. This is great for kayakers since it severely limits the powerboat traffic in the creek.

The shorelines of Windmill Point Creek and Little Oyster Creek are partially undeveloped and partially developed with private homes. Continue north and slightly east up the creek and go under the small bridge that connects the island to the mainland. Turn to the right after paddling under the bridge and explore the shoreline along the small bay. At this point it's difficult to know what is part of the island and what belongs to the mainland: the island is the shoreline on your right. Take time to enjoy the natural setting and the wildlife that lives there. There are numerous species of waterfowl including pelicans, osprey, herons, ducks, and geese.

As you continue around the bay and head back north again, there are large exposed sandbars that can be seen between the creek and the Chesapeake Bay, on the other side. Continue paddling past the bars and out of the bay, through the narrow passage.

Not far ahead, at the northern end of the island, you'll see an evenly cut channel that runs east to west. This channel is an old canal that was dug during the Civil War for use by Confederate blockade runners. A signal station was erected near the canal for the purpose of notifying the blockade runners of the Union gunboat positions. Paddle through the canal, into Oyster Creek, and then bigger water.

This is the part of the route when it becomes exposed, so make sure your skills match the conditions before continuing. This route is intended for expert paddlers. Turn slightly south to pass out of the creek and then make a right turn to round the northern point of the island. As you make the turn, you'll paddle between Little Bay and Fleets Bay. Continue paddling, with the shoreline on your right as you enter the Chesapeake Bay.

Wide, sandy beaches line most of the Chesapeake Bay shoreline. The paddle around North Point and down the eastern side of the island is tranquil and beautiful. Although this water can be very challenging, it is truly a lovely place to paddle. A handful of private residences are located on the waterfront, but there are also large stretches of natural shoreline.

At the southern tip of the island is Windmill Point. Sea turtles, dolphins, and porpoises can frequently be spotted in the summer months near here. It is also a fishing hotspot in the Chesapeake Bay. Speckled trout, rockfish, and croaker are a few of the early season species found there. Bluefish and Spanish mackerel arrive in the summer. A few local restaurants will even smoke the bluefish caught by their customers (with advance notice).

Once you round Windmill Point, continue northwest, up the western shoreline, into the mouth of the Rappahannock River. You will pass Windmill Point Marina and the small public beach. Continue along the shoreline and into the mouth of Little Oyster Creek. Once you pass into Little Oyster Creek, the mainland shore will be to your left. Head right, into Windmill Point Creek, and back to the launch. The entire circumnavigation is approximately 8 nautical miles.

MORE INFORMATION
Lancaster County, VA (lancova.com; 804-462-5220).

32

MILFORD HAVEN/GWYNN'S ISLAND

Choose from a variety of potential routes to explore beautiful and often-empty waterways.

Distance ▶ 7.0, 8.0, or 12.0 nautical miles

Cautions ▶ The shallow channel, known as Hole in the Wall, between Sandy Point and Rigby Island can be windy, wavy, and full of wakes from boats speeding by. Be mindful that the Chesapeake Bay can produce heavy wind and waves.

Charts and Maps ▶ NOAA Electronic Chart US5VA41M / Paper Chart #12235

LAUNCHES

Milford Haven Landing, Gwynn The main launch is from Milford Haven Landing, which will be your jumping-off point for either a round-trip or a one way trip to Whites Creek or Havens Beach. To reach the Milford Haven landing from VA 198 East, turn left on VA 223/Cricket Hill Road. Continue over the bridge to Gwynn's Island. Look immediately to your right. The launch is located in the parking lot of the Seabreeze Restaurant. There is no fee to launch, and there are no public restrooms. *GPS coordinates: 37° 29.562' N, 76° 18.607' W.*

Whites Creek Landing, Diggs To reach this launch, follow VA 198 to the end. Continue on VA 642. Turn right on VA 643, in the town of Moon. Follow VA 643 to VA 682. The launch is at the end of VA 682. There is limited parking and no fee to launch. *GPS coordinates: 37° 26.625' N, 76° 15.994' W.*

Havens Beach Landing, Diggs To reach this launch, follow the directions for Whites Creek landing, but take an immediate right onto VA 643 from VA 682 and follow it to the end. You will see a sign for Mathews Beach. *GPS coordinates: 37° 26.136' N, 76° 15.177' W.*

ROUTE DESCRIPTION

The second of the three big peninsulas that border the western shore of the Chesapeake Bay in Virginia is known as the Middle Peninsula and is nestled between the Northern Neck and the Virginia Peninsula. The Rappahannock River borders the peninsula to the north, and the York River borders it to the south. The Chesapeake Bay is at the mouth of both rivers.

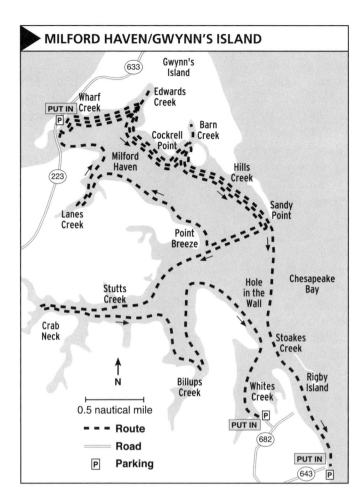

Mathews County is at the eastern end of the Middle Peninsula and borders the Chesapeake Bay and Mobjack Bay. It has more than 200 miles of shoreline, but less than 90 square miles of land. In addition to having shoreline on the Chesapeake Bay, the county includes land on three tidal rivers and has more than 50 navigable creeks, with plenty of water access. All this adds up to one thing: a very kayak-friendly county.

Mathews County is so boating-oriented that its visitor and information center created Mathews County Blueways Water Trail, with the help of many volunteers. This isn't just a few miles of waterways plunked down on a map, but instead is an interconnected system that includes five separate water trails on more than 90 miles of water. The trails, part of a network of recreational sites known as the Chesapeake Bay Gateways Network, are designed with small, hand-powered craft in mind and are geared toward both day trips and extended trips.

To say that the paddling in Mathews is exceptional is an understatement. As the visitor center itself says, "No one knows where the heck we are, and that means lots of uncrowded areas to explore." This statement pretty much hits the nail on the head in my opinion, as its diverse waterways are beautiful, interesting, and most of all, empty during much of the year.

One of my favorite places to paddle is on part of Gwynn's Island/Milford Haven Trail. Milford Haven is a sheltered waterway that separates Gwynn's Island and the mainland, is approximately 3 miles long, and opens up to the Chesapeake Bay on its southeast side. This is where I like to begin.

Milford Haven is between 0.5 and 0.75 mile wide and is widest on its southeastern side, where it opens into the Chesapeake Bay. Many creeks flow into Milford Haven and can be explored. It can be quite windy and wavy, especially as you near the bay.

There are many options for paddling in this area, including loop routes back to the Milford Haven Landing and one-way trips to other landings. When you launch, head left (southeast). You'll be in the busiest area of Milford Haven (near the bridge), and the tidal currents can be strong. It's a little industrial-looking at the start, but it will soon thin out and become more natural.

A good option if you're looking for a scenic route, with both calm creeks and more challenging open water crossings, is to follow the Gwynn's Island shoreline, taking time to explore its creeks. There's a cute bay (Wharf Creek) just after you start that normally has calm water and features less traffic than the main channel.

Continuing, you'll soon pass some buildings that mark the former location of a steamboat landing but now serve as a wharf where waterman unload their catches. The second creek is Edwards Creek (about 0.5 nautical mile long if you decide to paddle into it) and not much farther is Cockrell Point, which is a little more than 2.0 nautical miles from the launch if you take a direct route.

Continue past Cockrell Point to Barn Creek, which is, again, about 0.5 nautical mile long. Barn Creek is primarily residential and does make a nice side trip if you have the time.

As you continue paddling down Milford Haven, you will notice fewer homes, as the landscape gives way to marsh. This is where the natural setting of Middle Peninsula sets in. Sandy beaches and small islands will soon be visible in the distance. You will soon turn southward and pass a cut-through to the Chesapeake Bay at Hills Creek (available only during high tide). Be especially careful of tidal currents in this area as you continue south to Sandy Point, the southern tip of Gwynn's Island. It is a little less than 2.0 nautical miles between Cockrell Point and Sandy Point.

The area around Sandy Point is great for bird-watching. You could see eagles, terns, cormorants, and many other types of birds in this unspoiled area. It is also a great place for seeing dolphins. Sandy Point has a pretty little beach that boaters in the summertime flock to for fishing and swimming.

Looking south, you'll be able to see Rigby Island and the open water between it and Sandy Point. The closest land to Sandy Point is directly west at Point Breeze (the distance between the two is a little less than 0.75 nautical mile). This area is one of the most challenging, since the shallow channel (known as Hole in the Wall) between Sandy Point and Rigby Island can be windy, wavy, and full of wakes from boats speeding by.

From Sandy Point, you have several options. You can cross over to Point Breeze and paddle north along the shoreline of the mainland for a loop route, cross over to Point Breeze and then continue south to Whites Creek Landing, or paddle through Hole in the Wall to Stoakes Creek (on the west side of Rigby Island) and then south to Havens Beach.

Milford Haven Loop

If you decide to cross to Point Breeze and paddle back north along the mainland toward the Gwynn's Island Bridge and the Milford Haven Landing, you will be paddling along an area known as Crab Neck. This beautiful shoreline is mostly undeveloped, although there are a few scattered cottages.

After Crab Neck, you will find Lanes Creek, which is about 0.75 mile long. It has some residential development (primarily on its northwestern side) but is worth exploring.

After paddling up and down Lanes Creek, continue to the Gwynn's Island Bridge (VA 223) and make a careful crossing through this busy area to Milford Haven Landing. The total paddling distance for this loop is approximately 8 nautical miles.

A kayaker paddles near Milford Haven.

Continuing to Whites Creek Landing

If you decide to cross to Point Breeze and then continue southwest, you will enter the mouth of Stutts Creek and Billups Creek. The channel that crosses the mouth is quite busy during the summer months. Travel up Stutts Creek along the right shoreline. Billups Creek opens up to the south near Fanneys Point, but you can explore that on your way back.

Once you pass Fanny's Point, Stutts Creek becomes narrow until it's only about 0.25 mile wide. The shoreline is initially fairly low, but then becomes more elevated as a stretch of older homes becomes visible. This part of the creek is charming, sheltered, and quiet.

As you paddle back out of the creek, take the time to explore Billups Creek. To the east is Lilley's Neck, which is mostly marsh, but does have a few homes on its shore.

As you paddle out of Billups Creek, turn right and paddle around the northern tip of Lilley's Neck and then down its eastern shore. You will briefly paddle through Stoakes Creek before reaching Whites Creek. Continue about 0.5 nautical mile and the Whites Creek Landing will be on your left (at the end of VA 682). You will need to have a car waiting for you at the landing for this one-way trip. This one-way paddle is approximately 12 nautical miles.

Continuing to Havens Beach

If you make the channel crossing through Hole in the Wall from Sandy Point to Rigby Island, you will paddle through Stoakes Creek on the west side of Rigby Island, to the Rigby Island Channel. Check the tides before you leave to allow for the tidal flow. This channel will put you in the Chesapeake Bay once you pass Rigby Island.

Continue paddling south. You will soon see pretty sand beaches stretching along the mainland shoreline for miles. Be mindful that the open bay can produce heavy wind and waves. The Havens Beach Landing is located approximately three-quarters of a mile south of Rigby Island (at the end of VA 643). You will need to leave a car at the beach for this one-way trip. The total mileage is approximately 7 nautical miles.

MORE INFORMATION

Mathews County Blueways Water Trail (visitmathews.com/birding-wildlife-trails; 804-725-422).

33
EAST RIVER

Paddle up and down this river to enjoy
peaceful scenery and potentially see dolphins.

Distance ▶ 5.0 or 11.0 nautical miles

Cautions ▶ The East River is about a 0.5 mile wide near the mouth, where it meets Mobjack Bay. This is normally the roughest area of the river since it's more open to wind and waves. Unsettled weather can change conditions at any time and whitecaps aren't uncommon here.

Charts and Maps ▶ NOAA Electronic Chart US5VA26M / Paper Chart #12238

LAUNCH

Williams Wharf Landing, Mathews This place is one of the most amazing public boat landings I've ever seen. The wharf was first established around the time of the Revolutionary War as a trading port and warehouse facility. Believe it or not, it was one of the country's busiest maritime activity centers. Between 1802 and 1844, more than 10,000 ships used the wharf. Later, Williams Wharf became a bustling steamboat landing that served steamboats running the Baltimore-to-Norfolk route.

Today the wharf is a 4-acre waterfront space dedicated to hand- and wind-powered boats. More than $1 million was spent to preserve the wharf as a historic landmark and a space for environmentally friendly watercraft (no powerboats can launch there). It is beautifully maintained and has an enormous floating dock. It is located at the point where the East River is at its narrowest and is a great launching point for exploring both the upper and lower parts of the river. There is plenty of parking and permanent restroom facilities at the site. There is no fee to launch.

To reach it from VA 223 South, turn left onto VA 198 (Buckley Hall Road). The road joins VA 14 East. Stay on VA 14 when it splits from VA 198. Pass VA 615 (Town Point Landing) and turn right onto VA 614 (Williams Wharf Road), taking it to the end. *GPS coordinates: 37° 24.217' N, 76° 20.760' W.*

Town Point Landing, Mathews From VA 14, turn right onto VA 615 (Town Point Landing) and follow it to the end for this pretty little boat landing, with a ramp and soft launch. There is plenty of parking, but no restroom facilities. *GPS coordinates: 37° 24.930' N, 76° 20.231' W.*

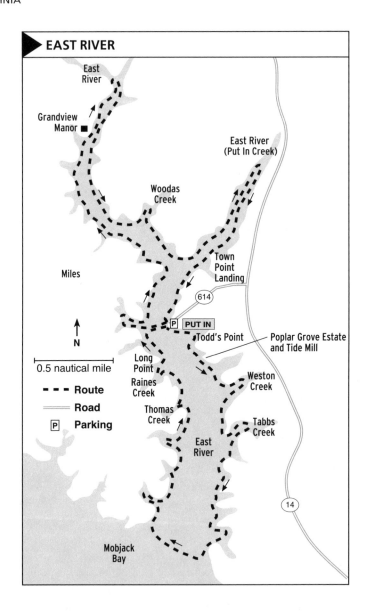

EAST RIVER

East River

Grandview Manor ■

East River (Put In Creek)

Woodas Creek

Miles

Town Point Landing

614

N

P PUT IN

Todd's Point

Poplar Grove Estate and Tide Mill

0.5 nautical mile

Long Point

Weston Creek

Raines Creek

Thomas Creek

Tabbs Creek

East River

Mobjack Bay

14

- - - Route
——— Road
P Parking

ROUTE DESCRIPTION

The East River runs along the Middle Peninsula, which is the second of three peninsulas that border the western shore of the Chesapeake Bay in Virginia. It is part of Mathews County, which has more than 200 miles of shoreline.

With so much shoreline, Mathews is very boater-friendly. So much so that a group of dedicated volunteers developed Mathews County Blueways Water Trail, a system of five interconnected water trails that cover more than 90 miles of water. The trails, part of a network of recreational sites known as the Chesapeake Bay Gateways

Network, are designed with small, hand-powered craft in mind and are geared toward both day trips and extended trips.

The paddling in Mathews County is exceptional. The area isn't crowded and has somehow managed to stay off the radar for many vacationers. You will still find boat traffic, especially during the summer, but not as much as you might expect in such a pristine and beautiful area.

The Middle Peninsula in Virginia is shaped like a crab claw, with the Mobjack Bay in the center of the claw. The Mobjack Bay leads into the Chesapeake Bay and on its northeastern side is the East River.

The Y-shaped East River hosts the shortest of the five Mathews Blueways Water Trails and is easy to navigate. It is a beautiful tidal river on which you can paddle past historic homes, a gorgeous wharf, and one of the last tide mills still standing on the east coast (with a fascinating history).

The river is about 0.5 mile wide near the mouth, where it meets Mobjack Bay. This is normally the roughest area of the river since it's more open to wind and waves. As you move up the river, it becomes more narrow and protected, but it can still be challenging, depending on conditions.

The river has a natural division between the top portion and the lower portion at a peninsula called Williams Wharf. The wharf juts into the river from the east.

There are two public launches on the East River, and both are lovely. They are fairly close together and are accessible off route 14. The first is Town Point Landing (VA 615). It has a boat ramp, soft launch, and plenty of parking. However, there are no restroom facilities. The second is Williams Wharf, a 4-acre launch for hand- and wind-powered boats, with restroom facilities.

You don't really need a specific route to enjoy paddling the East River. Mathews Blueways Water Trail goes up and down the river and into both sides of the "Y." Regardless of which launch you choose, you'll end up putting in around the split between the upper and lower portions of the river. You can choose which way to paddle and then do a round-trip.

Lower East River

To explore the lower section of the East River, launch at Williams Wharf and head south toward the Mobjack Bay. It's about a 2.5-nautical-mile paddle to the mouth of the river if you paddle straight. Unless you are paddling for a workout, I recommend taking the time to paddle through the numerous coves and creeks that appear around nearly every turn. You will find some beautiful modern homes, natural spaces, and older estates on this part of the river; it's very scenic.

The lower portion of the East River is wide. Start along the eastern (left) side of the river and paddle south. You will quickly pass Todd's Point and head toward one of the most historic sites in the county, the Poplar Grove Estate and Tide Mill.

A tide mill is a tidal-driven water mill. It works this way: A dam with a water gate (sluice) is built across a tidal inlet so that water can enter the millpond through the gate at high tide. Then the gate shuts the water in. When the tide recedes, the stored water is released, turning the water wheel. The original mill at Poplar Grove was built during colonial times. George Washington's troops at Yorktown are said to have eaten the meal ground at the mill. The original mill burned down during the Civil War, but was rebuilt shortly after and is the mill you can see today, one of only five remaining in the United States.

Poplar Grove is also home to a stately, historic eighteenth century mansion that is the birthplace of the only woman officially commissioned in the Confederate Army during the Civil War. Her name was Sally Tompkins and she is most famous for sponsoring a private hospital in Richmond, Virginia to treat wounded soldiers during the war. It's a more recent property owner, however, that might come as a surprise to most people: In 1980, just months before his death, John Lennon and Yoko Ono purchased Poplar Grove for use as their country home. After Lennon's death, Ono donated the estate to charity. The current owner purchased the property in 1985.

Continue a southerly paddle and explore Weston Creek and Tabbs Creek. There is a cozy inn on Tabbs Creek (The Inn at Tabbs Creek) and the paddle into their inlet is scenic and peaceful. As you continue on, you'll pass several more small inlets before reaching Mobjack Bay. If your skills are up to it, you can paddle into the bay and even continue to the Chesapeake Bay. Otherwise, cross the river near its mouth and head north up the opposite side of the river. Be sure to pay attention to the wind and tides. Remember, the East River is tidal and is also most exposed near its mouth. When the weather is good, this is usually not a problem, but with any body of water, unsettled weather can change conditions at any time, and whitecaps near the turn-around point aren't uncommon.

Be on the lookout for dolphins near the mouth of the river and on your trip up the western side of the river. Pods of dolphin have been known to travel up the river, especially in warmer months. Take the time to paddle into Thomas Creek and Raines Creek. The river crossing back to Williams Wharf is at the most narrow part of the river. A round-trip paddle from Williams Wharf to Mobjack Bay is between 5.0 and 9.0 nautical miles.

Upper East River

The upper section of the East River has a lot of residential development but is also very pleasant. Launch at Williams Wharf and cross the East River to Miles Creek. Paddle into the creek and by Zimmerman Marine, where you can see a variety of impressive boats being worked on. Continue up the river, past Long Point, and into the left arm of the "Y."

There are a few creeks along this sheltered part of the river that are navigable and fun to explore. Continue paddling past Grandview Manor, a 5,000-square-foot inn/guesthouse until you reach the river's headwaters.

On the way back down the river, stay to the eastern (left) side and enjoy the peaceful scenery. Woodas Creek is the largest creek in this part of the river. It's 0.5 mile long and makes another good side trip.

Williams Wharf is a rocky, yet well-maintained boat launch.

When you reach the intersection where the right arm of the "Y" turns sharply left, turn and follow the river northeast to explore this last section of the river. Some maps consider this part of the East River, while others call it Put in Creek. You'll find a shoreline of private coves and homes until you come to the Mathews Courthouse and the local water treatment plant. Turn around there and head back down the river to Williams Wharf. The total paddle distance is approximately 9 to 11 nautical miles, depending on how many side creeks you take.

MORE INFORMATION

Mathews County Blueways Water Trail (visitmathews.com/birding-wildlife-trails; 804-725-4229).

34
CHINCOTEAGUE ISLAND

Paddle between two pretty islands and observe herds of ponies at Chincoteague National Wildlife Refuge.

Distance ▶ 9.5 nautical miles

Cautions ▶ Be prepared to avoid the abundant amount of boat traffic on Assateague Channel. Toms Cove occasionally has difficult conditions, but the water is typically calm.

Charts and Maps ▶ NOAA Electronic Chart US4VA70M / Paper Chart #12210

LAUNCHES

East Side Landing, Chincoteague Island Two great launch sites provide access to the Assateague Channel. The first is called East Side Landing. It is one of the official launch sites for Virginia Seaside Water Trail, a series of paddling day-trip routes along the Eastern Shore of Virginia between Chincoteague Island and Cape Charles. There is a ramp, a floating dock, and parking, but usually no restrooms (on occasion there is a portable toilet). To reach the landing from Main Street on Chincoteague Island, turn onto Church Street. Follow it until it turns into East Side Road (VA 2103) and continue another 1.5 miles to East Side Landing (on the left). *GPS coordinates: 37° 55.162' N, 75° 22.193' W.*

Chincoteague Veterans Memorial Park, Chincoteague Island A second launch site is located 0.5 mile past East Side Landing, at Chincoteague Veterans Memorial Park. There is plenty of parking at the launch and a large ramp (a permit is required for boat trailers). The park has restrooms. *GPS coordinates: 37° 55.005' N, 75° 22.839' W.*

Snug Harbor Marina, Chincoteague Island A third launch area is also available in between the two at Snug Harbor Marina, on East Side Road (VA 2103). For a minimal fee, you can use the marina's facilities. *GPS coordinates: 37° 55.040' N, 75° 22.413' W.*

To launch a kayak on Chincoteague Island, you must purchase either a weekly ramp decal ($5) or a yearly decal ($20) from the town office or police station. Place the decal on your trailer or car in order to use the ramps. Kayaks do not need to be registered in Virginia, but the decal is required.

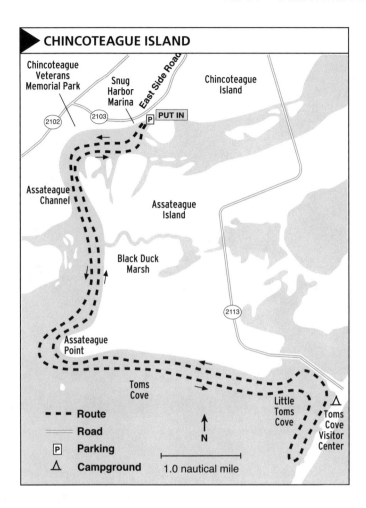

ROUTE DESCRIPTION

Chincoteague Island, the only resort island in Virginia, is located on Virginia's Eastern Shore, just south of the Maryland border. Chincoteague Island sits to the west of Chincoteague National Wildlife Refuge, separated by the Assateague Channel. The 14,000-acre refuge is famous for having herds of wild ponies (the same species as the ones who live on Assateague Island in Maryland—see Trip 28 and "The Wild Ponies of Assateague Island" on page 158) that have lived there for more than 400 years. Chincoteague National Wildlife Refuge offers ample wildlife watching, biking, hiking, miles of beautiful pristine beaches, marshland, and ample kayaking. The refuge is accessible by automobile from Chincoteague Island and can be visited for an $8 admission fee.

Although Chincoteague Island is a resort town, there are no high-rise buildings or a boardwalk. It is known for its relaxed atmosphere and its outdoor recreation.

The East Side Landing provides quite a few amenities for a day of paddling.

Chincoteague became famous in 1961 with the release of the movie *Misty of Chincoteague*, based on a 1947 children's book of the same name by Marguerite Henry. It tells the story of a family who lived on the island and their love and interactions with the wild ponies. The people and horses in the story were real, but the story itself was fiction. There was a real pony named Misty, whom Ms. Henry purchased after writing the book and owned for 10 years before returning her to the island. Ms. Henry wrote the book while staying at Miss Molly's Inn on Main Street, which is still in operation today.

The wild ponies aren't the only interesting wildlife on the island. Chincoteague is a bird-watcher's paradise, with more than 300 species of resident and migratory birds. Fantastic birding can be enjoyed all year on the island, considered to be one of the best places in the country for this activity.

Dolphins frequent the waters around Chincoteague. In the spring they bring their young into the bays and inlets and sometimes surprise kayakers with a brief visit.

Another lesser-known island resident is the Delmarva fox squirrel. This squirrel is light gray in color, has longer fur, and is larger than other squirrel species found on the east coast. It experienced a deep decline in numbers during the twentieth century and has spent many years on the endangered list.

There are many great options for paddling around Chincoteague Island, but a good start is to explore the eastern side of the island and the waters that separate it from the Chincoteague National Wildlife Refuge.

All three launch areas provide great access to Toms Cove, at which kayaks are permitted to be launched and landed. Landing is also allowed on the Atlantic beaches, which are technically part of the Assateague Island National Seashore, except in the areas where there are lifeguards.

Toms Cove is my first choice for paddling in Chincoteague, and this is where most people paddle. No boats of any kind are allowed in the impoundment and ditches on the refuge. Kayak camping is not permitted on the Virginia side of the refuge.

Be aware that there is a lot of powerboat traffic in Assateague Channel. You will also be entering the water in an environment of oyster beds, marsh, and mud flats; paddle around the oyster beds to avoid damaging your boat.

Launching at the East Side Landing puts you on a small creek that empties into the Assateague Channel. Make sure to note landmarks on your trip out since there are no channel markers. After you launch, cross the creek and start paddling southeast (to the right). Continue paddling down the shoreline until you reach the open water of Assateague Channel. Cross the channel, being extremely cautious of boat traffic, and continue paddling down the Assateague Island shoreline.

You will be able to see Assateague Lighthouse to the east. This 142-foot tall red and white lighthouse is an active navigational aid owned by the Fish and Wildlife Service. The United States Coast Guard maintains the light, but the wildlife refuge is in charge of the building's preservation. The lights can be seen for 19 miles at sea, and the large base is more than 27 feet in diameter. The lighthouse is open to the public.

Look for wildlife in this area, as you paddle along the shoreline and go around the southern bend (to the left) near the Chincoteague Veterans Memorial Park launch. Once you pass the area to your left, known as Black Duck Marsh, you will be headed toward Assateague Point. When you round it, you will see the expansive Toms Cove.

If conditions allow, explore Toms Cove. It often has calm water, since it's sheltered from the Atlantic. This is a great place for observing the wild ponies, wading birds, and cownose rays. Paddle along the northern shore of the cove and into Little Toms Cove. There is a sandy beach near the Toms Cove Visitor Center where you can land and take a break. The visitor center has restrooms, a bookstore, several exhibits, brochures, a marine aquarium, and a touch tank.

If you do see a herd of ponies, which is highly likely, you will be surprised at how tame they seem. Do not approach them directly, but you can paddle near enough to get great photos. Sometimes they will even wade through the water with you.

Every year the Chincoteague Volunteer Fire Company in Virginia buys a grazing permit from the Fish and Wildlife Service to allow them to house approximately 150 ponies on the island. In order to control the size of the herd (nearly 70 foals are born each year), they hold a pony auction every July. During this popular annual event, pony herds swim between Assateague Island and Chincoteague Island for the auction, after which the remaining herd makes the return swim back to Assateague Island. Literally tens of thousands of people come out to watch this local event.

If you land your kayak for a break, look for the prickly pear cactus in the dry sand and take a close look at it. American Indians peeled the pads and used them to dress wounds. They also drank tea made from the pads to treat lung problems. The cactus fruit was eaten fresh in the warm months and dried for use in the winter.

When you're finished exploring the cove, return to the East Side Landing the same way you came. An out and back with a bit of exploration in Little Toms Cove is about 9.5 nautical miles.

MORE INFORMATION

Town of Chincoteague Department of Recreation (chincoteague-va.gov/citizens/recreation; 757-336-6519). Chincoteague National Wildlife Refuge (fws.gov/refuge/Chincoteague; 757-336-6122).

35
ONANCOCK CREEK

This picturesque paddle will take you to the shores of a peaceful nature preserve that serves as a habitat for numerous plant and animal species.

Distance ▶ 8.0 nautical miles

Cautions ▶ You will likely encounter a handful of working watermen on Onancock Creek. Most are courteous to kayakers, so you shouldn't experience any issues if you are cautious when crossing the creek.

Charts and Maps ▶ NOAA Electronic Chart US5VA16M / Paper Chart #12228

LAUNCH

Onancock Town Landing, Onancock There's a public landing located near the wharf in the town of Onancock. A dock for launching kayaks is next to the Mt. Prospect Avenue Bridge. There is no fee to launch a kayak and parking is free. There are restrooms at the landing. To reach the launch from Route 13, turn west onto VA 179, which turns into Market Street. Follow it to the end. *GPS coordinates: 37° 42.705' N, 75° 45.292' W.*

ROUTE DESCRIPTION

Virginia's Eastern Shore is made for kayaking. You can't throw a stone without hitting water. On the Chesapeake Bay side of the peninsula, 32.0 miles south of Chincoteague Island, is a lovely and very picturesque town called Onancock. The town is located on Onancock Creek and has a deepwater harbor that flows into the Chesapeake Bay. The town streets are lined with charming nineteenth century homes trimmed out with gingerbread-like accents. It's a lovely place to paddle, dine, shop, and relax.

Onancock was settled in 1680 by English explorers, although it gets its name from the American Indian word *auwannaku*, meaning foggy place. Because of its deepwater access, the town was one of 12 original royal ports in the colonies. Its location up Onancock Creek also provided shelter for large ships during storms and is considered today to be a prime "hurricane hole" on the Eastern Shore.

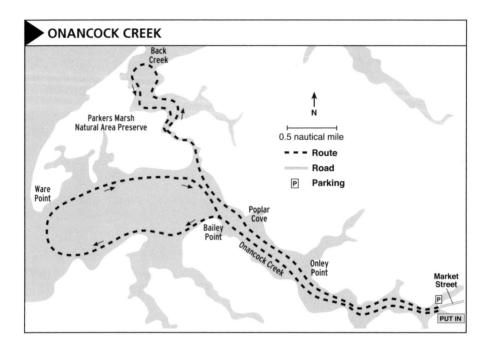

The town was a key trade center on the peninsula for more than 250 years and ranked among better-known ports such as Baltimore and Norfolk. As a popular stop on the Chesapeake Bay steamboat route, the homes along Market Street were originally built for sea captains and their families. The Onancock harbor today is a small working port and a tranquil stop for recreational boaters.

Beautiful and famous for its peaceful surroundings and wildlife, Onancock Creek is deep and wide, so you can launch and paddle even at low tide. Three creek branches stretch from the creek and poke into Onancock's neighborhoods. The town is even more charming from the water.

On the right side of the mouth of Onancock Creek is Parkers Marsh Natural Area Preserve, a natural area maintained by the Virginia Department of Conservation and Recreation.

Onancock Creek

The paddle to the mouth of Onancock Creek and back is approximately 8 nautical miles. As you're launching, the south branch of the creek will flow immediately from your left (south). Several branches along your route join Onancock Creek from both shores and make nice side trips if you have time for additional exploration.

Although Onancock Creek is protected, up the creek you may at times still face stiff winds coming off the Chesapeake Bay, resulting in small waves. If wind is an issue, paddle close to the shore to gain protection.

The first part of the paddle passes sparse residential development on both sides of the creek. When you reach Onley Point you are almost a third of the way to the bay. Continue paddling past the Peace and Plenty Farm Airport and enter into Poplar Cove, which has several residential homes and private docks that are clearly used for crabbing and recreation. You'll likely see osprey nests in this area.

As you pass Poplar Cove and make your way to Bailey Point (on the left shore), the creek will widen considerably as you start to approach the Chesapeake Bay. Parkers Marsh Natural Area Preserve will be visible on the right.

Parkers Marsh Natural Area Preserve is a wetland preserve that provides valuable habitat for numerous plant and animal species, with migrating waterfowl, shorebirds, and songbirds all making use of the protected space throughout the year. One rare species in particular, the sharp-tailed sparrow, has been observed nesting in the preserve, as have peregrine falcons. The marsh is designated an Audubon Important Bird Area (IBA) and is part of the Delmarva Bayside Marshes IBA.

An expansive salt marsh makes up approximately 75 percent of the preserve's 759 acres, and the thin forest areas that can be found on top of old dunes include loblolly pine and black cherry.

You can lengthen your trip by paddling into the preserve's coves. There are some lovely sand beaches on the Chesapeake Bay side of the preserve that you'll see if you decide to paddle out into the bay, and one near the mouth around Ware Point. There are no public access facilities on the preserve, but you can land a kayak on the beaches as long as you don't disturb any of the natural habitat.

One interesting thing worth mentioning is that the beach strand around the bay side of the preserve is home to one of the largest populations of the northeastern beach tiger beetle, a federally threatened species that is active along the intertidal zone during the day. At night, the beetles burrow under the sand along the beach.

Once you reach the mouth of the creek, you can either continue exploring the shoreline of the Chesapeake Bay (if conditions permit) or turn around and return to the launch.

Back Creek

The trip from Onancock to Back Creek and back is extremely scenic. You first paddle out Onancock Creek, then cut through the marsh on the eastern side of Parkers Marsh Natural Area Preserve and into Back Creek.

The first part of this route is the same as the Onancock Creek route. Once you pass Bailey Point and the creek opens up to the preserve, paddle up the right shoreline and into the next creek on the right. It is extremely helpful to take a look at an aerial view of the eastern side of the preserve on Google Maps so that you can see where the cut through from Onancock Creek to Back Creek is. A GPS device is also helpful. The cut-through is located at the end of the creek and makes a sharp left turn into the marsh. This is a lovely straight path for about a thousand feet, before it intersects with another creek. Turn right and follow the curvy path into Back Creek.

Kayak rentals are available in Onancock Creek.

The cut-through between the two creeks runs through a wind-swept marsh. It can feel very remote to paddle along this route alone; it will basically be you and the birds in a water-filled maze as you work your way to the reward of quiet Back Creek.

Once you reach it (the path will widen considerably), turn right and paddle into the main part of the creek. Turn left and paddle to the mouth.

There is no development on Back Creek, so paddling there is reminiscent of what Onancock Creek must have looked like back in 1608, when Captain John Smith first sailed into its serene waters. For further exploration, you can paddle the other side of Back Creek on your way back, before turning back into the curvy marsh to reach Onancock Creek. This route is also approximately 8 nautical miles round-trip.

MORE INFORMATION
Town of Onancock (onancock.com; 757-787-3363). Parkers Marsh Natural Area Preserve (dcr.virginia.gov/natural_heritage/natural_area_preserves/parkers; 757-787-5989).

36
TANGIER ISLAND

Kayak around this one-of-a-kind island to explore a place that has no cars and remains connected to its English ancestry.

Distance ▶ 2.0 or 8.0 nautical miles

Cautions ▶ In Mailboat Harbor, be mindful in the harbor of the many ferries and supply boats making their deliveries.

Charts and Maps ▶ NOAA Electronic Chart US5VA16M / Paper Chart #12228

LAUNCHES

Tangier Public Dock, Tangier Island Getting to Tangier Island can be half the fun. The island is isolated and can only be reached by boat (or by small private plane). There are two ferries to Tangier Island that allow kayaks on board, but they only operate seasonally (mid-May to mid-October). The first is the *Chesapeake Breeze* (804-453-2628, tangiercruise.com, $27 round-trip for same day service, $40 for overnight), which departs from Reedville, Virginia. The second is the *Steven Thomas* (800-863-2338, tangierislandcruises.com, $27 round-trip for same day service, $35 for overnight), which leaves from Crisfield, Maryland. Both ferries allow kayaks on board during the week for an extra $20. If you plan to go on a weekend, call ahead to see if space will allow.

Launching from the public dock where the ferries land is allowed but can be tricky, since the dock is several feet off the water. Another option is to bring wheels for your boat and walk down to the Tangier Island History Museum at 16215 Main Ridge Road. The museum has a dock from which visitors can launch and they also provide free recreational kayaks for visitors to borrow. There is no fee to launch. Restrooms are available at the public dock. *GPS coordinates: 37° 49.565' N, 75° 59.520' W.*

ROUTE DESCRIPTION

If Tangier Island is on your list of paddles, don't procrastinate. This fascinating yet quirky little island in the middle of the Chesapeake Bay is rapidly slipping into the blue. The combination of rising water levels and the fact that the land is actually sinking is putting Tangier in grave danger of disappearing forever. Although

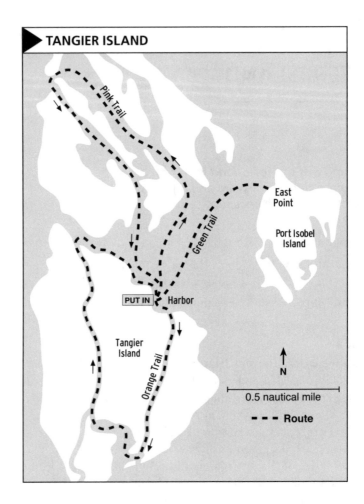

predictions vary, most experts agree that the island will be completely gone by the next century, and some believe it could be much sooner.

Tangier Island is approximately 3 miles long and 1.5 miles wide. It sits 12.0 miles off the Virginia coast and has approximately 500 permanent residents. The highest point on the island is only 5.0 feet above sea level.

Tangier was explored by Captain John Smith in 1608, when it was a fishing and hunting ground of the Pocomokewas. It was allegedly purchased in 1666 for the grand sum of two overcoats. People have been drawn to the island ever since for its abundant crab and oyster fishing and is today known as the soft-shell crab capital of the Chesapeake Bay.

Tangier consists of many small islands that are connected by wooden bridges and is made up of several low ridges (Main Ridge, Canton, and West Ridge) surrounded by marshland and tidal canals. The main harbor on Tangier is connected by a channel to the Chesapeake Bay on the west side and Tangier Sound on the east.

Many things about Tangier Island make it a great paddling spot. Aside from the obvious beauty of the island, the things that make it most special to me are its remoteness and its fascinating history.

When you reach the island, you immediately feel far removed from the mainland. In fact, I caught myself saying to a local resident, "when I get back to Virginia," forgetting momentarily that I was in Virginia. There are several key reasons for this. The first stems from the island's history.

The island's first settlers arrived more than 400 years ago and were primarily from Cornwall, a town on England's southwest coast. The island's unofficial history states that John Crockett and his eight sons were the first settlers to call the island home, reaching the island in 1686. Many of the island's residents today are decedents of the Crockett family and most still have English surnames, such as Crockett, Pruitt, and Marshall.

Due mostly to the island's isolation, Tangier's residents speak a unique and distinct English Restoration-era dialect. The community has attracted linguists from all over the country and has been featured in numerous documentaries. You can hear traces of the dialect when interacting with local business owners, but it is most pronounced when the local watermen talk amongst themselves. The uniqueness of the island isn't limited to language. Most of the island is listed on the National Register of Historic Places.

As you approach Tangier, the flat landscape is dominated by the island's water tower. When you get closer, you'll see that the narrow streets (which are not for cars, but instead bicycles and golf carts) are lined with tightly packed homes.

The island has survived four major epidemics. The most devastating occurred in 1866, when so many people died in a short period of time that due to lack of cemetery space, families buried their loved ones in their front yards. The dead were often buried in cement crypts that can be seen today in yards across the island.

There are no cars on Tangier Island. There is only one ATM, limited cell phone service, very limited Internet access, and no alcohol. The island itself can be explored in a couple of hours if you take your time (you can see most of the island from any given spot on Tangier), but those wishing to really get away from it all can spend the night in one of several inns. The island has great seafood and lots of ice cream. If you plan to eat and explore the island, bring cash, since many establishments do not take credit cards.

Tangier Island can be described as an island that time forgot or an island that has resisted change. However you look at it, Tangier is an excellent paddling destination, one that is quite different from many other spots in the mid-Atlantic.

It is possible to circumnavigate the island (about 8.0 nautical miles), but I prefer to paddle into the island and explore its many guts (narrow tidal straits), taking advantage of the many canals and creeks. The island is very boat friendly, so take your time and don't be shy to explore. One word of warning: be careful, especially at low tide, of very shallow water, since the marshes contain thick mud that can trap your kayak if you paddle into it. If this happens, do not exit your boat; instead, work yourself out of the mud using your paddle. Stepping into the mud can be very dangerous, and it is possible to sink into it like quicksand.

There are several self-guided water trails through and around Tangier. A water trail brochure for Tangier Island can be found at tangierisland-va.com.

Orange Trail

Orange Trail is the primary water trail that runs through the town. It is a 2.2-nautical-mile loop trail through what is known as the main gut of the island, the harbor and the Canton gut. Launching from the harbor or the museum dock, a clockwise start will take you through the Canton gut, around the point (through Cod Harbor) into West Ridge Creek, up the main gut, into the channel and back to the harbor.

On Orange Trail, you will paddle under five bridges; two (located on the main gut) are low and may have to be portaged at high tide. Look for stingrays in Cod Harbor, where the water is shallow and clear. You will also likely see authentic "shove boats," which are small, flat-bottomed boats that were used to deliver goods to individual homes before paths were built. While in the harbor, be mindful of the many ferries and supply boats making their deliveries. Expect to see working crab boats and the shedding houses for soft shell crabs.

A breathtaking view from Tangier Harbor.

Pink Trail

North of the main channel is marshland known as the "Uppards," an area once inhabited by approximately 600 people that now offers only ghostly reminders of its former residents. Pink Trail runs through this natural area, starting from the harbor and crossing the main channel. A counterclockwise loop takes you up Tom's Gut and near a pretty sand beach at the northwestern point of the route (you may have to do a short portage to reach the beach). It was near this spot that Hurricane Sandy pummeled the beach and unearthed human remains from a beachside graveyard. State archeologists have since relocated and reburied the remains, but the discovery drove home the fact that the island and its history are disappearing. Pink Trail is approximately 2 nautical miles.

Green Trail

A little less than a 1.0 mile paddle from the harbor on Green Trail is Port Isobel, a natural area owned by the Chesapeake Bay Foundation. Kayakers are welcome to visit the area, which has a walking path that can be explored through the marsh. Leaving the harbor, head northeast across what is known as Mailboat Harbor to reach Port Isobel. If you plan to take the walking path when you arrive, bring insect repellent.

MORE INFORMATION

Tangier Island (tangier-island.com).

AN ISLAND ON BORROWED TIME

It's hard to imagine when strolling around Tangier Island or puttering around on a golf cart, that in 50 to 100 years, the town's water tower may be all that's left of the island. Or is it?

Tangier Island doesn't receive much public attention, considering that it's an island slowly sinking into the Chesapeake Bay due to rising sea levels and erosion. Many people aren't aware that right in Virginia, is an island that used to encompass 2,062 acres but now squeezes by with less than 768, of which only 83 are habitable. People are also not aware that farms and livestock once thrived on the island, but with the loss of between 19 and 30 feet of precious land a year, this way of life has receded with the tide.

During the 1980s, a portion of the island's western shore was protected with a seawall made of boulders. This helped protect a small airstrip and the island's sewage-treatment plant from being swallowed by the bay, but attempts to expand this wall have never been executed.

The Fisherman's Corner restaurant on Tangier Island embodies the life of this seaside island. Fishing has been a way of life for generations here and restaurants such as these help support the local economy.

The island doesn't stand a chance without a seawall. One that runs the length of the island's eastern shore was approved with both state and federal funding. Only time will tell if this is a long- or short-term solution.

The problem faced by Tangier Island isn't new. In fact, many islands in the Chesapeake Bay have disappeared over the centuries. One example is Holland Island, which the community was forced to abandon in the 1920s. The last house on the island (which was built in 1888) finally collapsed into the bay in 2010.

The Uppards, a scenic area on the north end of Tangier Island, is an area that makes it easy to imagine what fate might await the rest of the island. Multiple families once lived there full time, but the area is now marsh and swamp with little remains of solid ground. Islanders recall days enjoying the Uppards, visiting friends, and duck hunting there, but now there are few signs that anyone lived there at all.

There's another reason living on Tangier Island could become a thing of the past. Younger people are turning their backs on the waterman's life and are leaving the island to receive an education and pursue modern conveniences. They want to go to college, join the military, or just plain have a car, go to the mall, and live like the rest of us.

Some younger residents still plan to settle on the island, but they are in the minority. Living a waterman's life, one of the only career paths available on the island, is hard work. So this leaves another pressing question: If the island does remain, will the next generation even want to live there?

37
OYSTER HARBOR (CAPE CHARLES)

*Take a short round-trip paddle or a long
one-way trip to explore nooks and crannies
while observing wildlife.*

      Distance ▶ 4.8 miles, 5.5 miles, or 22.0 nautical miles

      Cautions ▶ Wind can kick up the shallow water at any time of year resulting in whitecaps and choppy waves. At low tide, mud flats can appear and should be avoided.

Charts and Maps ▶ NOAA Electronic Chart US5VA14M / Paper Chart #12224

LAUNCHES

Oyster Harbor, Cape Charles The boat launch in the harbor is part of Virginia Seaside Water Trail and offers access to several great paddling routes. Owned by Northampton County, the boat launch area has a large gravel parking lot, portable toilets, three concrete ramps, a small fixed dock (to the right of the ramps), and a small beach from which you can launch. There is a fee to use the ramps. Oyster Harbor is tidal, so be aware of the tides before you head out. It is best to use the fixed dock to launch when the tide is high.

To reach the launch from US 13 in Cape Charles, turn onto Business 13 East at the traffic light. Continue for approximately 1 mile and then turn right onto Sunnyside Road. Continue for 2.3 miles and turn left onto Crumb Hill Road between two houses; there will be a sign for the boat launch across from Crumb Hill Road. Follow the road past the marsh and past the Anheuser-Busch Coastal Research Center/UVA. The boat launch is at the end of the road. *GPS coordinates: 37° 17.326′ N, 75° 55.415′ W.*

Red Bank Boat Ramp, Marionville For the long one-way paddle, you'll want to either place a car here or arrange for someone to pick you up. To reach it from US 13 in Nassawadox, Virginia (north from Cape Charles), take Red Bank Road east for 1.7 miles. Turn left on CR 715. Continue 0.1 mile to the boat ramp. There is plenty of parking and no fee to use the ramp. *GPS coordinates: 37° 26.750′ N, 75° 50.404′ W.*

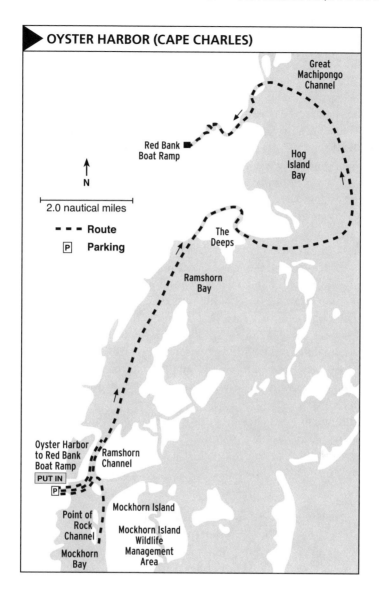

ROUTE DESCRIPTION

Oyster Harbor is an adorable little bay flanked with fishing boats and homes. It is located on the east side of Cape Charles, near the Mockhorn Bay. I strongly recommend using a GPS device in this area since tidal flats that are exposed during low tide can drastically change the landscape over a short period of time. Also, Mockhorn Bay, which is just outside the harbor, has many salt marsh islands that can complicate sight navigation. It is best to follow the marked boat channel out of Oyster Harbor and around the mud flats.

As with any area, be sure to check the weather conditions before you start your paddle.

South Route

Inexperienced paddlers can do a nice southbound out-and-back paddle out of Oyster Harbor. Begin by paddling east (left) out of the harbor, staying to the right side of the channel to allow boat traffic to pass, following the channel markers to the channel entrance through Cobb Mill Creek. Turn right into the Mockhorn Channel, once you pass through the entrance. You will be in Mockhorn Bay, opposite the northern end of Mockhorn Island.

Mockhorn Island was inhabited for centuries but it has now sat abandoned for more than 50 years. It's currently owned by the state, and as such, you are permitted to land your kayak there and even camp if you wish.

The island's history includes pirates—one of the area's best known pirates, Blackbeard, is said to have stayed there—confederate soldiers, salt works, and an exclusive hunting lodge. Ruins still stand but are off limits to the public for exploration. Today, much of the island is under water at high tide and a lot of the terrain is cordgrass.

Paddle down the peninsula shoreline, along the tidal fringe marsh, and explore the nooks and crannies, looking for wildlife. Stay on the right side of the channel. If the tide is high enough, you can explore some of Mockhorn Bay outside the channel, as several secondary channels lead into the bay, but make sure you don't get stranded if the tide is going out. You will not be able to walk on the mud flats, so do not attempt to.

After paddling approximately 2 nautical miles south into the channel, you will come to a channel marker at Point of Rock Channel. This is a good turnaround point for novices. By retracing your path back up to Oyster Harbor, you will cover approximately 6.5 nautical miles.

North Route

Beginning paddlers can also do a nice northbound out-and-back paddle out of Oyster Harbor. Begin by paddling east (left) out of the harbor, staying to the left side of the channel to allow boat traffic to pass, and follow the channel markers to the channel entrance through Cobb Mill Creek. Turn left into Ramshorn Channel, part of the Waterway Coast of Virginia (WCV), also called the Virginia Inside Passage. Elkins Marsh will be to your right.

Head north up the shoreline in Ramshorn Channel. As with the south route, the north route will take you past salt marsh islands and tidal fringe marsh. Continue a little over a mile north until you come to a wide channel on the left side. This is a good place for novice paddlers to turn around and retrace their route back to Oyster Harbor. The total distance for this route is approximately 5 nautical miles.

As with the south route, be aware that tidal mud flats are widely visible during low tide and should be strictly avoided. If you should become stuck in the mud, use your paddle to push yourself out. Never step out of your kayak onto a mud flat.

Oyster Harbor to Red Bank Boat Ramp

Advanced paddlers can make the 22.0-nautical-mile trip between Oyster Harbor and the Red Bank Boat Ramp, located north of Oyster Harbor. This is a one-way trip that requires you to either arrange for a driver to pick you up or to leave a second car at the Red Bank Boat Ramp. This route can also be completed as an out-and-back by turning around at any point.

A GPS device is a must for this trip. There are channel markers, but sighting can be difficult since landmarks come and go with the tide. Begin by paddling east (left) out of the harbor, staying to the left side of the channel to allow boat traffic to pass, and follow the channel markers to the channel entrance through Cobb Mill Creek. Turn left into Ramshorn Channel once you pass through the entrance. Elkins Marsh will be to your right.

Head north up the shoreline in Ramshorn Channel, part of the Waterway Coast of Virginia (WCV), also called the Virginia Inside Passage. You will pass tidal fringe marsh, salt marsh islands, and tidal flats at low tide (which must be avoided). Follow the WVC channel markers as you head north. Paddle through the channel and into Ramshorn Bay. Continue north through Ramshorn Bay and through Kitts Creek. From there, you will continue north into an area with a series of creeks that wind through a marsh called the Deeps.

The fixed dock to the right of the boat ramp is ideal for mid- to high tides. Paddlers may prefer to use the ramps, however, for which there is a fee.

You will find numerous side creeks off the main channel as you paddle through the Deeps. Be sure to keep to the channel, or if you decide to explore a little, at least be aware of exactly where the channel is (again, a GPS device is a must in this area). There are good navigational markers in the main channel.

As you exit the Deeps, look to your left, toward the open water. After crossing open water, where Hog Island Bay meets the Great Machipongo Inlet, turn north up the Great Machipongo Channel.

From there, follow this description from the Virginia Department of Environmental Quality website (deq.state.va.us). The references to the channel markers are important because of the combination of open water and tidal flats:

> As you pass marker #193, look to the North-Northeast (left and out toward the open water) for marker #11. Paddle toward marker #11 and then continue toward marker #12 and so forth as they lead up the Great Machipongo Channel. After passing marker #18 continue west northwest toward marker #1. Do not turn north toward marker #181 in the North Channel. After passing marker #1 continue up the channel. At channel marker #6 turn left.

Continue paddling up the creek and stay to the main channel while it twists and turns through the marsh as it leads up to the ramp.

MORE INFORMATION

Mockhorn Island Wildlife Management Area (www.dgif.virginia.gov/wmas/detail .asp?pid=6; 804-367-1000).

38
EASTERN SHORE OF VIRGINIA
NATIONAL WILDLIFE REFUGE

Paddle in a place considered to be one of the most important bird migration locations on the continent.

> **Distance** ▶ 2.5, 5.2, or 10.0 nautical miles
> **Cautions** ▶ Fishermans Inlet can be unsafe to cross if the water is flowing too quickly. Be aware of the boat traffic that often travels through the inlet.
> **Charts and Maps** ▶ NOAA Electronic Chart US5VA13M / Paper Chart #12224

LAUNCHES

Wise Point Boat Ramp, Cape Charles This is the best place from which to launch since the primary canoe and kayak launch cannot be used at low tide. To reach it from US 13 North, just past the Chesapeake Bay Bridge Tunnel, pass the Eastern Shore Visitor Center and continue approximately 0.5 mile. Turn right at the next road onto VA 600, pass your next entrance to the visitor center, on the right, and continue to the end of the road. Turn right (do not follow the large yellow and black arrows pointing left) and follow the signs to the Wise Point Boat Ramp by taking your second left and then the first right onto Ramp Road. If it is not low tide, you can use the canoe and kayak launch area on the right (there is no launch fee). If it is low tide, proceed to the Wise Point Boat Launch at the end of the road. There's a $10 fee to use the ramp, but at least you don't have to time your trip with the tide. The boat launch has two cement ramps and restroom facilities. There is also plenty of parking. *GPS coordinates: 37° 7.664' N, 75° 57.014' W.*

ROUTE DESCRIPTION

At the southern tip of the Eastern Shore is the final leg of Virginia Seaside Water Trail. It is located in the 1,123-acre Eastern Shore of Virginia National Wildlife Refuge.

The refuge is managed by the U.S. Fish and Wildlife Service and is considered to be one of the most important avian migration locations in North America. Every

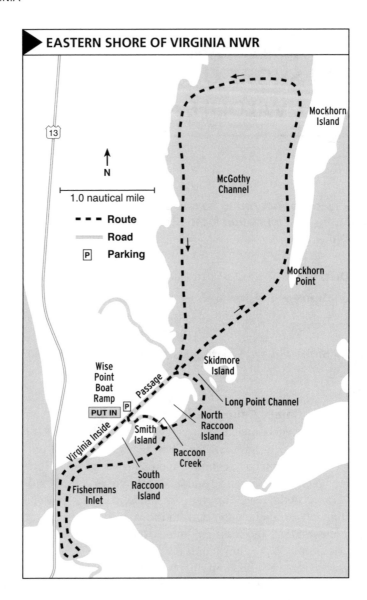

EASTERN SHORE OF VIRGINIA NWR

Mockhorn
Island

13

N

1.0 nautical mile

- - - Route
⎯⎯ Road
P   Parking

McGothy
Channel

Mockhorn
Point

Wise
Point
Boat
Ramp

Passage

Skidmore
Island

Long Point Channel

PUT IN   P

North
Raccoon
Island

Virginia Inside

Smith
Island

Raccoon
Creek

Fishermans
Inlet

South
Raccoon
Island

fall, millions of birds and monarch butterflies stop in the refuge on their way south. The protected marsh provides critical habitat for both the birds and butterflies so that they can take a break and refuel before continuing their long journey.

Although fall is truly a spectacular season in the refuge, with waves of brightly colored species passing through the area like clockwork, it is also a great kayaking destination any time of year, when the weather cooperates.

A good place to start your exploration of the refuge is at the visitor center, located off VA 600. This modern, well-maintained facility has interactive exhibits, maps, and restroom facilities. There is no fee to enter the refuge.

The Eastern Shore of Virginia National Wildlife Refuge is a little slice of paddler's heaven. There is abundant wildlife at all times of the year, with some permanent residents and many more that are seasonal. The protected passages and marsh offer paddlers the ability to view stunning wildlife that includes species such as flying squirrels, river otter, deer, swans, snow geese, loggerhead turtles, and the endangered leatherback turtle. At peak migration, more than 100,000 monarch butterflies can be seen in the refuge at one time, clinging to perches and floating on the breeze.

Many species of songbirds and migrant birds of prey travel through the refuge, including falcons, hawks, and eagles. The tiny and adorable saw-whet owl is also a resident during the winter months.

There are many great paddling routes in the refuge. My four favorites are part of Virginia Seaside Water Trail. They can either start at the primary canoe and kayak launch or the Wise Point Boat Ramp. If you are starting from the primary canoe and kayak ramp, you will need to wind your way southeast through the marsh to the Waterway Coast of Virginia (WCV), which is also called the Virginia Inside Passage, and then follow the route descriptions from there. The WCV is the narrow waterway that the Wise Point Boat Ramp is located on. It is a seaside waterway between the Delmarva Peninsula and the barrier islands.

South Raccoon Island

The first route is ideal for beginner paddlers. It is a short, 2.5-nautical-mile loop paddle that goes south around South Raccoon Island. Launching from the Wise Point Boat Ramp, paddle to the right, into the Virginia Inside Passage. South Raccoon Island, directly across from the launch, will be on your left. It is an uninhabited, marshy island that is renowned for bird-watching. Stay to the left side of the boat channel as you paddle down the passage.

At the southern end of South Raccoon Island is a beach. Kayak landing is only allowed on the beach between September 16 and March 31 since it is an active avian breeding ground. If you look south, you can see Fisherman Island National Wildlife Refuge and the start of the Chesapeake Bay Bridge Tunnel. Continue paddling around the tip of the island and head up the shoreline, keeping the island to your left. The beach continues for approximately another 0.5 mile. Be aware of the tidal flats between South Raccoon Island and neighboring Smith Island that become exposed at low tide.

The beach soon fades into a maritime forest with mostly pine trees. The shoreline will then jog to the left, where Raccoon Creek flows through the island. Look for the main channel of the creek and paddle left into it. Follow the channel through the island until you return to the Virginia Inside Passage. You will need to turn right in the passage to return to the Wise Point Boat Ramp.

North Raccoon Island

Another good beginner loop route is around North Raccoon Island. This route is a little less than 3.0 nautical miles long. Launch at the Wise Point Boat Ramp and paddle left into the Virginia Inside Passage. North Raccoon Island will be on your right. Stay to the right of the boat channel and continue to the northern end of the island.

Paddle around the top of the island and into Long Point Channel, keeping the island on your right, and continue down the coastline. As with a paddle around South Raccoon Island, be aware of exposed tidal flats between North Raccoon Island and neighboring Smith Island at low tide.

You will soon approach the maritime forest section (mostly pine trees) of the island. Soon after, you'll see signs of a clam farm along the coast. After passing the farm, look for the entrance to the main channel of Raccoon Creek and paddle to the right into the creek. Follow the channel across the island, back to the Virginia Inside Passage, and paddle across it, slightly to the north, to return to the boat ramp.

For a longer paddle, do a complete circumnavigation of Raccoon Island.

Fisherman Island National Wildlife Refuge

A great kayak route for intermediate paddlers is the trip to Fisherman Island, followed by the South Raccoon Island loop. This route is approximately 5 nautical miles.

Launching from the Wise Point Boat Ramp, follow the directions for the South Raccoon Island route until you reach Fishermans Inlet. If conditions allow (water sometimes flows too quickly for a safe crossing), make the 0.5-mile paddle across the channel to Fishermans Island. It's helpful to pick a landmark to paddle toward when making the crossing. Be certain to also look for local powerboats and large vessels crossing over the Chesapeake Bay Bridge Tunnel.

Upon arrival at Fishermans Island, you can paddle into the large inlet (US 13 will be on your right). Since the island is a wildlife refuge, no landing is permitted, but you can explore the interior by kayak. A creek twists and turns through the refuge and splits into several branches. If you decide to explore the nooks and crannies of the island, take care so that you don't get lost.

Although the island has served many uses over the years, the most recent purpose was as a harbor defense and detection base for submarines during World War II. In sharp contrast to the other Virginia barrier islands, Fisherman Island is growing rather than shrinking. In the late 1800s the island was just 25 acres but today is approximately 2,000 acres.

When you're done exploring the island, return the way you came. Again, selecting a landmark to aim for while crossing the channel is a good way to stay on course. Bring a GPS device with you to help find your way back. When you return to the tip of South Raccoon Island, continue up the eastern coastline and take Raccoon Creek to return to the boat ramp.

Egrets at Eastern Shore of Virginia National Wildlife Refuge.

Mockhorn Island

Mockhorn Island, one of two tracts of land in the Mockhorn Wildlife Management Area, consists of more than 7,000 acres of marsh and maritime forest and was once home to an exclusive hunting resort and several World War II lookout towers. A large portion of the island is underwater during high tide.

Ideal for intermediate kayakers, the Mockhorn Island route is a scenic 10.0-nautical-mile route that takes paddlers through the protected waters on the west side of the island. Turning left from the launch at the Wise Point Boat Ramp, paddle up the Virginia Inside Passage. As you pass North Raccoon Island on your right, stay near one side of the channel to allow boat traffic clear passage.

As you approach the top of North Raccoon Island, paddle across Long Point Channel passing Skidmore Island, on its northwest side. You should then be able to see across Magothy Channel to Mockhorn Point, on the southern tip of Mockhorn Island. Look for the island's two watchtowers and paddle to Mockhorn Point. When you arrive there, paddle north, up the western coast of the island for about 2.5 nautical miles, to a small cove called Cabin Cove. You should be able to see the remains of an old hunting club along the way. Many of the barrier islands were once inhabited, but today, only Chincoteague, at the northern end, still has a thriving community.

Since Mockhorn Island is owned by the state, it is legal to land on the island, and in fact, camping is also allowed. If you have the time, explore some of the island, although remember that access to the building ruins is prohibited. You will feel far removed from the bustle of everyday life.

When you're done exploring, paddle across the channel and then south along the peninsula shoreline. You will pass the Magothy Bay State Natural Area Preserve. Turn right to paddle back down the western shore of North Raccoon Island and back to the Wise Point Boat Ramp.

MORE INFORMATION

Eastern Shore of Virginia National Wildlife Refuge (fws.gov/refuge/eastern_shore_of_virginia; 757-331-3425). Fisherman Island National Wildlife Refuge (fws.gov/refuge/fisherman_island; 757-331-2760).

39

FIRST LANDING STATE PARK–
VIRGINIA BEACH

Paddle in the Atlantic Ocean along the Virginia Beach shoreline to get a view of dolphins or enjoy the calmer waters of a pair of bays.

Distance ▶ 11.7 or 19.0 nautical miles

Cautions ▶ In the paddle along the Atlantic Ocean shoreline, be prepared to encounter strong swells and currents, even on calm days. There are a few areas of caution to be aware of in the bay paddle. There is often a strong current in Long Creek, which is located on the northern side of Broad Bay, that is tide dependent. There is also a very strong tidal current near the route 60 bridge.

Charts and Maps ▶ NOAA Electronic Chart US5VA19M / Paper Chart #12254 and 12222

LAUNCHES

First Landing State Park beach launch, Virginia Beach Experienced paddlers can launch into the mouth of the Chesapeake Bay from the beach, near the visitors center. You will need to carry or wheel your boat about 200 steps from the parking lot down the wooden walkway that starts to the right of the visitor center. To reach the launch from US 60/Shore Drive, follow the road until you reach the park entrance at 2500 Shore Drive, following the signs to the camping area and visitor center parking launch. The entrance fee is $4 on weekdays and $5 on weekends, and the visitor center has restrooms and parking. *GPS coordinates: 36° 55.100' N, 76° 3.223' W.*

First Landing State Park bay launch, Virginia Beach First Landing State Park also has a boat ramp and is another great option, especially if you prefer to paddle in calmer water. To reach the ramp, take US 60 to 64th Street and head west on it until you reach the end. In the summer months, the launch can get quite crowded, especially during the middle of the day. There is a large parking lot and a restroom.

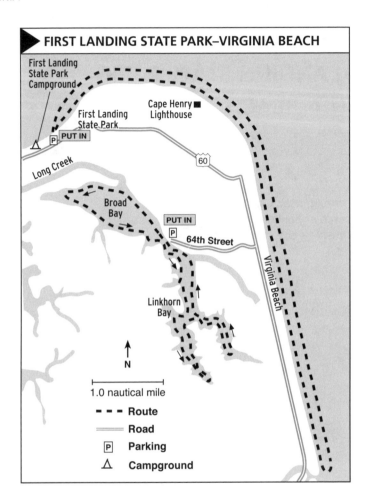

FIRST LANDING STATE PARK–VIRGINIA BEACH

Parking in the park is $5 on weekends and $4 during the week. It is free to launch a kayak. *GPS coordinates: 36° 53.406' N, 76° 1.043' W.*

ROUTE DESCRIPTION

If you're a fan of bottlenose dolphins—and really, who isn't?—then you may want to put the Virginia Beach area on your bucket list of paddles. Virginia Beach is known for having large pods of dolphins in the summer months and some resident pods year round. Just take a stroll down the busy boardwalk and look out in the water, and chances are you'll see them fishing or playing behind the surf.

This area features the 2,888-acre First Landing State Park, located around the corner, so to speak, from Virginia Beach, at the mouth of the Chesapeake Bay on Cape Henry, where it meets the Atlantic Ocean.

First Landing State Park is historically important because English settlers headed for Jamestown first landed there in 1607. Listed on the National Register of Historic Places, the park has lovely interior waterways, lagoons, and cypress swamps that have been used by American Indians, pirates, military ships in the War of 1812, Union and Confederate patrols in the Civil War, and schooners in the twentieth century. It is the first planned state park in Virginia and is the most popular park in the state, with over one million visitors annually.

Beach Launch

This paddle is not for beginners. Even on a calm day there can be strong currents and swells. It is, however, a great destination if you are comfortable in open water and are looking to get a fairly up-close view of dolphins.

The beach is wide, sandy, and clean. The launch is gradual and if the surf is calm, it is a lovely place for experienced paddlers to launch from, with nothing but open water in front of you. Paddling to the right will take you around Cape Henry, past the Cape Henry Lighthouse and into the Atlantic.

There are actually two lighthouses on Cape Henry, the original brick structure and its replacement, built in 1881. The original building was the first federally funded lighthouse in the country, with its construction authorized by George Washington and overseen by Alexander Hamilton. Used for almost a hundred years before the nearby cast iron lighthouse replaced it, the original is one of the oldest lighthouses in the country.

Virginia Beach has several military facilities. Cape Henry is home to Fort Story, the only Army training facility used for amphibious equipment training. It is also used to practice military cargo transfers between ships and shore, so there is often activity around the cape.

Naval Air Station Oceana, the east coast base for the Navy's fighter planes, is also located in the heart of Virginia Beach and is a hub of activity. Fighter planes regularly fly over the beach each day.

This paddle is a great way to get a somewhat close look at the bottlenose dolphins. Although it is illegal to deliberately paddle into a pod, you can keep a respectful distance and still get a good look. In addition to dolphins you will likely see osprey and occasionally bald eagles.

Bottlenose dolphins are some of the most researched marine mammals. They are highly intelligent, usually weigh between 440 and 600 pounds, and can eat between 13 and 33 pounds of food each day. Although they are known for their playful nature and often seem friendly to humans, they can also be aggressive at times—so observe them from a distance.

Take your time and paddle down the Atlantic coast as far as you feel comfortable. It's best to paddle just beyond the breakers, where you are most likely to encounter dolphins. The conditions on the water can vary greatly, depending on the surf, wind, and currents. It is approximately 9.5 nautical miles down to Rudee Inlet (19.0 nautical miles round-trip). The best time for seeing dolphins is May through September.

A tranquil sunset on Virginia Beach.

Bay Launch

The boat ramp is located in a pretty section of the park that is part maritime forest. The launch puts you on a body of water called the Narrows (kayak rentals are available near the launch during the summer months). The Narrows connects Linkhorn Bay with Broad Bay. Both are very nice areas to paddle, as the water is normally calm, with just a slight current and some waves caused by boat traffic. You will paddle mostly along the shoreline of the park (maritime forest, salt marshes, and sand flats) and past nearby neighborhoods. Egrets and herons are common residents in the bays, and occasionally dolphins make their way into the calm waters.

There are a few areas of caution to be aware of in this bay paddle. There is often a strong current in Long Creek, located on the northern side of Broad Bay, that is tide dependent. There is also a very strong tidal current near the US 60 bridge, so it is best to not access the Chesapeake Bay through Wolfsnare Creek; but a paddle in the bay is best accessed from the beach landing.

Two lovely loops around both Linkhorn Bay and Broad Bay will yield an 11.7-nautical-mile paddle, depending on how closely you follow the shoreline.

In addition to pleasure boaters, you will likely see people fishing or crabbing in the Narrows. The Virginia Beach area is known for its superb fishing. Croaker, spot, bluefish, Spanish mackerel, and flounder are just a few of the local favorites.

MORE INFORMATION

First Landing State Park (www.dcr.virginia.gov/state-parks/first-landing.shtml; 757-412-2300). Cape Henry Lighthouse (preservationvirginia.org/visit/historic-properties/cape-henry-lighthouse; 757-422-9421).

40
BACK BAY NATIONAL WILDLIFE REFUGE

Bask in the peacefulness of this remote wildlife refuge and enjoy seeing hundreds of species of birds.

Distance ▶ 7.4 or 12.6 nautical miles, with shorter options

Cautions ▶ Since the bay is very shallow, the wind can cause the water to become choppy, and paddling against the tide in wind can be quite challenging.

Charts and Maps ▶ NOAA Electronic Chart US4NC32M / Paper Chart #12205

LAUNCHES

Little Island Park, Virginia Beach Just north of the refuge, at Little Island Park, is a hand-carry launch. The park fronts both the Atlantic and Back Bay and has 144-acres and a fishing pier on the Atlantic side. The launch is about 100 yards from the parking lot and puts you in a small creek leading to the bay. Parking is $5, and there are restrooms. To reach it from Virginia Beach, head east on US 60. It will become VA 615 South/General Booth Boulevard. Stay on VA 615 by turning left onto Princess Anne Road. After approximately 1 mile it turns into Sandbridge Road. You will pass a sign on the right that looks like an entrance to Back Bay National Wildlife Refuge, but do not turn there; continue past it. Turn right onto Sandpiper Road and take it to the launch, on the right. *GPS coordinates: 36° 41.503′ N, 75° 55.523′ W.*

Back Bay National Wildlife Refuge Visitors Center, Virginia Beach There is a lovely launch site in the refuge near the visitor center, with restrooms and parking (arrive early in the summer since this is a popular place). To reach it, follow the directions above, passing Little Island Park, and take Sandpiper Road until the end. There is a $5 entrance fee. Enter the refuge and continue to the end of the road. The launch is next to the parking area on the right side. *GPS coordinates: 36° 40.351′ N, 75° 54.957′ W.*

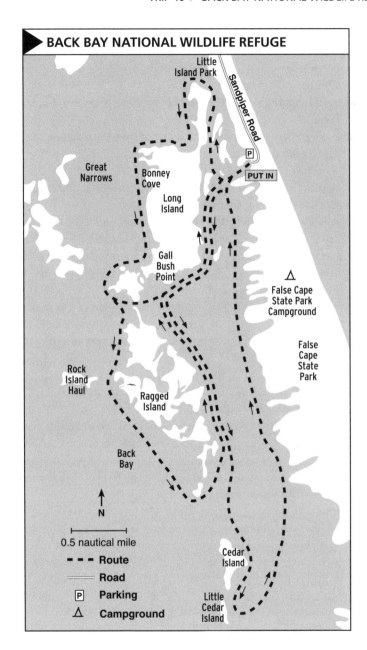

ROUTE DESCRIPTION

At the southern end of Virginia Beach is a vast and beautiful wilderness called Back Bay National Wildlife Refuge. Established in 1938 and managed by the U.S. Fish and Wildlife Service, the refuge is considered to be an important section of the

Atlantic Flyway for migratory birds. The refuge adjoins False Cape State Park and is immediately north of the Outer Banks of North Carolina.

The refuge's primary goal is to provide food and protection for waterfowl that migrate through the area or winter in Back Bay. As such, ten managed wetlands/impoundments are maintained in the refuge, providing nutritious food sources such as smartweed, three-square, and spike rushes.

The refuge encompasses more than 9,250 acres and is a paddler's paradise. Its namesake, Back Bay, is the primary feature in the refuge. Much of the refuge consists of emergent freshwater marshland located on small islands on Back Bay. However, there is also a thin strip of barrier island coast (in some places only 1,000 feet wide), as well as beach, dunes, fields, and woodlands.

Although it is located close to the highly commercialized Virginia Beach, the refuge feels remote and isolated. Literally thousands of tundra swans, Canada geese, snow geese, and multiple varieties of ducks are present in the refuge during the fall and winter migration. Approximately 300 species of birds can be found there throughout the year, including brown pelicans, peregrine falcons, and bald eagles. Multiple species of turtles (including snapping turtles) live in the refuge, as well as deer, gray fox, mink, raccoon, and otter. You may also see snakes, including black rat snakes, water snakes, the eastern hognose snake, and the poisonous cottonmouth.

There are many protected areas to paddle in Back Bay. It is a good spot for beginners to work on their skills at paddling through the protected marsh. As with most marsh areas, do not exit your boat should you get stuck in the mud; you can sink thigh deep in some spots.

The open waters of the bay are not usually conducive to a flatwater paddle. Since the bay is very shallow, the wind can cause the water to become pretty choppy. If you're working against the tide and wind, it can be outright challenging (bring a spray skirt). So plan your trip according to your skill level and be aware that when the winds are high, the water levels can be low. Because the water is so shallow, it doesn't take much to blow the water away, so to speak. Seasonal hunting is also allowed in the refuge, so some areas are closed during duck hunting season, which explains the duck blinds you might see.

My preference is to launch near the visitor center. It's a nice sandy launch and the chances of finding parking in the summer months are much greater than at Little Island Park. Sunscreen, insect repellent, and water should be in your dry bag as you head out. At the put-in, you will have great access to the entire bay. The options for paddling around the bay are endless; you don't need to follow a specific route. However, you should bring a GPS device with you since the marsh can get confusing.

Ragged Island

For a nice 12.6-nautical-mile paddle, head to the right after launching and paddle around the large primary island that is directly in front of you, Long Island. First, wind your way north toward Little Island Park and paddle around the tip of the island. Then head south down the western edge of the island, on the edge of the

Great Narrows, and into Bonney Cove, taking some time to explore some of the nooks and crannies.

Long Island is roughly connected to Ragged Island at its southern point. Continue south, between Rock Island Haul (to your right) and Ragged Island. Once you pass Ragged Island you will be in Back Bay proper.

At the southern tip of Ragged Island, head around the point and back up the eastern side. As you paddle north, with Ragged Island on your left, you will be heading through Sand Bay. False Cape State Park will be on the shore to your right.

False Cape State Park sits between Back Bay and the Atlantic Ocean on the barrier spit and stretches down the shoreline to North Carolina. It offers hiking, biking, boating, and primitive camping. Since it's not accessible by automobile, a tram (there is a fee) runs from April through October from Back Bay National Wildlife Refuge. But your best bet is to kayak there.

False Cape was named as such because from the Atlantic it looks similar to Cape Henry, located north of Virginia Beach, at the mouth of the Chesapeake Bay. This similarity is said to have fooled ships into trying to land on the cape, causing them to run aground in the shallow water. American Indians once inhabited the area and

Back Bay National Wildlife Refuge boat launch

early European survivors of one shipwreck (in the late sixteenth or early seventeenth century) allegedly started a community on the Cape called Wash Woods.

Wash Woods was home to 300 people and had a United States Coast Guard life-saving station, churches, a grocery store, and a school. Many of the town's structures were built from wood that washed ashore from shipwrecks. The town was abandoned in the 1930s, but several hunt clubs thrived in the area afterward. The park's current education center was built from a hunt clubhouse.

Once you pass False Cape, continue up the shoreline to return to the launch.

Long Island
For a shorter route, you can paddle the 7.4-nautical-mile circumnavigation of Long Island. Follow the Ragged Island route but slip through one of the passages at the south end of Long Island. Gall Bush Point marks the southern tip of the island, where you might see osprey nests.

Cedar Island
Another nice trip is a southbound out and back trip to Cedar Island. This will be between 9.5 and 11.0 nautical miles, depending on your turn-around point. Cedar Island and Little Cedar Island are south of Ragged Island, across from False Cape State Park. There is room to land a kayak on Cedar Island if you'd like to stretch your legs or explore a little. The island has some ruins of a home on it. It would have been an odd place to live given the issue of access.

Overall, Back Bay National Wildlife Refuge is an excellent paddling destination, with easy access and options for paddlers of all levels (weather permitting). Bird-lovers will find it especially exciting, but the vastness of the area provides many enjoyable routes and opportunities for wildlife viewing.

MORE INFORMATION
Back Bay National Wildlife Refuge (fws.gov/refuge/Back_Bay; 757-301-7329). False Cape State Park (www.dcr.virginia.gov/state-parks/false-cape; 757-426-7128). Little Island Park (www.vbgov.com/government/departments/parks-recreation/parks-trails/city-parks/Pages/little-island-park.aspx; 757-426-0013).

DARK DAYS FOR THE AMERICAN BLACK DUCK

The American black duck is a "dabbling" duck that lives in eastern North America. Dabbling ducks feed on the surface of the water and upend (tip their heads underwater until they are upside down) to feed on aquatic plants, and can dive to depths of nearly 13 feet. They also sometimes graze on land.

The American black duck has dark brown feathers but looks black from a distance. They are migratory birds and frequent Back Bay National Wildlife Refuge during the winter months. In fact, the park uses the arrival of the Black Duck as an indicator that the fall–winter migration is about to take place, since they are usually among the first of the cold weather visitors to reach the refuge and they tend to migrate prior to the onset of winter.

In addition to their dark plumage, the American black duck has a distinct iridescent wing patch or purple speculum that can be seen when they fly. Their heads, in contrast to the rest of their bodies, are pale gray and the underside of their wings are white. These ducks also have red feet. As such, their scientific name is "rubripes" meaning "red foot."

From the cockpit of a kayak, it can be difficult to tell the American black duck apart from the female mallard and several other ducks in the refuge with similar markings. The male and female also look alike, with the exception that the female is overall a little paler and has a greenish tint to its bill, while the male has a bright yellow bill.

The Back Bay National Wildlife Refuge offers the perfect winter habitat for the black duck since they prefer to settle in coastal marshes. They can also be found in bogs, woodland ponds, and in stream and estuary margins.

There is great concern over the long-term survival of the American black duck. Populations have steadily declined since the 1950s from around 200,000 down to approximately 32,000. Although studies indicate that the lifespan of the ducks has not decreased, it appears that their rate of reproduction has fallen behind their mortality rate.

It is not fully understood why their numbers are decreasing, but some findings from recent studies indicate that the introduction of hand-raised mallards into the wild have expanded these populations east into the black duck breeding grounds, forcing new competition for habitat. Another concern is the reduction in habitat through coastal erosion and development.

Although in decline, kayakers can still expect to see the American black duck in many mid-Atlantic coastal regions primarily between November and February. The highest concentrations are found during these months between Long Island and North Carolina.

Appendix A: Information and Resources

National Oceanic and Atmospheric Administration (NOAA)
Weather: weather.gov
Tides and currents: tidesandcurrents.noaa.gov
Charts: nauticalcharts.noaa.gov
Marine Mammal Stranding Hotline: 866-755-6622

United States Coast Guard
National Response Center: 800-424-8802
24 Hour Emergency Response: 800-410-9549
Staten Island, NY: 718-354-4037
Cape May, NJ: 609-898-6900
Rehoboth Beach, DE: 302-227-2440
Annapolis, MD: 410-267-8107
Baltimore, MD: 410-789-1600
Ocean City, MD: 410-289-1905
Portsmouth, VA: 757-398-6287
Cape Charles, VA: 757-331-2000

Shellfish Information
Mid-Atlantic Fishery Management Council: 302-674-2331
Marine Law Enforcement, New York Parks, Recreation and Historic Preservation:
    518-474-0456

First Aid Instruction
Appalachian Mountain Club (AMC): activities.outdoors.org
Stonehearth Open Learning Opportunities (SOLO): soloschools.com,
    603-447-6711
National Outdoor Leadership School (NOLS): nols.edu, 866-831-9001
Wilderness Medical Associates: wildmed.com, 207-730-7331

Kayaking Instruction
American Canoe Association: americancanoe.org
Appalachian Mountain Club (AMC): activities.outdoors.org

Organizations and Publications

Appalachian Mountain Club (AMC): outdoors.org

Paddling.net: paddling.net

Atlantic Coastal Kayaker: atlanticcoastalkayaker.com

Adventure Kayak magazine: rapidmedia.com/kayaking.html

Ocean Paddler magazine: paddlepressmedia.com/

Canoe and Kayak magazine: canoekayak.com

Appendix B: Float Plan

If we do not report by _____ A.M./P.M. on _____ (date),
please call _____ (agency/phone)
and report me/us overdue/missing and provide the following:

TOTAL NUMBER OF PADDLERS IN GROUP _____

KAYAKERS
  Names _____
  Ages/genders _____
  Phones _____
  Kayak colors (deck/hull) _____
  PFD colors _____
  Clothing _____
  Skill levels _____
  Medical info _____

GEAR CARRIED
  Signaling and communications gear _____
  _____
  Tent descriptions _____
  _____

LAUNCH SITE _____ DATE _____ TIME _____ A.M./P.M.
FINAL LANDING SITE _____ DATE _____ TIME _____ A.M./P.M.

VEHICLE(S), LICENSE # _____
_____

SHUTTLE VEHICLE(S) (IF ANY), LICENSE # _____
_____

PROPOSED ROUTE, CAMPSITES, ALTERNATIVES _____
_____
_____
_____
_____

Appendix C: More Reading

Sea Kayaking Manuals

Brown, Gordon. *Sea Kayak: A Manual for Intermediate and Advanced Sea Kayakers.* Pesda Press, 2006.

Dowd, John. *Sea Kayaking: A Manual For Long Distance Touring.* 5th edition. Greystone Books, 2004.

Hutchinson, Derek. *The Complete Book of Sea Kayaking.* 5th edition. Falcon Guides, 2004.

Johnson, Shelley. *The Complete Sea Kayaker's Handbook.* 2nd Edition. International Marine/Ragged Mountain Press, 2011.

Robison, John. *Sea Kayaking Illustrated: A Visual Guide to Better Paddling.* International Marine/Ragged Mountain Press, 2003.

Navigation and Safety

Broze, Matt. *Sea Kayaker's Deep Trouble: True Stories and Their Lessons from* Sea Kayaker *Magazine.* International Marine/Ragged Mountain Press, 1997.

Burch, David. *Fundamentals of Kayak Navigation.* 4th edition. Falcon Guides, 2008.

Cunningham, Christopher. *Sea Kayaker's More Deep Trouble.* International Marine/Ragged Mountain Press, 2013.

Ferrero, Franco. *Sea Kayak Navigation: A Practical Manual, Essential Knowledge for Finding Your Way at Sea.* 2nd edition. Pesda Press, 2007.

Local Guidebooks

Gaaserud, Michaela Riva. *Moon Maryland: Including Washington DC.* Avalon Travel, 2014.

Gaaserud, Michaela Riva. *Moon Spotlight Coastal Virginia: Including Colonial Williamsburg.* 3rd Edition. Avalon Travel, 2014.

Gaaserud, Michaela Riva. *Moon Virginia & Maryland: Including Washington DC.* Avalon Travel, 2014.

Gaaserud, Michaela Riva. *Moon Virginia: Including Washington DC.* 6th Edition. Avalon Travel, 2014.

Hayes, John and Alex Wilson. *Quiet Water New York: Canoe and Kayak Guide.* 2nd Edition. Appalachian Mountain Club Books, 2007.

Kenley, Kathy. *Quiet Water New Jersey and Eastern Pennsylvania: AMC's Canoe and Kayak Guide to the Best Ponds, Lakes, and Easy Rivers.* Appalachian Mountain Club Books, 2010.

INDEX

About the Author

Michaela Riva Gaaserud is a longtime sports and guidebook writer who has paddled throughout much of the United States and Canada, writing for national publications such as *Canoe & Kayak Magazine* and *Paddler Magazine*. This is her seventh guidebook. Other publications include *Sea Kayaking the Baltimore/Washington D.C. Area*; *Lake Placid: With the Olympic Village, Lake George and New York's Adirondacks*; *Moon Virginia and Maryland*; *Moon Virginia*; *Moon Maryland*; and *Moon Spotlight Coastal Virginia*.

About AMC in the Mid-Atlantic

Each year, the Appalachian Mountain Club's Potomac, Delaware Valley, New York-North Jersey, and Mohawk Hudson chapters offer hundreds of outdoor activities including hiking, backpacking, bicycling, paddling, and climbing trips, as well as social, family, and young member programs. Chapter volunteers maintain local trails, lead outdoor skills workshops, and promote stewardship of the region's natural resources. A complete listing of upcoming events is available on activities.outdoors.org.

AMC manages Mohican Outdoor Center in the Delaware Water Gap National Recreation Area, a four-season, self-service destination for hiking, paddling, skiing, snowshoeing, and camping, a short distance from the Appalachian Trail in New Jersey. Volunteers manage AMC's Fire Island Cabin, available on a self-service basis.

AMC is active in regional conservation issues, and is a leader of the Highlands Coalition, which works to secure funding for land conservation in the four-state Highlands region of Connecticut, New York, New Jersey, and Pennsylvania. AMC also monitors energy development proposals that have an impact on public lands in the region. It is leading the effort to establish the 100-mile Pennsylvania Highlands Trail Network.

To learn more about AMC's work in the Mid-Atlantic, visit outdoors.org.

AMC Book Updates

AMC Books strives to keep our books as up-to-date as possible to help you plan safe and enjoyable adventures. If after publishing a book we learn that trails have been relocated or route or contact info has changed, we will post the updated information online. Before you hit the trail, check for updates at outdoors.org/bookupdates.

While enjoying a trip from this book, if you notice discrepancies with the trip description or map, or if you find any other errors, please let us know by submitting them to amcbookupdates@outdoors.org or in writing to Books Editor, c/o Appalachian Mountain Club, 5 Joy Street, Boston MA, 02108. AMC Books is dedicated to being a recognized leader in outdoor publishing. Thank you for your participation.

APPALACHIAN MOUNTAIN CLUB

At AMC, connecting you to the freedom and exhilaration of the outdoors is our calling. We help people of all ages and abilities to explore and develop a deep appreciation of the natural world.

AMC helps you get outdoors on your own, with family and friends, and through activities close to home and beyond. With chapters from Maine to Washington, D.C., including groups in Boston, New York City, and Philadelphia, you can enjoy activities like hiking, paddling, cycling, and skiing, and learn new outdoor skills. We offer advice, guidebooks, maps, and unique lodges and huts to inspire your next outing. You will also have the opportunity to support conservation advocacy and research, youth programming, and caring for 1,800 miles of trails.

We invite you to join us in the outdoors.

YOUR CONNECTION
TO THE OUTDOORS

AMC's Best Sea Kayaking in New England

Michael Daugherty

This concise guide, written by a Registered Maine Guide, features 50 of the best sea kayaking adventures along the New England coast, from Connecticut to Maine. Each trip features a full description and map, notes on distance and time, launch site, tide and currents, "plan B" routes, and nearby attractions.

$18.95 • 978-1-628420-06-7

Quiet Water New Jersey and Eastern Pennsylvania

Kathy Kenley

Great for families, anglers, and canoeists and kayakers of all abilities, this trusty guide features 80 trips, covering the best calm water paddling in the region. Take a long paddle through Lake Aeroflex and connecting ponds, spot wildlife in South Jersey's Great Bay, or discover the beautiful French Creek State Park.

$19.95 • 978-1-934028-34-6

AMC's Best Backpacking in the Mid-Atlantic

Michael R. Martin

Within hours of New York, Philadelphia, and Washington D.C., thousands of miles of trails cross a wide variety of wild terrain. Whether you're looking for a two-day loop or a challenging weeklong trek, this three-season guide is an essential tool for finding the most exciting Mid-Atlantic backpacking experiences.

$19.95 • 978-1-934028-86-5

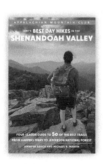

AMC's Best Day Hikes in the Shenandoah Valley

Jennifer Adach and Michael R. Martin

Bounded on the east by the Blue Ridge Mountains and on the west by the Appalachians, the Shenandoah Valley is a region of exceptional natural beauty. This guide offers the 50 of the best hikes that can be accomplished in the region in less than a day, from easy saunters of a few miles, to longer treks through rugged terrain.

$18.95 • 978-1-628420-17-3